9-24-76

Consumer's Guide to Fighting Back

Consumer's Guide to Fighting Back

Morris J. Bloomstein

DODD, MEAD & COMPANY, NEW YORK

Library of Congress Cataloging in Publication Data

Bloomstein, Morris J
  Consumer's guide to fighting back.

  Includes index.
  1. Consumer protection—United States.
2. Consumer education—United States.
3. Complaints (Retail trade) I. Title.
HC110.C63B55   381′.3   76-12428
ISBN 0-396-07321-2

1928274

To my beloved wife,
ELLEN,
whose anger over a torn couch
started the whole thing

Contents

Consumer's Guide to Fighting Back

CHAPTER
1

——————— Fighting Back ———————

Congratulations. You have been economically swindled, hood-winked, robbed. Repairmen have sneered at you; merchants have ignored your protests. You have felt helpless, with nowhere to turn. Now, you have made up your mind to fight back. Congratulations.

Declare war. To be a consumer today is to be at war with those who would take advantage of your right to proper goods and services.

Basically, there are two types of offenders: the arrogant, don't-give-a-damn ones, and those who cheat their fellow men. For them the cake is worth the candle. Consumers spend over $500 billion dollars a year on The American Way of Life. Refrigerators, cars, housing, food, drugs, an endless list of goods and services, all drain our dimes and dollars. If you are fortunate enough to always receive full value or are unwilling to defend yourself, there is no need to read further.

For the rest of you, the vast majority of Americans, make up your minds that if you go to war, you had better be prepared to use weapons you may have hesitated to use in the past.

Be prepared to be loud, for the silent ones are ignored. Persistence will be important, because the average seller, large or small, will try to brush you off. He knows you probably won't sue, since most complaints are small, and rare is the person who will hire a lawyer and involve himself with the courts for something that may involve more nuisance than it is worth. Besides, the other complications in your life are clamoring for attention, cooling the instant's fury, leading you to new crises, so that the old complaint fades into the elephant's graveyard of, "Ah, to heck with it."

Your weapons will be the nose to nose encounter, the argument you know will upset you (but which is vital), the constant needle of the telephone, and, perhaps most deadly, the pen or typewriter.

Just as you know the rules of baseball or canasta, so must you learn the rules of self-protection even before you take your first steps toward buying goods or services. You must learn them so that they are automatic. With whom may you safely deal? How do you nail down promises so that they are not shrugged off at a later time? What are the popular frauds that are aimed at your pocketbook?

Of course, you will not win every time. There may be situations where the seller is tougher than you are, doesn't care what forces are called into play against him, isn't concerned that he may have picked on the wrong person and has a whale of a fight on his hands. You may even be in the wrong.

But one thing is guaranteed. Your opponent (for that is what the seller is) will know that he has been in one helluva fight. Your batting average of satisfaction will shoot up; that, too, is a promise.

There may be certain situations where much money is involved, and you'll need a lawyer; the battle is beyond your capabilities without professional assistance. Do not hesitate to resort to this last extreme.

Each war will bring its share of disappointments, moments when, in the past, you would have quit the fight. Go on. The only battle worth the savoring and remembering will be that last battle, when satisfaction is achieved, is forced, is squeezed out of the hides of those who knew they could not lose while fighting you, the consumer-sucker.

Success will breed success; this, too, is a promise. An overall pattern will emerge to govern your actions, your order of procedure, until it will be ingrained in the consumer's corner of your mind. You will never again be stepped on, with impugnity.

Not every situation in your consumer-life can be covered, since the gamut of a lifetime of purchases is far too broad. But the everyday occurrences that will probably affect you are described herein. If your particular problem is not covered, seek the transaction described in this book most closely resembling your trouble and follow the general course of conduct suggested.

Most of the topics will be treated in four action sections.

First, there will be a discussion of preventive acts and safeguards as your first line of defense. How do you find out the reputation of the person with whom you are dealing? What should you know about your transaction? What must be put in writing? What are the earmarks of fraud?

Second, there will be a step-by-step description of the counterattack, how to promptly react to a violation of your rights as a consumer. Do you speak to an underling or do you try to see someone in charge? What tactics are available to you to speak to someone in authority? How far should you go in your demands? In person or by phone? When should you be the aggrieved Long-Time Customer, and when should you be the Bull in the

China Shop? One question may be answered now. When should you worry about the impression you're creating, or if you are offending your opponent's sensibilities? Never! "Don't tread on me!"

Third, there is the campaign and the siege. Sometimes you will win on the immediate counterattack, but don't count on it. Count on having to follow up the initial protest with calls, visits, handling the runaround, the delay, the return call that never comes, and the unfulfilled promise of correction. Patience and persistence will almost invariably win. Remember this during the long days of conflict, aggravation, and frustration. You will learn what to do when the calls and visits have been fruitless and you have had it up to here. Whom do you write to with problems involving national brands? What agencies, both private and governmental, are available to help you in continuing the fight to a conclusion? Where do you contact them and under what circumstances? What may you reasonably expect from them?

Fourth, in the mind of everyone who is not a professional in the consumers' rights field, there is a question, "What do I say when I write? What do I include? Am I saying too much? Too little?" This final action section will include suggested forms for putting your complaint into writing. No form will cover all contingencies in an actual situation. These forms are meant merely as guidelines. But as you play things by ear in your daily occupation, in your shopping, in your personal life, with the common sense that you use in each of these activities, you must remember that the most important factor the consumer can display is adaptability—reacting to change and making the necessary corrections in his responses. So it must be with forms. Vary them to meet your particular case, without fear of betraying your cause. If your protest has merit, and if you follow the *general outline and idea* of a form, your own version will suffice.

Remember, you are not alone. The abuse of the consumer makes kin of us all. But the trouble with consumer's rights is the consumer. If you will fight back for as long as it takes, as hard as it takes, and go to the trouble of informing yourself on the way to do it, you cannot lose. If you are aware of the risks, and of the fact that you have been taken, and if you can put aside the shame of admitting that you've been taken and avoid shrinking from the battle, you will not be stepped on!

CHAPTER 2

——————— How to Complain ———————

Those who allow themselves to be stepped on in silence deserve it. Of course, it is easier to give in to embarrassment, play the martyr, excuse your own do-nothing attitude on the ground that the corporate establishment cannot be fought. Now, you will no longer take things lying down; you will fight back! You will complain! MAKE UP YOUR MIND TO IT THIS MINUTE.

However, when it comes to complaints, some types will work better than others. Learn the rules. If you know them so they are part of your own unconscious personality, you won't have to hesitate or think before speaking. You will know. You will win.

Most of your complaints will be decided and settled at the very first stage—the one many people are afraid of—the direct confrontation between you, the consumer, and the store, manufacturer, or craftsman who has made such shoddiness your problem. This step, which should be made as promptly as possible after the transaction, may be broken down into two parts: the phone call and the personal visit.

The phone call is usually made first, and to the store, not to the manufacturer. The seller is usually more interested in retaining your patronage than a national organization is, and quite often his reputation in the community is important to him. By the nature of business, he must be more sensitive to your complaint, and he may even assist you, should this prove necessary, in complaining to the manufacturer.

In contacting the store, do not be surprised if, as often as not, you get a runaround, spend hours on the phone, are referred from one to another. Be persistent! Disgust and giving up only perpetuates the victim psychology that used to be yours. Besides, keep a written list of all these things. There will be a day of retribution.

The first and most important rule is to speak to the right person. If service is the problem, ask to speak to the service manager, or if the problem is with a product and does not involve service, the sales manager. Always ask for the manager, not just someone in the department. To speak to someone without authority is to waste your breath and beg for a brush-off. Don't ask for the person who handled the transaction; he or she is usually just interested in the cover-up. To get quicker service, call first, even though you know you'll have to bring the product in.

When you speak to someone, take down his name and make sure, by the way you repeat it slowly, that he knows you are writing it down. Pinned moths tend to worry, and—who knows?—even be more helpful. Besides, this information will be important if you ever get to the letter-writing stage.

Keep it short. Babbling brooks are fine, but not if you expect to get any satisfaction from a busy manager.

Speaking clearly (don't mumble through stage fright or nerves) tell the manager: (1) who you are (2) what you bought (3) approximately when, and (4) what is wrong with it.

"My name is Ellen Miller. I bought an electric tray from you last Thursday. There's a short in the tray and all we get are sparks.''

If haughtiness is the immediate reaction, an honestly expressed fear might be stated, not as a threat, but as a reminder of consequences.

''I'm just worried that a fire will start and somebody is going to be seriously hurt.''

''I'm just worried that if the leak continues, all of the new furniture will be ruined, and who will pay for it?''

''I'm just worried (fill in your own fear; he'll get the message).''

Remember, be subtle—no threats, no promise of consequences and/or a lawsuit. Let his or her imagination do a little work. The listener didn't get to that position by being a dummy.

Don't wait for the full unwinding of a brush-off. ''Well, we'll have to check into it. We'll call you. Etc., etc.'' Let the person at the other end of the telephone know what you expect—once again, subtly, tactfully, but no less firmly. Include a suggested time limit. ''May I expect a man here today to fix it? At what time?''

Notice the way that question is phrased. You are obviously waiting for an answer. You are also, though polite, intimating by your firmness that a put-off, a negative answer, will leave you unhappy enough to do something about it.

Then wait.

There may be a pause after your request and the normal tendency is to fill the void by adding another sentence or more onto your demand/request. Wait. When the person on the other end hears nothing, the psychological compulsion will require him to speak. Sometimes you will be lucky and the other party will agree that someone will be over at 3 P.M. that day. Don't count on it.

Being fairly lucky means that you will get a counter offer. "Sorry, we can't make it today. We'll have someone there in the afternoon tomorrow." Don't count on this either.

The usual response will be the put-off. "We'll call you as soon as we know when we can get someone out to you," or "There's a waiting list for repairs and we'll get to you when we can."

Don't accept this. A commitment is what you want. Don't hang up with a mumbled thank-you, feeling the same old frustration. Hang in there.

"So you'll be here today?"

Of course, this is not what he said, but he hasn't been able to brush you off and the pressure is building up in him too. Keep taking it step-by-step, with questions that demand a yes or no answer.

"What, not today? So you'll be here tomorrow?"

"Not tomorrow? Then surely on Wednesday?"

Human nature, at one point or another, tends to crumble in the face of a sustained attack, and you may get your "yes" to one of the alternatives. If you do, repeat the appointment so there is no question about the nature of the commitment.

If *no's* are constant, if the person grows growly in irritation, or if a firm statement is made that there can be no definite commitment, assume a firm voice and demand to speak to that person's superior, or whoever has the power to make a definite commitment. It might be wise at this point, before nasty words fly, to repeat the person's name, as if just checking, so that there will be second thoughts on his part before lashing out.

"Well, now, Mr. . . . uh, Reynolds, wasn't it? . . . I would appreciate speaking with your superior or anyone else there that *can* give me an answer to my questions. I intend to find out why a customer can't get service."

Sometimes you are told that someone will be over next Thursday, but they can't say when. The obvious problem is that you may have to wait around the entire day. Try to pin the promiser down, if not to a specific hour, then to a morning or afternoon, or find out if you may call the morning the repairman is due, in order to narrow down the interval in which he may be expected.

Sometimes you cannot even get an approximate date, despite all your maneuvering. Try to find out how long it generally takes, because if you are not serviced within that period of time, that will be another weapon to use at letter-writing time.

Let's face it. All of the above hints are merely ploys that experience has taught some of us over a period of time. They are not guaranteed to work, the world being the way it is, but you stand the best chance of getting satisfaction if these tactics are adopted.

The second step in the direct confrontation stage, the personal visit, follows along similar lines of conduct, and may even be used at once, without any telephone calls, depending on the proximity of the place of business to where you are.

Remember the rules.

1. Speak to the owner, manager, or person in charge, and persist until you get to that person.

2. Get the name of the person you are speaking with, and make sure he knows you are making a note of it.

3. Keep it short.

4. Keep it clear (organize what you are going to say in your own mind before you enter the place of business).

5. Convey only the relevant points (no arguments, no insults, nothing about what your spouse said, etc.). State who you are, what you bought, when you bought it, and what's wrong with it.

6. Don't permit evasions. Pin the person down by giving him one alternative after another as to when something will be done about the situation.

7. Keep quiet after each demand, thus forcing a reply.

8. If this person can't satisfy you, demand to see a superior, or a person who can satisfy you.

9. Don't worry about your persistence being obnoxious. To paraphrase a famous baseball player: obnoxious people finish satisfied.

10. One extra item is involved in a face-to-face confrontation. Some people come in with a hang-dog attitude, fearing to interrupt such important business personnel. Nonsense! Adopt an air, not necessarily of arrogance, but of impatience. You are the person who has been aggrieved, and your time is certainly as valuable as theirs. Be cranky.

Make a notation, when you get home, of each conversation you had, when, with whom, what was said, and what was promised. SAVE IT.

PUTTING THE COMPLAINT INTO WRITING

The next stage involves letter writing, and this, too, is broken down into two steps. The first letter is to the seller; the second is to the manufacturer, where applicable.

The first rule in letter writing is to make a copy of what you write. You may write a letter in ink or by typewriter (though a typewriter is preferable since it is easier to read and looks more businesslike), but whichever method you use, keep a carbon or a photostatic copy. A separately written, conformed copy of the original will suffice, but it is not as persuasive proof that an original was actually sent.

Now, why keep a copy? First, minds play funny tricks, and no matter how sure you are that the fact of this outrage will remain seared in your memory forever, time has a way of dulling little details, such as when ordered, when delivered or installed, the price, who you complained to, exactly what was said or promised, etc. Second, it serves as a record of what was complained of if the complaint must be restated to the president of the seller or a parent company, or a consumer or governmental agency, or even, if it comes down to it, a judge.

Don't bother with a fancy filing system. You can surely spare one small drawer at home. Throw all such copies into it. Obviously, if a copy is needed, a certain amount of rummaging may be necessary, but you will be sure to find it.

It has been the experience of many consumers that all claim letters should be sent by *certified mail, return receipt requested*. This is similar to registered mail, but costs less. Sending a letter in this manner may be far more expensive than by ordinary mail, but it pays in results. People have a tendency to treat mail they must sign for as much more important than the letter the postman drops in the mailbox. It is regarded as almost a semi-official piece of correspondence and will probably find its way to the desk of a much higher echelon than would otherwise handle it. You know they received it, and they know you know they received it, when they received it, and who received it on their behalf, and the lower echelons, at least, will have visions of lawsuits dancing in their heads.

What is the procedure for taking this simple step? If you live too far from a post office to get there regularly, one trip will suffice. The beauty of certified mail is that, with the proper amount of postage affixed, it may be deposited in the usual mailbox. Check with the postal clerk as to its cost, so that you will know for the future. In addition, he will give you a number of two sets of forms. The first is a fairly small white paper with a numbered stub attached, which also serves as a receipt from the post office (when mailed at a post office) of mailing. The second is a larger card which is affixed to the rear of the envelope and will be returned to you bearing the signature of the person who received the correspondence on behalf of the seller. Have the clerk show you what spaces are to be filled in by you, how to place the card on the back of the envelope, and where to affix the attached numbered stub from the small white sheet on the face of the envelope. It's much easier than it sounds and you should learn the entire process in no more than three minutes.

On the bottom of the letter, and on the front of the envelope, write: "Certified Mail, Return Receipt Requested." Do not bother paying additional postage for the "show address where delivered" service unless the seller has moved, and do not bother spending money for the "deliver only to addressee" service.

After the letter has been sent, staple the balance of the small white paper to the copy of the letter you have just sent. When the signed return receipt comes back, staple this also to the copy of the letter. Thus, your letter and proof of sending and delivery are all together, ready for production when required.

To whom should the letter be written? That depends on whether this is your first letter of complaint for this transaction, or whether you have been previously ignored and want to apply more heat.

If this is the first letter, write to the top man in the firm. You do not have to know his name; an address of "President" with the name and address of the firm following it will usually be sufficient. Going directly to the top is not only good strategy in your own case, but will serve to alert the very highest management that the lower strata of employees is not responding to the needs of the customers. Furthermore, examples are legion where a letter sent to a top executive and referred to a lower level for disposition is acted upon promptly. One never knows when that executive will casually ask for the disposition on that letter he sent along, does one?

If the problem involves a large manufacturer, the addresses of most corporations may be easily obtained from business directories or other reference works at the local library, *Standard and Poor's* being one of the best of such sources.

The letter will, in effect, include those points that you have learned to make by telephone or in person, but this time they are in black and white. There will be extras, as explained below, but this is by way of supporting evidence or to show the continuation of your grievance because of the company's failure to remedy the situation.

Be not humble; be not arrogant nor overly angry.

In the sections that follow, dealing with specific complaints as to specific products, services, or situations, there are suggested sample forms that will apply to many situations. Obviously, a single form will not cover the problems encompassed by a sofa that was torn when delivered, and an airline reservation that was not honored. However, most letters will have certain basics.

The complaint letter should contain:

1. Your name, address and phone number.

2. The store where the purchase was made and who the salesman was (even if only by description).

3. Date of purchase or installation.

4. What the product was, by name, price, serial number, model, etc.

5. Representations made to you (if not denied, this will lay some foundation for belief that what you say is so).

6. The problem.

7. Whom you have complained to so far and what was promised.

8. What was done or not done to remedy the situation.

9. How you have been inconvenienced and/or damaged.

10. What you request by way of remedial action (repair, replacement, refund—but nothing outrageous).

11. Copies (never the originals) of any supporting papers, such as bills, letters, etc.

Usually, you will get some sort of response, probably far more satisfactorily than from your conversations. However, let us assume that you either received no reply, an unsatisfactory reply, or that your letter is not answered within a reasonable time. The Blockbuster is then in order. The postage may make it somewhat expensive, but the results are often worth it.

A letter similar to the first one should go out to the same person or corporation as before, once again certified mail, return receipt requested, but this time with two additions. The first one is innocuous, and should merely be a reference to having sent a similar letter and whether a reply was received or what type of reply was received.

The second addition to the letter is the Blockbuster. At the bottom of the letter, in the lower lefthand corner, write, "CC" (meaning carbon copies) and indicate to whom you are sending such copies, one under the other. Incidentally, don't be ashamed or embarrassed. You should actually send the copies and attached documents to the individuals or organizations you are listing. These copies need only be sent by ordinary mail. Don't worry about being regarded by the sellers as a crank. In this day of Consumer Power, cranks seem to be given preference in the resolution of problems, if only to sweep them under the rug and prevent them from getting some activists or politically or publicity-motivated committee or organization down on the seller's neck.

Who should receive copies?

1. If your complaint has been with the store on a brand item, send a copy to the manufacturer. The maker may actually put pressure on the store.

2. The nearest Better Business Bureau office. They do not handle complaints about price, nor do they rate products, but they do deal with misrepresentations, unfair sales practices, and improper service.

3. Your local Chamber of Commerce.

4. Depending upon the severity of the situation, your senators, the congressman of your district, and the President's Office of Consumer Affairs.

5. The pertinent federal, state, or local government agencies or officials.

6. Voluntary consumer groups, such as Consumer's Union and Consumer Federation of America.

7. Does your local paper or TV station have a consumer reporter? Write to him.

You are surely asking, at this point, who do I write to? Where? Who handles what? These questions will be fully answered in succeeding chapters.

As a warning, even these remedies may not work, especially in the case of fraud. You may want to write letters addressed directly to the action organizations, and these are also covered in succeeding chapters.

CHAPTER
3

———— How to Obtain Help ————

Let's assume, to this point, that the worst has happened. You have either been ignored, insulted, sneered at, or have met with bland refusals. In some of the situations, let us further assume that you firmly believe that you have been swindled. Luckily, consumers are not friendless today.

There are two basic groups designed to assist you. Some are effective and diligent, some not, but they are all worth a try. The first group is comprised of governmental agencies, on a federal, state, and local level. Many overlap in their responsibilities.

The second group is composed of private agencies. Some of these are truly independent and exist for the sole purpose of protecting, advising, and alerting the consumer. The rest of them are industry-sponsored monitors, most of which are truly motivated to act on your behalf so as to maintain the reputation of a particular industry, instead of being mere apologists and cover-up artists.

The general discussion in this chapter is not designed to be the prime source of whom you complain to in specific situations. Each of the chapters that follow deals with specific problems, and the specific agency or agencies to contact are listed therein. Should a problem arise that is not covered in these chapters, however, you should have a knowledge of the broad spectrum of helpers that blanket the field and their general areas of responsibility. The addresses of each of the agencies discussed in this chapter are to be found in Appendix B.

On the federal or American government level, we have the following:

1. *Federal Trade Commission.* This group deals with deceptive and false advertisements, product labeling, unfair business practices, swindlers, warranty complaints, and similar matters. It also has new powers to arrange for the return of your money. Word that the FTC is on a tradesman's trail will often motivate him to adjust your complaint.

2. *Interstate Commerce Commission.* This agency regulates movers and public carriers, including trains and buses.

3. *Food and Drug Administration of the Department of Health, Education and Welfare.* They keep a weather eye on foods, drugs, cosmetics and medical devices, quacks and medical frauds, and hazardous household substances. The agency also ensures good water, food, and sanitary facilities on trains, planes, and interstate highways.

4. *The Chief Postal Inspector of the United States Postal Service.* He handles complaints about the multitudinous varieties of the use of the mails to defraud, of hazardous mail, and the flow of pornography.

5. *Office of Consumer Affairs,* the Director of which is the Special Assistant for Consumer Affairs to the President of the United States. This office analyzes and coordinates all federal agencies engaging in consumer protection, handles consumer complaints directly, and gives special attention to those pro-

grams aiding the needy, the old, the under-advantaged, and minorities. It also will refer complaints to a proper agency. Remember, there is quicker service on complaints that filter down from the top than on those that buck their way up from the bottom.

6. *Civil Aeronautics Board.* This agency has a specific Office of Consumer Affairs, and handles complaints concerning scheduling, advertisements, rates, bookings, and all other passenger-related problems of the airlines.

7. *The Department of Agriculture.* While this organization is not specifically designed to handle individual consumer complaints, it has the authority to issue orders banning deceptive or fraudulent practices in the marketing, distribution and/or labeling of fruits and vegetables. A little pressure from it may sometimes go a long way in ensuring the settlement of your complaint.

8. *Federal Communications Commission.* Many radio and television stations will take whatever advertising they can get, thus abetting all forms of fraudulent or deceptive hard-sell ads. This agency monitors the stations, investigates individual complaints from the public, including those of rates, practices, or service—but only after the complaint has first been made to the station.

9. *Office of Interstate Land Sales Registration of the Department of Housing and Urban Development.* This agency deals primarily with abuses in land sales, usually consummated from afar, by mail or other fast and hard-sell practices. It requires registration (including a multitude of details) from the promoters, and may initiate criminal and civil suits, should you become a victim of such an abuse.

10. *Department of Justice.* Although this Cabinet-level organization handles cases of violation of laws enacted for consumer

protection, primarily as referred to it by other governmental agencies, such as the Federal Trade Commission, the Chief Postal Inspector, the Food and Drug Administration, etc., it can't hurt to add it to any list of those who are being informed of your complaint, and may be just what is necessary to put that final bit of pressure on your seller–enemy.

11. *National Highway Traffic Safety Administration.* Primarily, this agency can help you with regard to cars that you may have problems with. The group is charged with the duty of seeing that all cars manufactured after January 1, 1969, conform to federal safety standards and similar regulations. It is armed with injunctive and inspection powers plus the power to fine civilly, up to $400,000. A seller's awareness of your letter of complaint to this agency may very well change an attitude.

12. *The Employment Standards Administration of the Department of Labor.* This office may sometimes help you with wrongful garnisheeing of your salary, if you are engaged in an industry that involves interstate commerce.

13. *Social and Rehabilitation Service.* This agency deals primarily with the aging, including their consumer problems. While it probably cannot help you directly, its duties are to strengthen and assist state and local agencies connected with the consumer problems of older Americans, and should be notified if your problem falls within its jurisdiction.

14. *Consumer Product Safety Commission.* One of the latest gladiators in the field, dealing in good part with the safety of products, for example, toys.

15. *Department of Housing and Urban Development.* This is quite often a source of information as to the reputation of a home improvement contractor, so that you may be warned in advance. Incidentally, it is better to contact the local office, since it knows the operators in its own district. You may find

the location of the nearest local office by checking in the telephone directory or consulting with your bank.

On the state level, in each of the 50 states, there is at least one agency—usually either a Consumer Affairs agency or a subdivision of the State Attorney-General's Office—that is specifically designated to handle the complaints of the consumer. Although they may be overworked, a surprising number of claims are either attended to, or in-depth inquiries are made. Many of these agencies are also designed to provide the information necessary to avoid problems. (Appendix B gives two separate lists: where to write and what numbers to call in each state. Although addresses and phone numbers change almost overnight in this burgeoning field of consumer protection, up-to-date information may be easily obtained from your telephone directory, or the mail will be forwarded to the new location.)

If your state is not listed, write to the Attorney-General of your state at your state capital, and it will be referred to the proper authorities.

Most of these offices, especially those connected with the various Attorney-General agencies, concentrate on claims of fraud. These are difficult to prove, as it is usually the word of the buyer against that of the seller. The more written corroboration or verification you have, the better—including copies of all contracts, correspondence, and so forth.

The Banking Department of each state, located in the capital, usually deals with problems involving your relationship with a bank, but also where you have been charged what you suspect to be an excessive credit fee. A few states even handle claims involving sales finance companies, and a simple letter or phone call to the Department will give you the answer as to whether the Banking Department of your state will investigate such a complaint.

Problems involving insurance, overcharge on credit insurance involving a debt, and similar matters, should be referred to the Insurance Department of your state, located in your state capital. *Warning:* Eastern State laws are much stricter and grant greater powers for regulation and action upon your complaints than the easier-going Midwestern states. Still, even in the West, it is worth a try.

There are many agencies on the state level that perform duties similar to those of federal agencies, and that are not hampered by any questions of whether the offending seller is engaged in interstate commerce. They all bear similar names, some with slight variations, but a letter addressed to such an agency at the state capital is sure to reach the proper hands.

For instance, there is the Public Service Commission. Primarily dealing with utilities, able to call them to account and take up specific injustices with them (including problems involving your gas, electric, and telephone service), this agency should be advised of your complaint, whether you have already informed federal authorities or not. They also quite often deal with problems involving public transportation.

In each state, there is something akin to a Department of Agriculture and Markets, also located in your state capital. Complaints as to food, adulteration, improper weights and measures, and fraudulent packaging of products, should be addressed to this agency.

Charity frauds are the province not only of the Attorney-General of the state, but what is, in each state, actually a Department of Social Welfare.

Most states have Departments of Health that not only have overlapping jurisdiction as to food complaints with the Department of Agriculture and Markets, but also deal with water supply, swimming areas, sanitation conditions at public and restaurant facilities, and the like.

On the city, county, and local level of governmental agency concerned with the consumer, it is difficult to cover the broad range of what is available. One writer has estimated that there are over 100,000 units of government in America—the federal government, the 50 state governments, and the rest local entities. And all with different names.

Still, the same problems must be dealt with everywhere. Read your telephone book. If in a city, look under the city listings, if a county, check the county listings. You will soon find names similar to the type of agencies that follow, and these are the ones to communicate with about your respective problems. If you make a mistake in which agency to write to, standard operating procedure will dictate that your complaint will be forwarded to the correct authorities. If this produces no results, call the Office of your Mayor to be directed to the correct agency.

There is usually a Department of Markets, dealing with food, weights and measures, mislabeling of goods offered for sale, service stations, and garages.

Departments of Health abound, dealing with sanitation, adulteration of products, etc.

In most cities and towns, there is some agency which, in effect, is a Department of Licenses. If your reading of the telephone book turns up anything like this in your locale, and if problems develop with a repairman or some other mechanic, call the Bureau and find out if such activity (such as a TV repairman) must be licensed. If so, direct your complaint to this agency. In addition, this is the authority that keeps a hawk eye, through licensing, on "going out of business" sales and "fire" sales, a very likely place to be handed the short end of the stick. Complaints will quite often result in hearings, and, upon threat of further action, many a recalcitrant merchant or artisan has been known to settle quickly.

Fraud requires a strong hand to stop it, and make restitution possible. If fraud is involved in your complaint, do not hesitate to go to your local District Attorney or Municipal Attorney. Bring all supporting documents. Almost every such office has a complaint bureau where you may be treated brusquely and rushed through a process. Don't let this disturb you. The time of the office is limited to getting an outline of the facts, not listening to the equivalent of *War and Peace*. Rest content in the knowledge that the office also has no time to fiddle-faddle with wrongdoers, but has developed a means of dealing with similar problems quickly.

Do not be overly selective in sending complaint letters. If you are going to strike, do it with a hammer, advising all the agencies on all levels that might help you in your plight, rather than risking selection of what might be the weakest office to enforce your rights. Keep trying, never quit. Never be silent. Even big government's inertia is afraid of today's consumer.

There is no one form that will apply to all notices to government agencies. The chapters that follow, dealing with specific problems facing the consumer, have forms of complaint letters aimed straight at that target. However, the following may serve as a guide for those situations not covered. This, of course, assumes that you have already sent a complaint letter to the seller of products or services.

(Name of Agency)
(Address of Agency)

Gentlemen:
   It is my understanding that you handle complaints of consumers with regard to (nature of problem; keep it *very* short). I am having a

problem with my (radio, roof, etc.), which was sold to me (repaired, etc.) by (name of firm), located at (address of firm).

After failing to obtain any satisfaction whatsoever, I wrote to them and am attaching a copy of the letter, outlining my complaint. I have received no response (or, they advised me they intend to do nothing to remedy the situation). I would appreciate your making an inquiry so that I, as a citizen, will have some recourse. Thank you.

Very truly yours,
Ellen Miller

This need not be sent by certified mail, return receipt requested, but by all means, retain a carbon or photostatic copy of the letter. The world will not come to an end if you change the wording of the letter to fit more naturally into your style, but *make sure you keep it short,* and when you say you are enclosing a copy of a letter or letters you have previously sent, be certain that you actually do so.

HELP FROM NON-GOVERNMENTAL ORGANIZATIONS

There is no end to groups who claim to help the consumer. Most are sincere. Some are industry-financed, but this does not mean that they are necessarily whitewash emporia. Many are set up to police their own industries, to keep the good name of the overwhelming majority of honest dealers, and sometimes to forestall government's taking a hand in policing unregulated fields.

However, some are in it for the battle, to promote their own murky purposes, and devil take the individual.

Most can help, and should be advised of the problem affecting the sphere they encompass, no matter what the organization's motivation.

First and foremost is the Better Business Bureau (See Appendix A for offices). It serves as a source of information on the reliability of merchants and it handles complaints based upon misrepresentation and fraud. It will not appraise or recommend products or dealers, nor does it handle complaints about prices. It will not give legal advice or recommendations. It will either give you the facts before a transaction, so that you can make up your own mind, or will act on your complaint. If the local bureau decides that the matter you bring before it falls within its jurisdiction, it will ask you to write, sending you a standard form to fill out in most cases. Quite often, if you have a legitimate complaint, the B.B.B. will help you to settle the problem quickly, although it has no police or legal powers. The B.B.B. often works closely with government agencies and newspapers plus TV and radio stations in an attempt to stop fraudulent practices and advertising. It will not take up a complaint unless you have attempted to settle your problem with the dealer first.

While the Better Business Bureau is sponsored by the businesses of the community, without regard to specialty, there are many industry-sponsored organizations that must be kept in mind when your immediate antagonist does not rectify the wrong done you. For the addresses of these organizations, as well as all others mentioned in this chapter, see Appendix C.

Major appliances in general—Major Appliance Consumer Action Panel (MACAP).

Retail stores—National Retail Merchants Association.

Discount stores—National Association of Discount Merchants.

Furniture—Furniture Industry Consumer Advisory Panel.

Furniture manufactures—National Association of Furniture Manufacturers.

Interior Decorators—National Society of Interior Decorators.

Interior Designers—American Institute of Interior Designers.

Mail order problems—Mail Order Action Line Service.

Credit and billing problems—Association Credit Bureau.

Door-to-door sales—Direct Selling Association.

Jewelry—Jewelers Vigilance Committee.

Travel Agencies—American Society of Travel Agents.

Fabrics—International Fabricare Institute.

Veterinarians—American Veterinarian Medical Association.

Hospitals—Joint Commission on Accreditation of Hospitals, or American Hospital Association.

Nurses—American Nurses Association.

Nursing Homes—American Nursing Home Association.

Doctors—American Medical Association, or your County Medical Society.

Dentists—American Dental Association, or your County Dental Society.

Podiatrists—American Podiatry Association

Surgeons—American College of Surgeons

Lawyers—American Bar Association.

❋ Large corporations, including automobile manufacturers, also have central complaint bureaus. Many of these, too, are listed in Appendix C. ❋

Then there are the consumer advocates. For centuries, the accent has been on "caveat emptor," or "let the buyer beware." Today, the entire orientation of our society is in the other direction, that is, "let the seller beware." These consumer advocate organizations have taken their proper place in the forefront of this movement, after having spent years crying in the wilderness.

Many of these organizations and much of the activity of the remainder are involved with comparative shopping advice (which car is safer; is the more expensive brand Y any better than the cheaper brand X, ad infinitum).

But we all get "stuck" sooner or later, and many of the agencies listed below are designed to act upon your complaint. Which agency best suits your need? Succeeding chapters on individual complaints list the choices you have. If your situation is different, or you still remain in doubt, check with your clergyman (most of them do have. at their command information as to which agency would help you); your Community Welfare Council, listed in your telephone directory as Community Council, Community Services Council, Council of Social Agencies, or some similar name; your local newspaper; your congressman; the Consumer Action Department featured by many local newspaper, television, or radio stations, or your union.

Still, there are some outstanding national consumer organizations that you should feel free to contact. (First see if they have a local chapter by checking your telephone directory.)

The Consumer's Union is a non-profit group that tests products, publishes the monthly *Consumer Reports,* warns of the latest frauds (in law or in fact), and will use a variety of pressures in a case that looks as if it would affect a number of citizens. By and large, however, it is an educational organization. Should it become interested in your problem, however, its intervention will bear a great deal of weight.

The Consumer Federation of America is a clearing house for information to local consumer groups, and should be contacted with your specific complaint. It is well-known and effective.

Other general consumer's organizations that may be contacted are:

National Consumer League—not only works for consumers, but for better labor conditions.

National Consumer Congress—this is one of the most recently formed groups, arising out of the meat boycott of 1973, and it is attempting to prove it has muscle.

Center for Auto Safety—one of the prime movers in forcing the wave of auto recalls, this group forwards your complaints to the appropriate agencies and recommends the most effective, direct action.

National Consumer Federation—a group with much union backing, composed of representatives of most of the national and local consumer groups. It, too, would refer your complaint to the proper and most effective agency to handle your specific problem.

International Consumer Credit Association—some help may be derived by advising this agency of credit abuses perpetrated against you.

National Safety Council—handles, in part, complaints as to unsafe products.

Family Service Association of America and *National Foundation for Consumer Credit* (check if there is a local office in the telephone directory)—voluntary community groups that advise on a wide range of topics, including contracts, what to do if your salary is garnisheed, and how to handle the unpleasant consequences of debt.

Consumer Association of Canada—for our north of the border friends.

In many cases, if all else fails, your local Small Claims Court may be your best bet, although collections of judgments rendered by this Court are scandalously small. To find out how to make the best use of this "remedy," write to the Small Claims Study Group.

Take the time to fight, and never concede defeat. These are the two main ingredients of building the winning habit, the feeling that if you refuse to allow yourself to be stepped upon, you will not be stepped upon. Make the time to write as many letters or make as many calls as it takes to win. Don't give up because one agency turns you down, or another cannot help, or a large corporation holds you beneath contempt. Whether hard or easy, eventual victory and vindication are sweet.

CHAPTER
4

───How to Be a Smart Buyer───

PICKING THE SELLER

Most men will want to know with whom they are playing poker before getting into a game. Hardly a woman would dream of going to a doctor who had not been given rave reviews by one of her friends. Why is business different? After all, the jungle of commerce is the tradesmen's turf, not yours. Don't you think you should have as much information as possible on a prospective opponent before engaging in combat for your dollar?

Small purchases obviously do not require such scrutiny. For anything beyond small change, however, do not be taken in by plausible salesmen, glittering fixtures, and the like.

First, learn to rely on your *common sense*. If you are excited because the price is so low that the seller must be losing money on it, don't worry; he's not losing any money on it—you are.

We are not talking about the salesman's pitch, the seller's inflation·of the merits of a product. That, unfortunately, is the acceptable norm in our marketplace. We are not concerned here with quality, whether an item is a good buy, or even the wisdom of a purchase. You're an adult, and all your adult life has been spent making decisions of this type. No, we are speaking of those who go beyond the bounds of legitimate commerce, those who hold out the beautiful lure, the appeal to greed, the come-on, to those poor souls who always seek something for nothing, the impossible bargain. Notice how these poor souls always get burned because of their own cupidity, but never blame themselves? Common sense.

Do you make a practice of buying from street vendors? They may be legitimate, but let the warning sign flash before your eyes. To whom will you complain tomorrow? Buying a watch or radio, or any other expensive item, from a street vendor is issuing a license to steal. Perfume pitchmen, quite often, will sell you bottles of colored water, no matter how well wrapped. Some shady jewelry stores have sidewalk solicitors, which common sense brands as a trap. If you plan to buy jewelry from a store, don't consult the appraiser that the seller recommends—get your own. Common sense.

Reputation is your second clue to honesty or reliability. If you're dealing with a contractor or mechanic, he surely should be willing to give you the names of several (not one) previous customers, so that you can check what sort of a job he does and how he lives up to an agreement. Don't be embarrassed. If he is legitimate, he will gladly do so. If not, you had better learn about it right now. And if you get the names, don't forget to call the customers. Merchants in your town should know the contractor (the lumberyard, paint and hardware store, etc.) and how good his name is.

If the seller is a store, it is quite probable that one of your neighbors, friends, or acquaintances has dealt with it. Does the store live up to a deal? Does it stand behind its merchandise? Does it give an unrealistic delivery date, and are there troubles with delivery and installation? Is the store known for its hidden charges which turn a "bargain" into a "full retail price plus" deal? How long has it been in business? Questions may be endless, but quite often you will find the general impression of a friend whose judgment you trust will outweigh all questions combined. By all means, go and use your own judgment, but forewarned is forearmed.

The third guidepost, especially if the prospective purchase or proposed contract involved is a substantial one, is to consult with the Better Business Bureau nearest you. On contacting the B.B.B., do not expect any advice on value or service, only information on complaints that have been received, the firm's reputation for reliability and honesty, any reports of unadjusted delay in deliveries, information on how long the company has been in business, and other similar knowledge. This is valuable information, indeed, but expect no conclusions. It is up to you to decide from the facts.

THE ORDER

Now, let's get down to specifics. You're out to buy, the money ready in your hot little fist, you've checked on the best and most reliable places to buy, you're aware of your rights generally, nobody is going to take advantage of you, and the buying fever is rising. Cool it.

The watchamacallit you see is gorgeous, true, but what's the story? The price? Warranty? Delivery? Little things like that.

GET IT ALL WRITTEN DOWN. It may be called an order, purchase ticket, contract, or something else, but the seller will write down as little as possible so as not to bind himself, should the unforeseeable occur. It must strike you, then, that it is to your benefit to have as much in writing as possible. Don't be impatient to complete the deal, or let the salesman's impatience to get to the next customer deter you from insisting on a fully set-out agreement. It is only at this one point in time that you can really guard yourself. And get a copy!

Never sign any blank contract. Would you sign a blank check for a stranger?

Certain questions should be kept in mind when discussing the prospective purchase with the seller. When will it be delivered? If a definite date can be given, make sure it is put into writing. If the item is damaged or doesn't work, or is unsatisfactory to a reasonable person, under what terms may return be made? May the item be returned for cash? Credit only? Exchange only? Can it be returned at all?

What is the price? Are there any other charges? What about delivery charges, credit service charges, and similar charges? How much for these items? Write it down, please, mister. Does the price include installation? Building and town fees? Is there a credit for a down payment indicated on the paper? What about a trade-in?

An honest salesman will usually not avoid a direct answer, nor will he usually refuse to put a promise into writing. An attitude of either deviousness or you-must-trust-me calls for a hasty retreat from the obvious dishonesty.

THE WARRANTY

Who makes good on the item? The seller? The manufacturer? Both? Fine, let's see the warranty or guarantee that goes with it. (A warranty is a promise of what will be done should something be or go wrong with the product.) No, Mr. Salesman, don't tell me about it, I'm sure that it's in writing. Ah, here it is.

Don't be rushed into a cursory reading or no reading at all of the warranty. Money doesn't come that easily and you had better check it out NOW.

Any reasonable warranty should cover the following:

1. Is it the retailer or manufacturer who stands behind the product?

2. If repairs are needed, will they be made in your home? Must you return it to the seller, the manufacturer, or a designated repair agency?

3. Does the guarantee cover the entire item or just certain parts? Against only certain risks?

4. Who pays for labor?

5. How long does the warranty run for?

6. What do you have to do? Notify in writing? Do you know where to send the item? What if you move?

You may be sure that unlike the contract, the longer the warranty is, the more loopholes it contains to render it worthless. Go for the simple, no-escape warranties.

In fact, a law enacted in 1975 provides for two types of warranties: a "full" or a "limited" warranty. Both must make clear to whom the warranty flows; the products and parts covered and those that are not; what the one who issues the warranty will do in the event of a defect or breakdown; who pays for what; the time period of the offer; how long repairs or replacement will take; how we may invoke the benefits of the warranty; and what remedies we have if the warranty is not lived up to.

Most full warranties bar any charge for transportation of the item to a place of repair, and provide for repayment or replacement if the item cannot be fixed after a reasonable number of attempts. They apply to anyone who has the product, instead of just the original purchaser, so the gift you received would be covered.

Anything less than these standards would constitute a limited warranty.

Furniture is almost never guaranteed by either the maker or the seller. If a salesman blithely assures you of a guarantee, challenge him to write it on the sales slip and have him *sign the slip*. "Lifetime" guarantees on furniture are usually a phony come-on, and should signal a hasty exit.

Refrigerators usually have a warranty for the first year, and the refrigerating system itself is usually covered for an additional four years. Check the warranty.

The above few items are meant to bring this point down to specifics. If what you are about to buy costs more than a negligible amount of money:

1. Don't be rushed.

2. Insist that all essential elements of the agreement and all promises be put into writing.

3. Read the warranty slowly and thoroughly.

Look, they want your sale. Do what's best for you and be sure. The time to make sure is *before* you sign your name on a paper, not after.

PRICE

Although the question of price may seem to you to be part and parcel of your agreement to buy, even respectable sellers use gimmicks to add that little extra to the price, and thus to their profit. Do you have any idea how much money dribbles out of your purse or pocket during the course of the year by these innumerable penny-losses? But you can protect yourself.

This is not to say that a store cannot re-price items. Such a practice is perfectly legal in most localities and is often based upon increased costs to the store. No, there are more devious methods of robbing you.

Scales are often the chosen weapon of your enemy. Most large stores today have customer scales where you can check the amount allegedly contained in pre-packaged, pre-weighed goods. Use them! Differences of 50 percent have been found, which occurred "by accident." If the man behind the counter is doing the weighing, don't let a scale be used that you cannot see. In many communities, "blocked" scales are illegal.

No matter how small the quantity of a weighable item, insist that it be weighed. The difference in price is better in your pocket.

While watching the scale, make sure it is set so as to start at zero, and double check that it stops before the counterman whips it off and quotes you a "rule of thumb" price—usually *his* thumb added to *your* item's weight.

How valid are the advertised prices? If the price (for instance, in a supermarket) is stated on a sign in the window, a display, or a newspaper or flyer ad, but is not stamped on the item as well, watch it! There is a good chance that you will be charged a higher price at the check-out counter, the regular price, not the "special" price.

Most areas have laws on the books with regard to accurate price labeling, but the variety of such laws run into the thousands and defies description here. "Made to sell for X dollars" means nothing except trouble for you.

If you see tiny print in an exciting ad, take the trouble to read it. If it states, as is quite often the case, special conditions that you consider unreasonable, for instance, "this offer is good on Thursday only, between 7 and 8 A.M.," pass that store by. Another gyp joint has given itself away.

How high is up? There is a type of firm that uses range advertising. "ONLY $7.95—and up." Up to what? You had better have second thoughts before you wander in and become just another victim of a con-artist salesman. This is true not only for products but for services. Many jurisdictions have strict rules against this very type of unfair advertising.

Other examples are too numerous to mention, for the fraudulent mind of man is wonderful in its complexity and scheming. Reducing salons that advertise saunas, show saunas in the accompanying picture, proudly trumpet a price of $9 per month, and then, when you have made the commitment and the trek, levy an extra charge for the sauna, are one example.

Have you heard about the photographers who advertise a picture of your cute baby for $1, and then, presenting you with the 5 × 7 you have chosen, tell you that the $1 was for a wallet size and this one costs $4.95? They're around. The come-on price again.

Does the price cover installation? Service charge?

Buyer beware, indeed.

Well, you've caught someone fooling around with a scale or the price. What do you do?

The best defense is to stand up to the seller right then and there. Submerge your fear of making a scene. Insist that the item be reweighed. Call faulty scales or mismarked merchandise to the attention of the manager, and demand "how come," preferably in a loud voice. In short, if you are dealing with a halfway respectable organization, insist on your rights then and there.

The odds are, however, aside from supermarkets, that you may be dealing with sharpies. Above all, don't justify a do-nothing attitude in your own mind by the fact that if they could have been stopped, they would have been long ago. Not true. Sometimes an accumulation of gripes will cause a governmental agency to take action, and sometimes, in truth, no one had the nerve to complain before.

With prices, you are dealing mostly with a local problem, so forget about federal authorities. Also forget about letters to the firm; it will do no good.

Write to your local Better Business Bureau, County or District Attorney, and to either the equivalent of your State's Department of Agriculture and Markets (if a question of weights or packaging is involved) or to your State, City, or County Agency that deals with consumer problems. These, you may recall, can be found by looking at the phone book for your city or county listings, and noting an agency that is usually self-descriptive as representing the consumer, or by calling the Mayor's Office for the name and address of the appropriate agency. As for state consumer agencies, see Appendix B.

A sample letter addressed to this problem might read as follows: (Subject to the modifications involved in your own problem.)

Department of Markets
(Address)

Gentlemen:
I would like to register a complaint with you about (name of seller) located at (address). It is the only such store near my house, and I would have hardship shopping elsewhere.

There are two scales in the store, and neither is set at zero, but at some weight above that. On (date) of this year, I bought a package of Brillo which was advertised in the paper this week by them for (amount) but which was marked at a price 15¢ more than advertised when I went to the store, and which they insisted I pay.

On one occasion, their advertised "special" (give details) was not available in the store, though I arrived there on the morning of the first day of the sale, and no "rain check" could be obtained from them for a time when they would have the item.

I feel that they are defrauding the public, myself included, and I ask that you make an investigation.

Thank you.

Very truly yours,
Ellen Miller

cc: Better Business Bureau (Appendix A)
    State Agency (Appendix B)
    District Attorney

Don't dawdle either. Go right home and write that letter of complaint while you are still burning, and before you get cold feet.

Remember, the name of the game on television may be "The Price is Right," but when they are playing with your money, the game should be called "The Price Had *Better* Be Right."

DELIVERY PROBLEMS

Some ahead-of-his-time-consumer once pointed out that there is many a slip 'twixt the cup and the lip. How many have never heard of or experienced a situation where you just can't get delivery of what you've ordered or bought; or, if delivered, it arrives damaged or in non-working condition; or, if what arrives is in fine shape, it is not what you ordered?

This is one of the most frustrating problems you will experience. Quite often, the seller had promised you the moon to make the sale, will already have all or part of your money, and consequently has no real motivation to rectify the situation. Vague promises are quite easily made by the seller in these situations, as is shifting the blame.

Non-delivery or outrageously delayed delivery feeds on your desire for a product you have emotionally committed yourself to owning. Many times, the seller has no real wish to delay delivery, but his acquisition of the item from the manufacturer cannot be guaranteed. In his haste to make the sale, he will promise a delivery date he knows he cannot possibly comply with.

Since furniture is the number one source of non-delivery complaints, let us use this field to see what may be done. You may thereafter adopt similar tactics with regard to your own purchase.

As has been stated, your first line of defense is inquiry and the sales agreement. Even in the furniture industry, famous for delivery delays, there are certain firms (quite often widely advertised) that are notorious for their conduct.

Check with your neighbors or, if this produces no results, consult with your local Better Business Bureau office (Appendix A). This type of information quite often forms the backbone of one of their files on a store. Complaints of rash delivery promises, inordinate delays, or non-delivery will be furnished and then you have no one to blame but yourself if you deal with the offending firm. Of course, if people haven't taken the time to complain to the B.B.B., or if, as happens in the best of organizations, there is a slip-up and you are not apprised of complaints the local office has actually received (this situation is very rare), then you have to protect yourself.

Don't be so excited with your purchase that you forget the protection afforded you by the sales agreement. One of the most important factors is: "When will I get it?" If you get a runaround—even orally—on this vital question, forget it unless you *must* have the item and don't care when you get it.

Salesmen, however, are usually smooth enough to indicate some delay but will pooh-pooh it, and will advise you confidentially that they will expedite it just for you. Smile knowingly and press further. When? You must know, because you have plans of your own (which your tone indicates are your own personal affair).

Finally, you will get a date. Orally. Ask for it in writing on the bill of sale, contract, or whatever the firm calls it. A hurt look will usually appear on the salesman's face, and a line to the effect that his word is to be trusted (or that it is not possible to give an exact date) will be trotted out. Don't accept it.

Be patient, but insist that you must have it in writing to protect both of you. You may even be willing to accept a later date as an outside date, but it must be in writing.

Realize that such a date is not that legally binding, unless the statement is written somewhere on the contract "time is of the essence," a magical legal phrase meaning no extension of time will be granted. So why insist on it? The two reasons for the date are that (1) the seller only has a "reasonable" (comparatively short) time after the stated date to live up to its agreement or you can start making it hot for him, and (2) a date on an agreement will give you something to hang your hat on if and when you complain to an outside agency. A further hedge is to put down the least possible down payment. If you are eventually stuck, why be stuck for more than is necessary? This will also serve as an incentive to the seller to have the goods delivered so that he can obtain the rest of the money.

There will come the day when the delivery date has arrived, and you cover your shyness and/or embarrassment by saying to yourself, "Gee, I don't want to push them. I'll give them another two weeks before calling." Wrong. Push. As Leo Durocher observed, "Nice guys finish last." Firms tend to get rid of pests by taking care of their complaints as soon as possible.

When you call, be firm, be the injured party. Put them on the defensive and don't be content with speaking to the switchboard operator.

You will then hear (as you will in subsequent calls) the sad song of the furniture seller. The store blames the manufacturer; the manufacturer blames the component supplier, or the union (strikes, etc.), or even acts of God.

Keep calling. Don't get tired and don't give up. Of course, you may compromise if you are desperate enough. If prompt delivery is a must, you may want to accept something that is in the warehouse or that you have seen in the showroom's stock.

If you can wait, and you refuse to be stepped on, the day will come to start making complaints to others besides the seller.

Letters of complaint (or carbon copies of the same letter) should be sent to the Better Business Bureau office nearest your home; the Federal Trade Commission and the Office of Consumer Affairs in Washington; the pertinent industry organizations and consumer groups, with, of course, a carbon copy to the seller. If an inordinate amount of time has passed, and the seller turns ugly, refusing to refund your deposit or give you any idea when to expect delivery, a letter to your local District Attorney or County Attorney, carbon copy to the seller, will be in order.

Let us continue with our example of delay of furniture delivery. The Furniture Industry Consumer Advisory Panel should be one of the groups to be notified, but one problem with this group is that if the product is manufactured by a non-member, the letter may only be referred to the manufacturer. However, the list of other addressees on the copy of the letter received by the seller should indicate you mean business, and will usually produce results.

A sample letter might read as follows:

Furniture Industry Consumer Advisory Panel
209 South Main Street
High Point, North Carolina 27261

Gentlemen:

I wish to complain about non-delivery of furniture that I ordered seven months ago.

On December 28, 1975, I bought a bedroom suite of furniture from (name of firm) located at (address). I am attaching a copy of the sales agreement I received at that time. Please note that I paid $150 as a down payment, and that the company promised to make delivery by February 18, 1975.

When no delivery had been made by February 25, I called the store and spoke to the manager, Mr. Johnson. He told me that they expected the shipment any time, and that the factory, the Leroy Company of Winston-Salem, North Carolina, had had a strike and there were some delays. I have been calling every week since then, but now the manager refuses to speak to me and the switchboard girl says if and when they get the shipment, they will call me. They have refused to return my deposit.

This is obviously not the best advertisement for the furniture industry or for the businesses in my community. I am mailing copies of this letter to the appropriate authorities and organizations, and request that action be taken immediately.

Very truly yours,
Ellen Miller

cc: Seller
Better Business Bureau (Appendix A)
Federal Trade Commission (Appendix B)
Office of Consumer Affairs (Appendix B)
National Association of Furniture Manufacturers (Appendix C)
Manufacturer
District Attorney (see your telephone book)
Other consumer groups (Appendix C)

Of course, this is just a suggested form. Change it around to fit your own facts, but don't get much more long-winded. Remember, no diatribes, no threats, just the facts in as few words as possible. Don't forget to send out the carbon copies (or photostatic copies) to those organizations listed after "cc:" and don't forget to attach a copy of the sales slip to *each*. Keep a copy of the letter and the original sales slip for yourself. While nothing is sure in this life, the odds are that something will pop and you will get satisfaction, either because of the edginess of the firm when it sees who is being notified, or by action of one of the organizations.

If the time period for delivery of the item is much shorter, and there is little question that you will not receive the merchandise (such as lost film), you are in trouble if you have already charged payment on your credit card. Don't hesitate to notify the credit company immediately. You may not be charged. A recent change in the law as to merchandise ordered by mail (if not C.O.D.) gives you the option of cancellation if the order is not received by you within 30 days.

The next problem is goods received in a damaged condition, or that won't work once installation has taken place.

Most deliverymen have a slip with they extend in such a manner that you cannot read it, and brusquely tell you to "sign right here," or if they are a bit less brutish, they will tell you to sign just to show receipt. They will attempt to rush you so you will not bother to either inspect the goods or look at what you are signing. Don't fall for this.

Take your time and inspect the goods. Take your time and read what you are being asked to sign. If you are met with a growl or mutterings that the deliveryman has no time to waste on this, face him down and tell him to get his boss on the telephone because you want to find out just why he can't wait, or tell him to take it back. He will do neither, but will subside and grumble.

If you discover damage, either tell him to take it back, or make note of the damage on the receipt. Even if you don't get a copy of the receipt to keep, the firm cannot claim you acknowledged that the merchandise was delivered in perfect condition. That, friends, is what was printed in small type above the line you were being asked to sign on. If you were to make a claim afterward, it would be flaunted in your face—or the judge's face, if you had to sue. You are paying out a good deal of hard-earned money. Take those extra few minutes to check things out.

And don't accept the oral excuse that although it might be

damaged, just sign for it on the line and someone will be there tomorrow morning to fix it. Come, now!

Sometimes blemishes are missed on a first inspection through excitement or for some other reason. Pay by check, if possible. Checks can be stopped, and many firms will then do something about the condition. You would otherwise be ignored if they already had your cash.

Call to confirm delivery time and make sure you are at home on that day. If you are not, if you trust the doorman of your apartment house or your neighbor to accept the item, it might be signed for and the money paid over without a proper inspection.

With damaged or defective merchandise, many firms will pick up, exchange, repair, and make good with very little prompting, but there are plenty of those other firms that make a book such as this necessary. The runaround prevails. "You signed for it that it was received in perfect condition." Or "Sorry, lady, our repairman only can get to your area once in a while, and we don't know when he is going there again." Or "Sorry, it's not our fault. Contact the shipping company." Or "Are you sure you didn't break it yourself?"

Strike fast and hard. Use the same form of letter as for a non-delivery, but change it to show delivery and what was wrong with it. Send copies to the same sort of organizations. Unlike non-deliveries, however, address the letter to the seller, and send the carbon copies to the others.

A sample letter with regard to a damaged washing machine might read as follows:

(Store Name)
(Address)

Gentlemen:
    I wish to complain about a General Electric Washing Machine I bought from you on (date). Attached is a copy of the sales slip. It

was delivered on (date) and installed by your mechanic. I signed for it without trying it because your man said that if there is anything wrong, the company would send somebody there immediately to repair it.

After he had left, I tried it and not only didn't it work properly, but my basement floor was flooded. I called your service department right away and spoke to a Mr. (name). When I told him my problem, he first insisted that I must have done something wrong, and then said he couldn't possibly tell me when he could get a repairman to my house. I called him again for the next few days and he, in effect, hung up on me.

I ask that you do something about this immediately and I am notifying the organizations listed below so that investigation may be made as to whether fraud is involved.

Very truly yours,
Ellen Miller

cc: General Electric Company (obtain address from librarian who will have access to this information or booklet that came with machine)
Better Business Bureau (Appendix A)
Federal Trade Commission (Appendix B)
Office of Consumer Affairs (Appendix B)
District Attorney (telephone book)
Major Appliance Consumer Action Panel (Appendix C)
Other consumer groups (Appendix C)

Amazingly, one of the worst damaged-goods offenders is the Post Office, not because of their procedures, but on sheer volume, and the fact that the sender and his packaging methods are not under the control of the Post Office.

For those who send packages rarely, and are thus unfamiliar with the safest packaging procedures (sending many items in wrapped shoe boxes, orange crates, etc.), the Post Office sells padded bags in various sizes, and also fiberboard boxes (which still require cushioning inside with newspapers).

Another safety factor in shipping via the Post Office is "special handling." This is faster and safer than parcel post, and cheaper than first class mail.

Let us assume the worst has happened and your parcel has been damaged. Your local Post Office should be consulted, but don't expect any real satisfaction unless the item was insured. Instead, complaints should be made in writing to the United States Postal Service, Consumer Affairs Office, Washington, D.C.

"We now come to the situation where what is delivered is perfect—but it is not what you ordered or you thought you purchased.

Of course, not all substitutions of merchandise may be remedied. Earl Wilson, the columnist, reported the case of a man who had purchased tickets to a show that had a scene in which an actress went topless. Unknown to him, a theater party that night also had tickets for the same show and had requested the management to arrange for a cover-up. After the show, a bitter letter of complaint was fired off by the irate ticket holder, but to no avail.

A much grimmer cause for complaint prevails when you have seen an item in a shop window far from your home, the salesman brings out a sealed box, implying that this is fresh merchandise, and when you open the box at home it is different, cheaper, and not at all what you bought. The moral remains: have the salesman open the box in the store, check it out, then have him reseal it. Do not be put off by his petulant expression or sneer. If he makes too big a fuss, demand to see the manager. Watch how quickly your previous requests are complied with.

The usual case of a switching of merchandise occurs as a result of human failure. With the departmentalization prevalent in many large firms today, which creates a chasm between order-taker and order-filler, a certain number of orders will not be filled correctly. The order is not written up properly before being sent to shipping (due to inexperienced or sloppy sales personnel or simple human error) or once it gets to shipping, careless personnel, the rush of business, or any one of several reasons will cause the wrong carton to be pulled out of the wrong bin or section and sent to you. On occasion, the seller may be out of an item, a color, or a size, and so the nearest thing to it will be forwarded, rather than go through the entire tedious process of contacting you with all its attendant complications.

Remember, much of this occurs because businesses have come to expect the consumer, as a rule, to be lazy or to shrink from making waves, or, at the most, to place one abortive phone call (where you hang up while waiting endlessly for the right party to complain to).

The first line of defense is to demand that the carton be opened while the deliverer is still there and to send it back (no other way) if it doesn't match what you ordered, or if you have not been so fatigued by the wait for the item that you will accept practically anything.

Let's be honest. Most times you won't do this, being harried at the moment with other things, or so excited that you finally received the item, or because the carrier is an independent parcel delivery service.

If the item is small enough and the seller is close enough, bring it back immediately. Don't dilly-dally; unless the store thrives on a reputation of satisfaction rendered to the customer, it will rarely pick up the item (too much red tape). If the parcel is large or the distance far, by all means call—but do not rely on that alone. Place your position on record in writing at once, certified mail, return receipt requested. A sample letter might read as follows:

President
(Name of Store)
(Address)

Gentlemen:
   On (date) I bought a card table and set of four chairs from your store. A copy of the sales slip is attached. A parcel service delivered it today and when I opened it, it was not at all what was ordered. As can be seen from the order, I had bought and paid for a Gardex table, olive color with four matching chairs. I received a blue Cardex table, but the chairs were white. Naturally, this is not acceptable. At the present time, because of home responsibilities, I cannot bring it back, and I ask that you have the items picked up immediately and the proper items delivered. If you do not have the proper merchandise in stock, I want an immediate refund.
   I called your store immediately after receipt and spoke to a Mr. Clark in the department where I had bought the table and chairs, but he was most unhelpful, insisting he couldn't help me, and he didn't know to whom I might speak who could help me.
   I think you will agree that this raises a question about your store's reliability, and I ask that this matter be attended to at once. I live in a three-room apartment and this unwanted item is taking up space for which I must charge you storage, should this proceed to Court.
   In the meantime, I am letting the organizations listed below know of this matter, should I be required to proceed further.

Very truly yours,
Ellen Miller

cc: Your local Better Business Bureau Office (Appendix A)
    Local Chamber of Commerce (telephone book)
    State Consumer Agency (Appendix B)

   Follow up, if necessary, by phone and letter. The important point to keep in mind is that you have not lost until the moment when you decide to quit.

CHAPTER
5

———————— **Food and Drugs** ————————

When dealing with the purchase of food or drugs, you are usually dealing (in the absence of fraud) with a large store, whether it is a market or drug store. In this case, "big" is not necessarily the equivalent of "good." In a more dignified manner, these stores can be as much like hucksters as anyone selling merchandise.

In such a situation, your first line of defense is self-defense. Look, examine, think, be suspicious—or suffer the consequences. If you wear eyeglasses, don't forget to bring them with you when you go shopping, for some of the most enlightening tip-offs to your own well-being are in small print on labels.

It has been estimated that prices may vary as much as 400 percent in the various drug stores, and that mark-ups over wholesale by the pharmacies can vary from one to the other as much as 750 percent. One answer is comparison shopping. After all, no laws are broken by any store that charges more than the next store, and if you don't defend yourself by knowing what the going rate is, you are taking money out of your own pocket.

Many communities now require a listing in the store of the most popular drugs, and what the charge is. Don't be bashful; ask your druggist if your community requires this, and, if so, ask to see it. Since the probabilities are that you would only be interested in one or two items at a time, the process is painless. Many chain pharmacies (Walgreen's, for example) are extending this practice to all of their stores across the nation, required or not.

Eyes should be used to see more than price. Let's discuss what can be seen before we discuss what can be done. In many communities, "open dating" of perishable foods is required, and rightfully so. Eggs, bread, cottage cheese, cakes, cream cheese, milk, are just some of the items that bear the last day of sale or use on the wrapper. If you don't bother looking, don't bother complaining. Also look for recommended storage conditions. Don't become confused—pick those items with the *later* date stamped on them, not the earlier one. The earlier dated items are the older items.

Many stores seem to have a knack of running out of "advertised specials" before you—or anyone else—can get to the store. Don't be switched onto something else; and don't just give up. Usually the advertisement is in a flyer. Clip out the ad, go to the courtesy desk or the manager, and have him endorse a "rain check" on the ad. That is, he will okay the purchase for the advertised price at a time later than the end of the offer. You will almost never encounter difficulty in having this done for you, and it only takes a moment or so.

Speak up in a drug store when ordering medication. Demand that the brand name and the strength be placed on the label. Many druggists assert that this shouldn't be done for a variety of reasons, but don't believe it. If you are told the practice is illegal, ask them to show you where it says so. Usually, such bluffers fold.

"Fortified" foods deserve your scrutiny. If the claim is made, a recent ruling says the label must list the nutrient content. How much are there of the seven vitamins? How much of minerals, fats, carbohydrates, proteins, calories? The label must now bear the truth, unless the item contains less then four nutrients. Don't get hooked on a fancy description (for fancy prices) unless the label bears it out.

High-flown names on packaged meats also mean nothing. Also, watch the chopped meat. If you take it home and it remains its "fresh" reddish color for a prolonged time, "color" is just what was added. Take it back for a refund or replacement. If they know they're caught, and you are willing to protest to the proper authorities, watch how obliging the manager becomes.

The government is now prosecuting with a vengeance your right to know about other foods.

Bacon: All curing agents must be listed. The package of bacon must show a full representative slice, not just a bit of meaty edge.

TV dinners: They must now contain at least three foods, one of them including a substantial portion of protein. The label must describe all three, in descending order of weight (although the amounts need not be listed.)

Packaged main dishes: Many of these imply something that is not contained therein. "Pepper steak," right? So where's the steak? All actual ingredients should now be listed, and if something is to be added, it must say so.

Delicatessen: Hot dogs that aren't made of beef can't be called "beef hot dogs." If other animals are used, the hot dogs must be so labeled. This is not to say that other things cannot be added, but the label must indicate this (up to 15 percent poultry, water, curing agents, sweeteners, soy binders, etc.). If the meat is labeled "frankfurter," "salami," "baloney" and so forth, the muscle part of the beef must be used. Otherwise, it must be designated with the word "by-products" or a similar term.

Use your glasses to read the label on bottled water also. If certain governmental standards are not met, the label must state, "Contains excessive bacteria," or "Contains excessive chemical substances." All right, you ignore the warning on cigarette packages, but for your family's sake, don't miss *this* warning.

Watch for juice products that have funny names. Any non-carbonated juice product that falsely appears to be a natural fruit or vegetable juice because of color, flavoring, or labeling, must have as part of its name a statement that the product contains no natural juices.

Rules are being made to help the ladies, too. It has been estimated that cosmetics cause more than 60,000 injuries per year, from rashes to eye damage, from burns to hair loss. Now, since March 31, 1975, cosmetics must list all ingredients except fragrances and flavors. Once you know what you are allergic to, the rest is easy.

You've used your eyes and your common sense; you still have problems with the product. What do you do?

Let's start with canned goods. Although the government advertises some of the instances of poisoned canning it uncovered, many are not revealed because of the fear of starting a panic, or you may have missed that little article in the paper, the one day it was printed. If a can is bloated or doesn't look right, *don't* give it the "taste test." Survivors are few. And don't go by brand names. "Oh, this firm is so big, the product must be all right, or they would have taken it off the shelves." That's almost as dangerous as the taste test. Save the can, save the label, save as much of the product as you can, and bring it back to the store. Presumably, the seller is interested in avoiding lawsuits, and will inspect the rest of its stock on the shelves. However, first write down the details, including the distributor's name at the bottom of the can (to report to the authorities, as we will see in a sample letter).

After contacting the seller, do yourself and your fellow citizens a favor and report the occurrence to the authorities. Far and away, the most important agency to report to (whether you have obtained satisfaction from the seller or not, but especially if fair dealing has been denied you) is the Food and Drug Administration. It is growing more important each year in protecting the consumer concerning foods, drugs, and cosmetics. It investigates and fights adulteration, short weight, and mislabeling. True, the FDA will not act on your specific problem (to obtain redress for you), but your complaint will be promptly investigated and you may be sure that such a seller will tread the straight and narrow thereafter. *Note:* When you write to the FDA (you may phone, but you are better off to put it in writing), a copy sent to the seller may result in rather hasty action by the seller to satisfy your complaint.

Write to the nearest field office of FDA, or to headquarters (see Appendix B.) In your report, use the following guide.

Your letter should include:

1. Your name, address, telephone number.
2. What seems to be wrong.
3. A description of the label on the product, including any code marks that appear on the container. Many cans have them embossed on the lid.
4. The name and address of the store where purchased.
5. Date of purchase.

In addition to sending a carbon (or photostatic copy) to the store, send copies to the manufacturer, packer, or distributor shown on the label.

Furthermore, save whatever remains of the product (or even the empty container) for your doctor or possible FDA inspection. Hold any unopened container of the same product bought at the same time. If any injury is suspected, see a doctor immediately.

With medicines, you usually know something is wrong because of an unusual reaction. Call your doctor; don't worry about appearing foolish. You are playing with your life. The medicine itself may be all right, but the deleterious action may be a side effect. This, too, should be reported to your doctor (who should, in turn, report it to the FDA and the American Medical Association. If you believe he won't bother, you should do it.)

FDA is also interested in veterinary products, such as drugs, animal feed, pet foods, and such. Notify your vet if an unexpected reaction, injury, or death results, and he will notify FDA if he feels the product is responsible.

A suggested sample letter to FDA might read as follows:

District Office
Food and Drug Administration
U. S. Department of Health, Education and Welfare
(Address)

Gentlemen:

I would like to make a complaint with regard to certain food I recently purchased.

On (date) I bought two cans of pork and beans at the (name of store), located at (address), and paid 69¢ per can. When I got home, I opened one of them and found that it tasted terrible. I then noticed that the other can was swollen. I was sick for two days.

Both cans had labels with the brand name "Carleton House Pork and Beans," with the distributor listed at the bottom of the label as Fillmore Distributing Corp., Talmadge, Pennsylvania. I had already thrown away the lid of the open can, but the closed can has the numbers "14726-55" on its lid.

I brought the open can back to the market, but the manager didn't seem to care. He just said, "Well, these things happen," and offered me a refund. He didn't even offer to pay my doctor's bills.

I am afraid that if the same situation exists with regard to the other cans of this product, others will be made sick. Please investigate this. I still have the closed can.

> Very truly yours,
> Ellen Miller

cc: (Store)
    Fillmore Distributing Corp.

You may notice the notation at the bottom that indicates carbon copies are being sent to the store and the distributor. Do not forget to mail these copies, and don't forget to keep a copy for yourself.

In addition, the Food and Drug Administration will immediately follow up on claims of "quackery." People love magic cures and there is nothing to feel ashamed of if you have been bitten by such cures. After all, the men who push them are past masters at the art of selling to the public.

Some types of quack ads involve false health claims as to drug or food supplements; instant relief from colitis by the use of certain laxatives that only tend to make matters worse; drugs that "melt away" fat without dieting; lotions that would sprout hair on a billiard ball, in effect, and will cure a man's baldness; "face peels" that will restore that youthful look, but are usually harsh chemicals that may cause permanent disfigurement; and, worst of all, cures for cancer.

There are very definite signs of a quack product. Does it claim to be a "secret remedy?" Is it sold door to door, or by traveling lectures conducted by a "health advisor"? Is the claim made that the product's proponent is battling the medical profession which is trying to suppress this wonderful discovery? A sure sign is if the product is being promoted by a sensationalist magazine, faith healers, or a "crusade organization" of laymen.

These are the warning signs; don't ignore them. Let's assume, however, that you have been bedazzled and have been taken for some of your good money or, even worse, that the product has made you sick.

In this case, don't even bother advising these pushers. Notify the Food and Drug Administration (Appendix B) and the Better Business Bureau Office nearest you (Appendix A). If you are made sick, see your doctor and inform your County Medical Society (the address is in your telephone book). If the advertising and/or sale took place by mail, notify the United States Postal Service (Appendix B).

Other complaints dealing with foods, drugs, or cosmetics may be made to other agencies, in addition to the Food and Drug Administration. The Federal Trade Commission (Appendix B) should be advised of suspected false advertising, while problems involving meat and poultry products should be addressed to the United States Department of Agriculture (Appendix B).

You may have a situation, however, where the product is made within your state and is sold only in your state. Under these circumstances, you should notify your State and Local Departments or Boards of Health. When it comes to sanitary facilities in restaurants, your local Board of Health is your best bet.

If you have problems involving pharmacies and drug quality and price, your State Board of Pharmacy in your State Capital should be advised in writing.

In this field of foods, drugs, and cosmetics, as always, don't be on the defensive and don't give up—attack.

CHAPTER
6

———— Dangerous Products ————

There is, however, one aspect of the consumer's war where defense is more important than attack. If a product can harm you, perhaps kill you, your own awareness in avoiding injury or illness is infinitely more important than achieving satisfaction at a later time from the seller. Let us examine the innocent-appearing product that may endanger you and how to guard yourself.

A roll call of items found to be dangerous would encompass practically every activity known to man—or worse, to children. Toys, butane lighters, gas ovens, space heaters, ski boots, TV sets, autos, children's sleepwear, lawn mowers, power tools, mattresses, cribs, toasters, children's car seats, dishwashers, and aerosol cans are just a random sampling of the traps that await you.

Of course, many of the items that might be classified as dangerous have already been discussed, such as drugs and items pushed by quacks.

Some might say that if an item is dangerous, it will be recalled. As in the case of cars and TV sets, this is not necessarily so. And if you haven't read about the recall on other items (small appliances and canned goods, to mention just two), who will pluck them out of your house or pantry before you are hurt?

The key is alertness and informing yourself. One of the greatest protectors you now have is a new agency, created on May 14, 1973, known as the United States Consumer Product Safety Commission, which has the authority to set mandatory safety standards for thousands of consumer products, or ban products that are unreasonably dangerous. It has the right to impose civil penalties and commence criminal prosecution, which is a far greater deterrent than a slap on the wrist, such as a cease-and-desist order. The cease-and-desist order, in effect, says that even if the offender is caught in the act after numerous people are hurt, the company is only required in the future to stop doing whatever it was doing.

The Consumer Product Safety Commission (hereafter referred to as CPSC) has been extremely active in the field and, as part of its basic research, has published a *Consumer Product Hazard Index,* consisting of 369 product categories, with associated types of injuries. A listing of the top 15 is included at the end of this book as Appendix D.

The CPSC has also issued a *Banned Products List* which is obtainable free from the agency by writing to it in Washington, D.C. 20007. It might be wise to enclose a stamped, self-addressed envelope with your request.

However, you cannot rely on a product being banned, or standards for safety in manufacturing being set, or the moral responsibility of large chain stores, to fully protect you. Many stores still have banned goods on their shelves, eager to unload them quickly so as to avoid a loss; thousands of units of products made before any standards were set await your unsuspecting purchase, and five of the largest chain stores have been found to still be selling, each to a greater or lesser degree in each item, dangerous children's sleepwear, lawn mowers, power tools that are not double insulated, mattresses, and toys. So beware.

It is part of our heritage and culture to be alert for those items that may be dangerous to children. More than six million injuries each year are related to children's products.

Let's first look at the toy situation, wherein some 700,000 injuries per year occur (not including bicycles.)

When shopping for toys in general, some simple rules should be observed.

1. Do not choose a toy you secretly would like to play with; find one suitable for the child's age and development.

2. If the packaged toy has a warning that it is not intended for children under a certain age, believe it!

3. When buying a toy for an older child, remember that a younger sibling or friend may lay hands on it, and avoid toys that would be dangerous for such infants.

4. If the toy includes fabric, check to see if there is a label reading: "non-flammable," "flame retardant," or "flame resistant."

5. For stuffed toys and dolls, see if the notice indicates the item is washable and/or made from hygienic materials.

6. If you're buying a chemistry set or an electric toy for an older child, show him or her what to do. Don't let the child remove or replace electric components.

7. Toys have a habit of coming apart in the most dangerous way possible, so check from time to time for developing sharp points, jagged edges, or loose small parts.

An additional set of rules is necessary for infants, toddlers, and young children. Make sure that the toy is not so small that it can be swallowed. It should have no detachable parts that can lodge in the throat, ears, or nose. It should not be easily breakable into small or jagged pieces. The original toy should have no sharp edges or point, or be put together with easy-to-get-at straight pins, sharp wires, or nails, as in dolls. Avoid items of glass or brittle plastic. If the child is young enough to instinctively put things in the mouth, make sure the item is not painted, or that it bears the label "non-toxic."

Some baby bouncers, in which the toddler bops around on what is, in effect, a walker, are dangerous and may pinch or amputate tiny fingers or toes. Look for three things on such items. The "X" part of the frame should have guards; spaces should be wide enough not to catch hands or feet, and spring coils should stretch no further apart than ⅛ inch.

Easily broken rattles constitute a clear danger, for the beads inside may be swallowed.

With regard to electrical toys, look for warning labels concerning hazards, and buy toys with safety plugs.

Toy chests have proved death traps for many children who become caught inside. Make sure the chest has adequate ventilation, no automatic locking device, a light lid, and that the hinges are not likely to squeeze or pinch fingers or feet.

More than a million bicycle and tricycle-related injuries are tallied in hospitals each year. For a tricycle, see that it is properly and tightly assembled, with free-spinning pedals. Double-check for sharp edges and rough metal surfaces.

For bicycles, the seat should be adjusted to such a height that the rider's feet can touch the ground on both sides. Watch out for sharp edges and projections, especially on a part the child would hit if thrown forward in a fall. Make sure the pedals have skid-resistant surfaces to prevent slippage when footwear or pedals are wet.

Watch out for toy balloon kits wherein the balloon is blown through tiny plastic straws. Children have choked on them, many of the ingredients are inflammable and some are toxic.

One of the most important rules with regard to toys for young children is to first remove AND GET RID OF plastic film packaging. Many a child has been smothered to death when its face or head has been covered by this clinging substance, or it has been swallowed.

More than 1500 toys have already been ruled unsafe and dangerous, but thousands more have gone undetected, and many of the 1500 are still on sale.

A child snuggles into a bed and is safe from the day's dangers. Right? Wrong.

A flammable fabrics act was passed several years ago for children's nightclothes up to size 6X, and has recently been extended to size 14. Ignoring the technicalities of the act, if compliance were assured you would have some measure of security. Don't count on it.

Read labels. Does the item ("such a bargain!") tell you that the product complies with the Flammable Fabrics Act? If not, forget it. Some responsible companies have gone beyond the minimum requirements of the law, and will state this, in effect, on the label. Give such an item preference, even if it costs a few cents more. After all, what investment in time and money, not to mention love and patience, have you already made in the child?

And if your child wears larger than size 14? Take nothing for granted in this field. Read the labels and save your child's life.

What if the goods have been hanging around on a dealer's shelf, and were made before July 29, 1973? There is no requirement that such a garment must be flame retardant. Read the label.

Lastly, if there is no label as to the nature of the material, avoid it like the plague.

Now, the clothes are safe. What about the crib in which the infant sleeps?

As of February 1, 1974, certain mandatory federal safety regulations went into effect to protect infants from strangulation, suffocation, falls, and other hazards, by regulating side-rail height, amount of pressure needed to unlock the side-rails, narrow slat spacing, and smoothness of finish. Labels will inform you of such compliance. Look for them.

However, the new law does not cover all of the hazards. Retailers may have pre-regulation stock on hand, and palm it off on the unsuspecting, non-label reading public. Beware of crib sales with no reason given for the sale.

Another hazard is the crib made of plastic. Though complying with flammability standards previously established by the government, these cribs go up in flames much faster than wooden cribs. Worse, burning droplets of plastic fly all over, spreading the fire beyond control.

To protect your child from the dangers inherent in both the new and old standard cribs, keep in mind the following safety factors:

1. Try to avoid plastic cribs.

2. Look for the label, which should say on both the crib and carton: "This crib is in accordance with new safety standards."

3. If you suspect that the crib you are buying is one of the old-standard ones, buy bumper pads with at least six straps, fitting around the entire crib.

4. Be sure the mattress fits snugly. If you can insert more than two fingers between the mattress and the crib, you are buying trouble.

Children's car seats are also dangerous, though new legislation is designed to minimize the risks. Be sure to inquire about safety features when you compare varieties.

Color television sets have proven a great problem in recent years. While new standards may be set that do away with many of the hazards, remember that this will not remove the fire and shock traps now sitting in your living room. The government, in past years, has only had jurisdiction over radiation emission from the set.

Even with regard to radiation, there is no automatic recall of dangerous sets. There has been some publicity in the media, but you may have missed it. Whether or not you suspect your set of emitting dangerous radiation, why take chances? Call the dealer you purchased it from, or the local branch of the manufacturer, to find out if your model number is on the danger list. If you do not receive a satisfactory response immediately, call or write the Major Appliance Consumer Action Panel (Appendix C).

The danger inherent in fire and shock from existing TV sets may be realized from the fact that in America today there are 115 million TV sets, 5 million more than the number of telephones. If even a small percentage constitute a danger, it can immediately be seen that the problem is substantial. Under "voluntary" industry reports to the government, there have been claims of such hazards present in 140,000 sets in American homes.

Fire hazard has been associated almost entirely with portable or table model color sets, while shock hazard spans the range of outstanding sets. Many portable TV sets are made of plastic, with the ignition point of such plastic being very low, the rate of burning being rapid, and the dense noxious resulting smoke capable of causing death from smoke inhalation.

Sets with an "instant-on" feature, stressing no warm-up wait, seem to be viewed with alarm by the experts as a possible cause of fire.

If you have been notified by the maker or dealer that your set has been recalled because of possible shock or fire danger, unplug it immediately (it may still be dangerous while just in an "off" state) and bring it to an authorized station for repairs.

If the set smokes or seems to heat up excessively while being used, unplug it and bring it in for repairs.

If your set is plugged into an outlet controlled by a wall switch, use the wall switch to turn the set on and off, thus reducing wear and tear on the set's on–off button. Don't continually plug and unplug the set when leaving the house or going to bed, because the power cords are built for stationary appliances, and a constant plugging and unplugging could damage the cord and increase risk.

The papers and television have been full of automobile recalls by the factories, but such recalls aren't always automatic. If you have a question whether your model is a potential death trap, send 50¢ to the Superintendent of Documents, Government Printing Office, Washington, D.C. 20402, for the *Motor Vehicle Safety Recall Campaign List*. If your vehicle appears on the list, return it to the dealer for repairs, or to the factory for correction.

Dishwashers and toasters are potential hazards. One of the consumer groups, the Consumers Union, in a rating study, has found that some makes can operate with the door open, releasing hot water and causing burns and eye injuries.

Aerosols are the current scare item, due to a tendency to explode when exposed to heat (or even strong sunlight) and cause a wide dispersal of inherently dangerous contents, such as drain cleaner, paint, and garden sprays. Improper use, through the failure of adequate warnings on the dispenser, have resulted in injury and death.

The difficulty in laying out a course of action for fighting back in this type of situation is the probability that, despite your caution, you bought the item and *have already been injured*. If the injury is even moderately serious, do not take things into your own hands. Consult an attorney immediately. This will usually not cost you any money because if your claim is well-founded, the lawyer may take the case on a contingency basis— that is, he will participate (to a reasonable degree) in any recovery of money for your injuries, medical expenses, loss of earnings, and other losses.

The consumer's war in this field is divided into three fields of attack.

1. If no injury has occurred as yet, but you want the purchase price returned and the product taken off your hands.

2. If the seller and/or manufacturer has refused to do anything with regard to your complaint of a dangerous condition.

3. Allied with the other two, if you are public-spirited enough (and you should be, considering the beating that you and other consumers are taking from the irresponsible manufacturer and seller) you should alert the proper authorities, so that others will not be hurt.

To quote another worthwhile campaign slogan: "The life you save may be your own."

In order to obtain repayment, redress, or repair, there is no question that you should approach the seller first, or even the seller and the manufacturer at the same time. The element of danger is now present and should be stressed. Under the circumstances and the present publicity dealing with dangerous products, you should receive a much faster and more satisfactory response than you would with a merely damaged article.

If you don't get fairly prompt action, start writing immediately—primarily to the action organizations, both governmental and private, with carbon copies to the seller and manufacturer. This will serve not only to obtain redress of your own grievance, but will alert those who must stop the danger to others.

Considering its responsibility for maintaining the safety of a vast array of merchandise, and its eagerness to perform the task (the chairman is said to have once worked all night on a problem, after receiving a letter of complaint) you can't go wrong in addressing most written complaints, in the first instance, to the United States Consumer Product Safety Commission. Certain problems must be referred elsewhere, and, with regard to certain other items, the CPSC has joint jurisdiction with other groups.

The CPSC has 14 field offices, in New York, Atlanta, Boston, Chicago, Dallas, Denver, Kansas City (Mo.), Los Angeles, Minneapolis, New Orleans, Philadelphia, San Francisco, Seattle, and Cleveland. It might be better, however, to write to the main office, Washington, D.C. 20007, and your letter will be referred and possibly acted on a bit sooner by the local office (Big Brother is watching).

The CPSC, among other things, has jurisdiction over toys, flammable fabrics, television sets, appliances, children's car seats, spray adhesives, children's sleepwear, lawn mowers, power tools, mattresses, health and safety aspects of shoes, butane cigarette lighters, ovens, bicycles, and a host of other products.

It appears to have concurrent jurisdiction (the best advice is to write to CPSC and send a copy to the agency or agencies having co-jurisdiction) with the Environmental Protection Agency, Washington, D. C. 20460, and the Food and Drug Administration (Appendix B) with respect to aerosol dangers.

The Food and Drug Administration and the Federal Trade Commission (Appendix B) quite often have concurrent jurisdiction over health and cleanliness products, such as bubble baths that result in infection and irritation.

All other complaints concerning dangerous foods, drugs, and allied products should be addressed to the Food and Drug Administration (Appendix B). This group has been active lately with regard to baby shampoos that contain bacteria and antibiotic ointments for baby skin rash that precipitate allergies and deafness.

The National Highway Traffic Safety Commission (Appendix B) should be notified with regard to claims about defects in cars and motorcycles.

Bets should be hedged. Copies of each of the letters to a governmental agency (with the bottom of the letter showing such forwarding of the carbon copies) should be sent to those who are in the forefront of the non-governmental agencies supporting the consumer.

The Consumers Union (Appendix C) is sincerely concerned and should be informed by carbon copy, especially with regard to dangerous items. It was this group that first broke the news on defective dishwashers that scalded people, although the government later pooh-poohed it. Copies of letters of complaint with regard to vehicles should be sent to Ralph Nader's Center for Auto Safety (Appendix C). In fact, a perusal of Appendix C will suggest other industry and consumer groups to contact that would be involved with your particular problem. Don't be afraid or lazy; send carbon or photostatic copies to everyone who might help.

Many of these dangerous products are advertised in magazines and other publications, some of them quite prestigious. The advertising media is not concerned with verification of the safety of the products advertised in their publications, although many publishers have offices that check out the claims actually made in the ad. In two recent examples, some of the best known magazines took advertising for lamps that had exposed contact points (resulting in shocks and possible fire,) and a TV antenna that was a shock hazard. These items were obviously hazardous except to those who made money from their advertisements. The CPSC has no control of such advertising media.

It would be helpful, therefore, if you were touted onto a product by reading about it in a publication, to send a copy of the complaint letter to the publication.

Publishers are nervous today about any adverse publicity forming the basis for governmental regulation and letters such as yours, possibly resulting in a threat to the manufacturer to have his advertising outlet closed, would probably help your claim. "Take care of it, settle it, we don't need this person making any more waves."

Once again, under the assumption that the danger or defect has not already caused an injury, and that calls and personal visits to the seller have proved unavailing, a letter in a form similar to the following would be in order:

United States Consumer Products Safety Commission
Washington, D.C. 20007

Gentlemen:
I wish to make a complaint about my (make of set) color television set that I bought on (date) at (name and address of store). I am attaching a copy of the bill of sale, showing the model number and the terms of sale.

On (date) the set started smoking heavily and then stopped playing. I called the service number I had been given by the salesman and when the repairman came around, he supposedly fixed it, but warned me not to keep too many applicances on at the same time, but wouldn't tell me what could happen. The next night, I felt the set starting to get hot and turned it off. I called the store and spoke to Mr. Adams, the manager, but he refused to take the set back. He said he could only send a repairman around after the set broke down.

Since then, I have asked around and found that fires have started in two other such sets, and I am afraid for the safety of my family.

I would appreciate your doing something about this dangerous condition, and I ask you to do anything possible to get the store or manufacturer to take the set back and return my money. Thank you.

Very truly yours,
Ellen Miller

cc: President, Manufacturer
President, Store
Better Business Bureau (Appendix A)
Consumers Union (Appendis C)
U.S. Office of Consumer Affairs (Appendix B)
Your State Consumer Agency (Appendix B)
Your State Attorney General (Appendix B)
Major Appliance Consumer Action Panel (Appendix C)
Any other consumer groups from Appendix C you may care to advise.

In looking over the list of carbon copy receivers, don't get panicky. Including the original to the addressee, and a copy for yourself, 11 copies would be needed in this particular case. You may think of the time and money to be spent in photostating (the best method for this number of copies) addressing envelopes, and postage, but how much time and money have you already invested in aggravating yourself over having been "taken"? Do it! Make the copies. Send them out. You can never tell which one will win the battle for you. Remember once again, you are never beaten until the moment you admit that you are.

"Dangerous products" constitute one of the few instances where it would be wise to complain *after* your satisfaction is obtained. If you saw your neighbor about to be hurt, and you had it in your power to save him, which of you would not do so? In writing a letter about a potentially harmful product, even though you haven't lost a dime, you are helping to save neighbors.

A simple letter is sufficient. In most cases, it will go to the Consumer Product Safety Commission; if it is not within the Commission's jurisdiction it will be forwarded. Let us take the example of the TV set referred to in the previous letter, and further assume that the store, upon the first occasion, immediately took the set back and refunded your money.

United States Consumer Safety Commission
Washington, D. C. 20007

Gentlemen:

I bought a color television set recently, the attached copy of the bill of sale giving all details as to the seller, model number, etc. On (date) the set started smoking heavily and then stopped playing. The store took it back immediately and refunded my money.

Since then, two people I have spoken to have said they know of fires arising from the use of such a set.

I call this to your attention so that a dangerous product on the market will be prevented from causing death or injury.

Very truly yours,
Ellen Miller

Please notice: No carbon copies, except one for yourself, and no frills. Put the information into the hands of those who can eliminate the danger.

Remember, with products that may prove to be dangerous, your personal inspection is your first and almost sole line of defense against death or injury. If there is doubt, don't buy it. The second line of defense, personal contact, writing, etc., is a far-distant second at best.

CHAPTER
7

—— Buying New and Used Cars ——

The purchase of a car usually requires more caution than most other purchases, simply because you are investing a greater amount of money. Investigation before investment is very much in order.

Let us first examine your defenses and attacking potential in buying a new car. As you know, most cars are sold by the manufacturers through independent middlemen—the dealers—some of whom may be guilty of sharp business practices, some of whom may be guilty of fraud or just plain negligence, but all of whom are astute businessmen, far more knowledgeable than you in the field of buying and selling automobiles.

It would be simple if you could just visit your nearest dealer and be assured of satisfaction. Unfortunately, this may not be so. Before you make a visit to any dealer, check his reputation in the community. Friends, neighbors, casual acquaintances, as usual, are your best sources of information. Back this up with an inquiry of the dealer's reputation as it may be reflected in the files of your local Better Business Bureau.

If you find a dealer with a poor reputation, but one who

seems to be offering a cheaper deal, you are practicing false economy. Basically, all dealers will offer you a similar price, within a range of a couple of hundred dollars. While this difference is not to be sneezed at, if you consider the total amount of money you are investing, there may be more important considerations.

In selling you the car, the manufacturer also gives you a warranty, this is, a guarantee that certain repairs on the car as well as replacement of parts will be made within a stated time period at no cost to you. It is rare for a new car to be sold in flawless condition today. In fact, in recent years, Consumers Union found that about one-third of all new car purchasers were dissatisfied with the vehicle's condition as received and—what is more important—a large percentage of this group was still unhappy after the authorized repair agency had allegedly attempted to correct the condition.

The new law concerning warranties applies to the purchase of new cars. American Motors has opted for a "full" warranty, giving you the right to a new car or refund should the defect not be repairable after a reasonable number of tries, but the others have only offered "limited" warranties. Though limited, the new law opens doors to lawsuits in state courts against the offending manufacturers, with the possibility existing that the car companies may have to pay the legal fees.

The trick, in other words, in selecting a dealer is to find one that will "do the right thing" in honoring your warranty, in making further service adjustments or repairs, and will not attempt to steal you blind (as only a few dealers have been known to do.)

While theoretically most makers' warranties are honored by all dealers who sell that make (the factory pays them for the work), in practice you will probably be at the mercy of the dealer that sold the car to you.

Keep all this in mind when selecting a dealer, but *still* comparison-shop.

You are probably all old enough and experienced enough to know about bargaining over the price of a new car and the value of the trade-in on your old one. Let us, however, examine some of the hidden and semi-larcenous tricks that you may be subjected to concerning price.

Federal law requires every car to carry a sticker listing the manufacturer's suggested selling price (subject to a great deal of downward revision by knowledgeable bargaining), cost of optional equipment attached to the car, freight charges, and dealer's preparation charges. If it is not on the car, demand to see it, for this is your only yardstick as to price. Many dealers affix the oficial list on the car, but also add a sticker next to the first one, with regard to added charges for items such as dealer-applied undercoating and waxing. You have a perfect right to refuse these extras if you don't want them.

Many times the dealer will insist that he is entitled to a five to twenty-five dollar fee for office, clerical, or dealer conveyancing, a fee for the paper work necessary in the sale. This is not an illegal charge, but it certainly is subject to argument. This is the very same charge that has always, until recently, been absorbed by the dealer as part of his normal cost of doing business.

Most contracts for the sale of a car permit an increase to be tacked onto the agreed price if the wholesale price (that is, the cost of the car to the dealer by the factory) should go up before delivery. This is reasonable, except for a couple of gimmicks you should be aware of. If the dealer asks for additional money on this basis, ask to see the *dated* factory-to-dealer notification or an article on the price rise in a recognized trade periodical, such as *Automotive News*. Furthermore, make sure that the dealer was billed by the factory for *your* car *after* the effective date of increase. If you are refused on these reasonable requests to see documents backing up the increase, you may be fairly certain that a small swindle is taking place. Refuse to pay the increase, demand your money back, and if you can get away without further trouble, consider yourself lucky. If you don't get your money back, write to the Dealer-Complaint Department of your State Motor Vehicle Bureau (only a few states do not have such a department) and also to your State Attorney General, and your local District or County Attorney.

The same remedy should be invoked if the dealer starts to give you double talk about the reappraisal clause contained in most contracts. This deals with the credit you are to receive for the trade-in of your old car. The claim will be that, since your old car is several weeks older than when it was initially appraised, it is now worth less on a trade-in under this reappraisal clause, and you consequently will have to pay a larger net amount. Don't believe it. Most dealers take this into account when they make their first appraisal. The reappraisal clause should only refer to those cars that are damaged or break down between the time of contract and delivery of the new car.

A sample letter of complaint might read as follows:

Dealer Complaint Department
Motor Vehicle Bureau
(Address)

Gentlemen:

On (date), I signed a contract for a new car with (name and address of dealer), a copy of the sales contract being attached hereto. As can be seen from the agreement, I agreed to pay (amount) and the dealer agreed to take my 1972 Pontiac Grand Prix in as a trade-in, for the agreed price of (amount).

Yesterday, Mr. (name of the dealer) called and told me three things. First, the car was ready. Second, the price has gone up because the factory is now charging them more for the car. Third, since my old car was three months older than at the first appraisal, they will allow me $350 less for it on a trade-in.

They refused my request to see any documents backing up their claim of the increase in price, they did not seem to be interested in the fact that my car was in just as good condition as when they first saw it, and they refused to give me my money back.

I feel I am being made a victim of sharp business practice, if not outright fraud. I ask that you investigate this immediately.

Very truly yours,
Ellen Miller

cc.: State Attorney General
District Attorney

Now everything has been agreed upon and you're signing the order. Don't be so excited that you forget to read what you're signing.

Printed contracts are not sacred. If you have agreed orally on anything else, demand that it be added in writing. Although this may be a malapropism, I am sure you will understand me when I say that oral promises aren't worth the paper they're written on.

Don't sign any documents, don't pay any deposits, and don't surrender your old car keys or registration until all details are down in writing, including an acceptable price commitment, and the contract or sales order has been signed not only by the salesman, but by an official of the dealership as well.

The reason for the signature by the authorized representative of the firm is that unless he has signed, the agreement may be cancelled by the dealer at will. Let's assume that you sign under the promise that you will be notified within a reasonable time whether the representative has signed. What do you think the dealer is doing during the weeks that you wait? If the market gets better—so that he can get a better price—he will have no hesitation in notifying you at the last minute that there is no deal, unless it is at a higher price. If you haven't heard within a reasonable time, you should call them. Don't be put off. You want the countersigned copy in writing, or your money back, or you will have to go to the authorities.

If the new car is being ordered from the factory, remember that the date given for delivery on the order or contract is only an estimate, and doesn't really bind the dealer. A verbal promise of delivery on or before a specific date is not binding unless it is a written part of the contract *in so many words*. The mere statement, "delivery for August 22, 1975," means nothing. The phrase "time of delivery is of the essence" must follow it to have the effect of a cut-off date, or something along the lines of: "If dealer fails to deliver this car by August 22, 1975, the buyer may cancel the contract and get his money back immediately."

Never sign a blank contract. (It should be mentioned, if you haven't gotten the message already.)

Read the warranty, line by line. You will find that a warranty on a new car does more to limit the manufacturer's liability than to assure you of satisfaction. See if there is a requirement (as there often is) that you give your new car certain specified maintenance at stated intervals before they will honor the warranty, and be sure to keep careful records of such services, because you may be asked to exhibit them. A good place to write this information down is in the owner's manual, because most such manuals have room for exactly this type of record.

Many problems arise with respect to unreasonable delay of service, unsatisfactory service, and the fact that, though you have complained about major defects prior to the expiration of the warranty, these major defects are not properly checked into by the service department of the dealer until after the warranty expires (when the dealer can charge you directly at a price higher than he would receive from the manufacturer). Such complaints, as filed with the Better Business Bureau and the Consumer Federation of America, are legion.

When dealing with a service department, you have to protect yourself from the very beginning. Whether you bring in your car during the warranty period or after, hand the service manager a copy of the list of things you want done on the car. Make sure the date you bring it in is on the sheet, and keep a carbon or photostatic copy for yourself. If you know the name of the man you are dealing with, or see the name stitched on his work clothes, write it on the back of your copy so there will be no question later as to who you dealt with. In any event, ask him to initial his copy and return it to you upon completion of the work. When picking up the car, check the items stated on the invoice presented to you against your list. If the items seem to tally, keep the sheet anyway, so that if anything goes wrong, you will have proof.

If something has not been done, or has been done improperly, don't just take it lying down. Bring it back to the service manager and explain the problem.

If the car is once again not repaired properly or if the service manager refuses to do anything about your complaint, call the factory zone service manager. Zone officers are usually listed in your owner's manual. Ask this individual to arrange a meeting between himself, yourself, and the dealer service manager in order to straighten the matter out.

Incidentally, it is sometimes possible to have repairs paid for by the manufacturer even after the expiration of the warranty, on a selective basis. This is possible, though unpublicized, because the factory has experienced certain failures with a component that they have either hushed up or there has not been enough of an incidence of the problem to necessitate a recall. If your problem involves a component it does not hurt to ask for correction of your problem at the expense of the factory even after your warranty has expired.

If you still receive no satisfaction with the ordinary non-repair or improper repair, it is time to contact the factory.

A typical letter may read as follows: (Most factory addresses may be found in Appendix C.)

Owner Relations Manager
(Name of Manufacturer)
(Address of Manufacturer)

Gentlemen:

Approximately two months ago, I bought one of your cars from (name and address of the dealer), a copy of the bill of sale being attached hereto. As can be seen from it, the vehicle is a (Make and Model) and its identification number is (get this number from your ownership certificate or automobile registration).

About a month after purchase, I brought the car back for correction of certain problems. I gave a list of the problems to the service manager, Ken, and he initialed it. I am attaching a copy of the list. One of the problems was (set forth in as few words as possible). After getting the car back on (date), I noticed that the problem had not been corrected. I called Ken the next day, but he said he could do nothing further about it.

I immediately called the factory zone service manager, whose address I found in the owner's manual. I spoke to Mr. James, who told me he could do nothing about it, and referred me back to my dealer.

As must be apparent, this item falls within my warranty, and it is dangerous to let it go uncorrected.

Please arrange to have this matter taken care of immediately.

Very truly yours,

Ellen Miller

cc: (Dealer)
    Office of Consumer Affairs (Appendix B)
    Chairman, Federal Trade Commission (Appendix B)
    State Attorney General
    District or County Attorney
    State Consumer Agency (Appendix B)
    Center for Auto Safety (Appendix C)
    Better Business Bureau (Appendix A)
    Consumers Union (Appendix C)
    Consumer Federation of America (Appendix C)

Send the letter to the company by certified mail, return receipt requested. The other copies may go by ordinary mail. A good deal of work and copies involved? Yes. A good deal of your money and possibly your life involved? Yes. Do it. Don't be lazy. The next time around, you will probably be treated with kid gloves.

If, improbably, none of this works, don't hesitate to consult an attorney.

To do your fellow citizen a good turn as well, report possible auto safety defects to the National Highway Traffic Safety Administration (Appendix B). A copy of the above letter should suffice.

Another problem that may arise with regard to your car involves recalls. They are not automatic. If you know that your model has been recalled, *you* call the dealer. Don't wait for him to contact you. Again, if you are not sure if your car has or has not been recalled, send 50¢ to the Superintendent of Documents, Government Printing Office, Washington, D.C. 20402, and ask for *Motor Vehicle Safety Campaign List*.

Getting satisfaction with regard to the used car you may purchase will almost certainly be far more difficult than with regard to a new car. It is almost a truism that there is a greater fringe of "sharpies" among used car dealers than among new car dealers. Walk into a deal very carefully.

The first pitfall involves advertising for such cars. Read between the lines of the ads. Have you ever seen an advertisement in a paper that offers a repossessed car where all you have to do is pick up the payments? Nine times out of ten, this is a come-on and once you are on the dealer's lot, you are switched over to a "better buy" which will be just an ordinary used car at ordinary or inflated prices. If you respond to such an ad, ask the dealer for proof of the offer. If he refuses, notify the Better Business Bureau and do not buy anything at that lot.

Another favorite gimmick is the advertisement that proclaims, "No cash down—three years to pay!" When you go there, you will find that a down payment is needed, but you will be steered to an accomplice loan company that will lend you the cash for the down payment. Of course, the balance will have to be paid out over three years. Presto! You will now have two loan payments to make each month instead of one. Don't buy it.

If you decide to buy a used car from one of these dealers, of course you will haggle about the price. Don't be impressed by any "official used car price guide," flourished by the salesman. There is no such thing. There is always fluctuation in the market, so the book can only give you a rough idea of the fair market value.

Especially if buying a late model used car, check the recall lists first. Many owners of cars that have been recalled for dangerous defects sell them instead of returning them to the new car dealer or factory for repairs. Many irresponsible dealers then resell them with the same old defects.

Before buying, check out the car first. No reasonable dealer will refuse a road test or having the car checked out by your own mechanic.

There is no substitute, however, for using your own eyes. What is the condition of the car and how many miles has it been driven? Has the odomter (mileage indicator) been turned back so that you may be fooled into thinking the car has been driven less than it has been? Under the Federal Motor Vehicle Information and Cost Savings Act, the seller must disclose in writing, at the time the contract is signed for the purchase of the car, the actual mileage that the car has been driven at the time you buy it, or, if this information is unknown (such as in the case of a broken odometer), a statement to that effect. A notice must be placed on the left door frame telling the prospective buyer the number of miles driven until the repair of the odometer, and the date of repair.

If you discover that the odometer has been turned back, jimmied, or that the correct mileage has been otherwise covered up, a suit may be started in Federal or State Court for the actual damages or $1500, whichever is greater.

If you still have doubts as to a dealer's truthfulness, ask the salesman for the name and address of the previous owner. If this is refused, something is probably being covered up, and you should avoid the deal. If given, by all means call the last owner. Not only may you find out how many miles the car was driven until he sold it to a dealer, but you should also ask him about any prior accidents to the car, or if there were any serious defects when he sold it. The last owner has already been paid and has nothing to lose by being truthful.

In using your eyes, check for old lubrication stickers. More than one turned-back odometer has been given the lie by such a sticker found in the glove compartment or under a seat.

Is there a low mileage indicated but the floor pedals are worn down to the metal? Worse yet, are there brand new pedals? Beware of 30,000 to 40,000 mile cars with five brand new tires. Have your mechanic check the speedometer fitting on the transmission. If dirty, fine. If wrench marks, look out.

Now you've decided to buy the car. A recent test proposed to verify someone's credibility was phrased: "Would you buy a used car from this man?" Unfortunately, many used car salesmen would elicit a "yes," based on their smoothness and line of patter, when what is called for is a resounding, "maybe, but cautiously."

There will be any number of verbal promises. Don't let them just slip away and be forgotten at the time you make up a sales agreement. As he's talking, keep a pad and pencil near you, and take notes of what is being promised. The point of all this is that when it comes time to draw up the agreement, make sure that each and every promise is put down on the agreement in writing. Don't be jollied out of it; insist or no deal (if the item is that important to you) or be prepared to forget the item. Demand, at the time you sign any paper, that you get a copy of what you signed right then and there. Turn thumbs down on any proposal that a copy be sent to you or given to you at the time of delivery.

If there are any blank sections on the agreement, make sure that they are filled in by the dealer, or crossed out, or marked "void." If you leave a deposit, get a proper receipt.

Are you getting a warranty? If the car you are buying is a late-model vehicle and you are being offered the balance of the new car warranty, make sure you find out exactly what the remaining portion of the warranty is and have it so stated in writing. Not only should you get the unexpired term of the warranty in writing, but you should obtain an acknowledgment in writing from the dealer (which he will presumably have gotten from the person who sold the car to him) that the former owner has fulfilled the maintenance requirements which, you may remember, certain manufacturers insist upon as a basis for honoring the warranty.

Experience has shown that unless you are getting the balance of a new-car warranty, the obtaining of a used car guarantee from the dealer is practically useless. One of the cutest gimmicks usually pulled is a guarantee whereby you and the dealer share fifty–fifty in the cost of certain limited repairs for the first 30 days. Pure thievery. What is done is that the dealer has the right to arrange for the repairs, and has his dummy give a figure of twice the amount of what the repair would actually cost. For instance, assume a repair that any honest shop would do for $100. The dealer will have his "friend" give you an estimate of $200. You would therefore pay $100 and assume that the dealer is matching your payment. Forget it. The mechanic accepts your $100 as full payment, and the dealer hasn't contributed a dime.

You are in even worse trouble if the mechanic decides to make some profit on you, and the estimate for the $100 job soars to $400. You now will pay $200, double the value of the work. The best deal, if you can get it, is for the dealer to pay 100 percent of the cost of these limited repairs for 30 days. Don't count on getting it, though. That is why it was pointed out to you earlier that you should have an independent mechanic look over the car before you sign any papers. Whatever the cost is, it will come to far less than being cheated after the sale.

Contracting the authorities is practically the only way to deal with unscrupulous used car dealers.

A sample letter of complaint might read as follows:

District Attorney
Frauds Division
(Address)

Dear Sir:

On June 1, 1975, I bought a 1971 used car from (name and address of dealer). A copy of the sales agreement is attached. As can be seen from the agreement, I was given a guarantee for 30 days on certain items. It was also represented to me, as can be seen from the paper attached to this letter, that the car had been driven 40,165 miles. Unfortunately, I did not have a mechanic check it out before I bought it.

After driving the car home that night and parking it, the car never again did run normally, but could only creep along at some five miles per hour. The dealer shrugged his shoulders and, without having his mechanic look at the motor, told me on June 2 that there was nothing he could do about it, and whatever it was, it wasn't covered under any guarantee.

I thereafter had my own mechanic look at the car and, per his report that I am attaching, he told me that the car had obviously been in at least one major accident, that the motor block was cracked and the entire motor rendered useless, and that the mileage had been obviously changed, the old mileage having been at least 100,000 miles. In fact, he found a lubrication sticker in the glove compartment, which I now have in my possession, showing more than that amount.

I feel I have been cheated and defrauded and I request an investigation.

Very truly yours,
Ellen Miller

cc: (Dealer)
    State Attorney General
    State Consumer Agency (Appendix B)
    Better Business Bureau (Appendix A)
    Consumers Union (Appendix C)

Consumers Federation of America (Appendix C)
National Highway Traffic Safety Administration (Appendix B)

If nothing happens in a reasonable period, contact an attorney. In buying a used car, many people buy lawsuits as well.

CHAPTER 8

Appliances
—— and Other Merchandise ——

As with almost everything we buy today, major appliances, small appliances, and similar purchases are often defective and are difficult to have repaired or replaced once they break down.

Among major appliances, refrigerators and ranges are the ones most complained about. Assuming that you have pursued your first line of defense by buying from a reliable dealer, look beyond the immediate purchase of the item to the days following, covered by the warranty or guarantee (the same thing). The warranties define your rights. Refrigerators, for instance, usually come with a warranty for one year, with four more years of protection for the refrigerating system itself. You must read the warranty carefully, however, for what is "usual" does not bind the seller or manufacturer. Don't be afraid to ask questions if you don't understand the warranty. If the warranty is very long, what is happening is that the duties and obligations of the seller and/or manufacturer are being limited. You are not getting more protection, but less. It would be better to steer clear of such an item, since a major appliance (or a small appliance, for that matter) is costly to begin with, and the cost compounds with extensive repairs.

Read the entire warranty. After all, what the large print giveth, the small print taketh away.

You will not be able to get satisfaction, or satisfactory answers, on all of the following items of inquiry as to the warranty or guarantee, but bear them in mind. When the crisis arises is not the time to start asking for such information.

1. Who will "make good"—the retailer or manufacturer?

2. Does the product have to be returned to the seller, manufacturer, or a designated repair service, or will the work be done in your home?

3. Is the entire item guaranteed? Only certain parts? For how long?

4. Who pays for labor? If the warranty only mentions "parts replacement," the cost of labor comes out of your pocket.

5. Is the guarantee prorated? If you have a warranty for one year, and the item breaks down after eight months, do you only get a credit of one-third of the price (since one-third of the year is left)?

6. What is the product guaranteed against?

7. Does the guarantee run from the date of sale or of manufacture?

8. If the warranty covers both parts and labor, read further. Does the coverage for labor run for as long as for parts?

9. Is the warranty extended only to the original purchaser? The item may be an appliance which you would pass along with the sale of a house.

10. Does the warranty or guarantee require "regular maintenance procedures" before the seller or manufacturer will honor it? What are they?

11. Is there a registration card to be completed and mailed back to the manufacturer or repair service on purchase of the item? If so, do it!

12. Is the warranty full or limited?

Remember, a warranty or guarantee is only as good as the company that gives it. The clearest, most generous warranty from a fraud is just a piece of paper. It is also a mistake to rely on guarantees stated in advertisements alone. Of course, a court may force a firm to live up to its ad without any other warranty, but do you really need a lawsuit?

A new problem has arisen in recent years. Upon the expiration of the original warranty by the manufacturer, many stores have been doing a growing business in the sale of service contracts for appliances and small equipment. Many of them extend for up to two to three years. Complaints are coming in constantly about the failure of such stores to live up to the contract by delay, inefficient repairs, or just doing nothing. Another catch is that the service must often be performed in another city at a repair shop that the store has retained to perform under the extended warranty. Naturally, this not only causes hardship, but extensive delays and deprivation of the use of the item.

Now that you've bought the item, let us examine the problem of obtaining repairs under or outside of the warranty. Complaints range from outrageous charges for just making the service call (before even looking at the item) to arrogant scheduling when you call for an appointment (whereby you are not given even an approximate time, sometimes not even the day, and quite often are scheduled for an appointment that is not kept); from what seems to be undue cost of labor and parts to inefficiency that can also lead to repeated service calls.

Some of this must be put up with. Difficulties in making appointments may often be traced to unexpected delays on prior scheduled calls. High labor costs may often be the result of regional union wage agreements and will probably increase.

However, there comes a point where enough is enough. With regard to major appliances, the industry has formed a fairly efficient organization known as Major Appliance Consumer Action Panel, also known as MACAP (see Appendix C for address). This panel deals with consumer complaints on all brands of major appliances. However, it will handle the complaint only if the consumer has already contacted the manufacturer and is unhappy with the results. Part of MACAP's efficacy is due to the fact that complaints received by it are sent to top management, and approximately 90 percent are cleared up by the manufacturer or dealer.

However, especially where there are no service contracts or warranties still in effect, the majority of repairs are handled by independent service agencies—small businesses unaffiliated with large manufacturers—and MACAP has no control over them at all.

Now for action. Remember, with major appliances, call the dealer, call or write the manufacturer if you receive no adequate response from the dealer, and if your contact with the manufacturer still leaves you unsatisfied, a typical letter of complaint might read as follows:

Major Appliance Consumer Action Panel
20 North Wacker Drive
Chicago, Illinois 60606

Gentlemen:
  On March 17, 1975, I bought a (make) refrigerator, bearing model #___, Serial #___, from (name and address of dealer). I'm attaching a copy of the sales slip. Two days after it was installed, there was a loud bang inside and the whole thing stopped working, spoiling about $50 worth of food.

I called the number that the dealer had given me for service, as shown on the sales slip, and got an answering service. I called for the next two days and left my name and number, and finally, on the third day, I received a call and an appointment was made for the next day. I took off from work especially to wait for the man, but he never came, nor did I receive a phone call. I lost $38 in pay. After several more days of calls, a new appointment was made and I had to take another day off. This time, on March 31, a mechanic and a helper showed up and told me, after a five minute look, that they could find nothing wrong with the refrigerator and it must be my wiring. I wrote to the (manufacturer), a copy of the letter being attached, and received a printed form letter that the matter was being looked into (a copy of the form being attached hereto). Nothing has been heard from the company since, and I am still left without a refrigerator.

I would appreciate your investigating this matter and letting me know immediately, as things are getting desperate in my house and I can't afford to buy another refrigerator.

Very truly yours,
Ellen Miller

cc: Manufacturer
    Dealer
    State Attorney General
    District Attorney
    State Consumer Agency (Appendix B)
    Better Business Bureau (Appendix A)
    Consumers Union (Appendix C)
    U.S. Office of Consumer Affairs (Appendix B)

Naturally, it will take time to send out nine copies of the above letter and keep the tenth, and to make copies of the attachments for all of the letters, and to write out the envelopes and attach postage. But how much aggravation have you had to date? How many expenses have you had on phone calls, etc.? How much did you pay for the appliance? Don't put it off for tomorrow! Now! Today!

In buying small appliances, you will find that most warranties cover parts and labor for varying periods, from 30 days up. Some manufacturers will even exchange a poorly functioning appliance for a new one at no extra cost during the first year, though the warranty may not call for this relief. Try it; you have nothing to lose.

A few tips:

1. Bring the portable appliance to a service center, but check if they have a "bench charge," that is, a fee for examining and estimating.

2. If you must send the appliance to a service center, pack it well, together with a letter in detail, and insure the package for its full value.

3. If in a hurry, ask for a specific date of completion, and to be notified of a delay.

4. To prevent an expensive repair on an item having little remaining value, ask the repairman to call you if the repair exceeds a certain amount.

Before purchasing the small appliance, a word of warning is in order. See if the seal of Underwriters Laboratories (UL) is on both the appliance and its cord, indicating that they have been checked for fire, casualty, and electrical safety. Items tagged thusly are your best bet whatever the price.

TIRES

Buying a tire often means trouble. Most labels, such as "premium," "first line," "second line," have no meaning but are terms invented for advertising purposes. The Federal Trade Commission now requires tire ads to state that such labels are not based on industry-wide standards. Still the flim-flam goes on.

"Sale" tires are another gimmick. If the tire fails (and it

usually will) and you survive (and you sometimes will), when the tire is brought back, a measurement is taken of the tread and you are given a prorata share of the "sale" tire which turns out to be minuscule, only as against the purchase of a regularly priced tire. You thus will wind up paying more than if you had bought a good tire in the first place.

If any dealer offers you a life-of-the-tread guarantee, ask to see his data sheets on test results from the manufacturer. If he has nothing to show you, the guarantee is worthless.

Incidentally, when you buy a new tire, make sure the dealer has your name and address (some don't bother) because if there is a tire recall, you want to be informed of the defect that might threaten your life.

If you have a defective tire, two federal agencies should be informed, but unfortunately, they will only act for the future safety of other purchasers. However, letting the seller know that the federal government is onto them (along with local consumer agencies) may be the lever to get you results.

If you have a defective tire, advise the National Highway Traffic Safety Administration of the U. S. Department of Transportation (Appendix B for address) and your local office of the Federal Trade Commission (Appendix B) as well as the dealer, manufacturer, Better Business Bureau, and Consumers Union (or any other state consumer group or agency you know of, or to be found in Appendices B and C).

Give the circumstances, as in previous sample letters, mention that you have the tire in your possession, but add one thing to permit all addresses to check out the tire in question. On each sidewall, there is a set of letters, followed by nine or ten numbers. The last three digits disclose when the tire was manufactured. Enclose this total number in the letter.

FURNITURE

The purchase of furniture has made many persons sadder but wiser. Furniture is almost never guaranteed by a manufacturer or retailer. If the salesman mentions a warranty, get it in writing. Be extra-suspicious of lifetime guarantees.

Much of what goes wrong with furniture, aside from delivery and improperly filled orders involves deceptive advertising and labeling. The Federal Trade Commission has been given power to act upon some of the deceptions and has recently ordered binding arbitration between a furniture company engaged in interstate commerce and a consumer, an historic "first." The FTC has set up "guides for the household furniture industry," and has banned wood-appearing plastic, leather-appearing vinyl, furniture that is labeled Danish, but was made in North Carolina, and other misleading items, unless the furniture is labeled as to its true nature. Also banned, as is quite often the practice in ghettos, is the labeling of repossessed furniture or trade-in furniture as "floor samples" or "demonstration pieces."

Not covered, however, are mattresses, bedsprings, metal cots, cedar chests, musical instruments, radios, TV's, venetian blinds, pictures, lamps, clocks, rugs, draperies, large appliances, such as air conditioning, and other things that would ordinarily go to fill out a roomful of furniture. A sample letter to the Furniture Industry Consumer Advisory Panel was given earlier. The same letter may be adapted for a situation wherein you have been deceived, possibly defrauded. The same organizations should be notified.

HEARING AIDS

One of the biggest fields for fraud and sharp practice has grown up in the hearing aid industry. Some one-half million hearing aids are bought each year in the United States.

In a recent test conducted in a major city, three volunteers were tested beforehand, two of whom had perfect hearing and the third with a total hearing defect that could not be helped by the assistance of a hearing aid. Five stores chosen at random sold hearing aids to all three, with glib assurances of necessity and beneficial results.

Once again, the first line of defense must occur before you buy the appliance. Firstly, get medical advice from an otologist or audiologist. Though this may cost a modest medical fee, you may be able to avoid the trap of an unnecessary aid, or be able to bring to a dealer specific instructions as to the type of hearing aid you require. Remember, not all of them perform the same function. Some of these tests are rendered free, such as those through the Veterans Administration.

The important questions in purchasing such appliances are:

1. Will my particular hearing deficiency benefit from a hearing aid?

2. Will a hearing aid enable me to hear AND understand sounds in a group of people?

3. Will a hearing aid enable me to hear and understand when there is background noise present?

Your ear doctor should be consulted about such questions, as well as the store that sells you a hearing aid.

Beware of the following common deceptions.

1. Direct or implied representations that hearing aids will help *all* people in *all* situations.

2. Newspaper ads that promise a ''free gift'' or ''valuable information'' without mentioning that a response from you will cause a high-pressure salesman to visit you.

3. The promise of a ''free replica,'' this merely being a plas-

tic non-working model brought by the same high-pressure salesman.

4. Blurbs that this hearing aid works on a ''new scientific principle.''

5. Claims that the aid may be worn invisibly.

Although there are licensing laws for hearing aid distributors in at least 24 states, the risks of being taken or lied to are still high. As stated before, the Federal Trade Commission usually can do nothing to help you in your own individual case.

A sample letter of complaint might read as follows:

Attorney General of the State
Fraud Division
(Address)

Gentlemen:

I have suffered from a hearing problem for some time. On June 1, 1975, I went to the (name and address of firm), without having seen a doctor first, and they examined me and sold me a hearing aid for $375 on the assurance that it would help me. It did not. I am attaching a copy of the bill of sale.

I then went to Dr. (name and address of doctor), and he advised me that I had a defect which no hearing aid could help. I'm attaching a copy of his note to this effect.

When I brought the hearing aid back to the store and showed them the doctor's note, they refused to refund my money. I ask your help in investigating this matter and helping me get my money back.

Very truly yours,
Ellen Miller

cc: Licensing agency (if your state has one; find out from the Better Business Bureau)
Seller
Federal Trade Commission (Appendix B)

Consumers Union (Appendix C)
State Consumer Agency (Appendix B)
Better Business Bureau (Appendix A)
U.S. Office of Consumer Affairs (Appendix B)
Other consumer groups as you may choose to write to from Appendix C.

Only a few dealers will defraud you or make misrepresentations. Keep three other items in mind. First, it is common practice for the seller to take an impression of your ear canal. The normal cost of this, quite properly, is $10 to $15.

Second, insist that the aid be bought on a trial basis only. Most reputable dealers will rent you the aid for $1 a day for a month.

Last, during the trial period, return to the otologist or audiologist to see if it is working correctly.

CHAPTER
9

—— Those Who Provide Service ——

Centuries ago, when life and thingamajigs were simple, most people did everything for themselves. Today, we buy another man's time and knowhow, and the purchase of services vies strongly for our dollar.

Use the standard rules in selecting those who offer services. Check on honesty, reputation, and efficiency.

If repairs are involved, choose an authorized service representative, not the general neighborhood handyman. In the long run, you will save money and have fewer headaches. To find an authorized repairman, check the use and care booklet for the item, the Yellow Pages, or the nearest dealer who stocks such an item. If there is a breakdown during a warranty period, make sure the repair shop you call does "warranty repairs" because not all of them do.

Get the prospective charges itemized and in writing and ask for a receipt after the repair. You will need it if trouble crops up. If the cost of repair includes a guarantee on new parts or workmanship, make sure this is specified on the receipt (and for how long).

If the repairman does not have an essential part, and must come again to your home, make sure you will not be charged another travel fee.

AUTOMOBILES

One of the most notorious sources of repair complaints is the automobile. It is true that many of the problems are not caused by fraud, but by incompetence, lack of enough mechanics, insufficient training of repair personnel, and the like, but a substantial minority of the charges are based on fraud. The interior of an automobile engine is a mystery to most people, and there are repair shops that are not loathe to perpetrate misrepresentation and outright highway robbery.

Since the ways of cheating are legion, only two examples are given here to illustrate the problem. Incidentally, a certain transmission repair shop was found to have committed both.

The first is "salting." Metal filings and other foreign objects are slipped into the transmission oil pan and shown to the customer as evidence of malfunction and the inevitably large repair bill. Then there is "bench selling" where sections of the motor are taken apart and spread on the bench, but not before worn parts lying around the shop are substituted for good parts taken out of the car. Presto, Mr. Customer! Large repairs needed. Large bill.

Most complaints involve the following categories:

1. Reluctance or unwillingness to make warranty repairs.

2. Lengthy waiting periods for scheduling or actual repair work, especially for manufacturer recalls.

3. Disputes over what repairs were made, or even if they were needed.

4. Repeated repairs for the same problem.

5. Inability to get satisfactory responses from the dealer or

manufacturer.

Parts of these problems and what you should do to get action have already been discussed.

First, know your repairer. If you have found one to be consistently trustworthy and efficient, treasure him as a jewel for "they don't hardly make that kind anymore."

If you are in the position of most people—that is, shopping around for proper repairs to your car—and if you are in doubt about one or two garages that you had in mind, ask your friends or neighbors who might have used them, and by all means call the local Better Business Bureau office to find out if they have any files on the reputations of the repairers.

Watch for garages that display the emblem of the National Institute for Automotive Service Excellence, the Independent Garage Owners Association, or the National Automobile Dealers Association since firms that display such emblem or emblems usually have mechanics of some ability.

Watch out for "flat rate" repair offers because shops offering them are quite often clip joints, and are to be avoided.

If a major repair is involved or claims to be needed, always get at least another estimate from a different shop.

If you make the plunge, be sure to have the repair shop or the garage write out an invoice (get a copy) spelling out the exact trouble. If the transmission will not go into reverse, make sure the invoice reads "Fix reverse" instead of "Fix transmission," which is vague and offers the garage an escape hatch later if things go wrong. All parts for which you are charged should be listed on the invoice, and if there is a claim of a new part, ask for the return of the old one. Leaving the old part in and charging for a new part has long been a favorite dodge of some garages.

Make it clear (in writing on the invoice) that no work is to be done on your car beyond the first written estimate unless you are notified in advance and given an opportunity to approve it.

A special problem arises if you are on the road and have to pull into a strange gas station or garage for emergency repairs. Most are no more liable to swindle you than the ones in your own home town, but there are some who are specialists at fleecing you.

The means of defrauding you are too long to list in this book, let alone in this chapter. Just a few examples, however, may give you some idea of the problem. Switching wires so the motor will run roughly; pouring oil into your engine from an empty oil can; if two gas pumps are joined, filling from one and charging from the higher amount already recorded on the other; ruining batteries by putting in baking soda to make them foam; puncturing or slashing radiator hoses, tires, and fan belts—these dirty tricks are all merely tips of icebergs.

Since you do not live in the town where the station or garage is located and cannot check on reputation; since most of the cheaters are located along lonely stretches of roads; and since most people are loathe to contact authorities in a town or county they will probably never visit again, one of the few remedies you have is, once again, the first line of defense—watching out for yourself.

A few simple rules may save you much grief. Watch all operations performed at any service station unless you are familiar with the personnel and they know you. If you have some idea that your oil has been incorrectly checked, ask to have it dipped agan and watch carefully that the mechanic or attendant pushes the dip stick all the way in before withdrawing it. Be alert at any gas tank filling procedure. Do not leave your car unattended at a garage or station, but if you do, to go to the rest room, telephone, or for any other reason, lock the car. Most important of all, before you start on a trip, have the car thoroughly checked out by your own station, so you will minimize the chances of permitting yourself to fall into the hands of such swindlers. If the garage or station sells gas, take the name of the gasoline company that is represented there, along with the name and address (or physical location) of the place. It may be useful in the next step.

First lines of defense, preparedness, are all very well, but the enemy attack took you for a bundle of money. In short, you have complaints about the repairs (allegedly made) and the garage or station refuses to attempt to remedy the situation.

In dealing with an authorized representative and repairer for a particular brand of motor vehicle, you should still contact the manufacturer. It has a vested interest in reducing any bad word-of-mouth advertising about its dealers. If the repair is made by one of what appears to be a chain of specialty auto repair shops, the odds are that the individual garage is merely a franchise of the central organization and you should notify the central organization of your complaint. It, too, has a vested interest in avoiding bad word-of-mouth advertising. Get the address from your local library (your librarian has several books with an organization and address format), or call the local Better Business Bureau.

It goes without saying that the Better Business Bureau should be notified, as well as Consumers Union (which has done much good work in this field) and the Consumers Federation of America (also very active for the consumer in this area).

If fraud is suspected, contact both the local and state law enforcement anti-fraud agencies. Another good idea is to advise the gasoline company, if applicable, that either enfranchises, has a contract with, or owns the garage or station. In this Day of the Consumer, they are all "running scared." The Federal

Trade Commission receives numerous complaints about each car, but may not be able to help you with your specific problem; still, advise them.

A sample letter might read as follows:

District Attorney (or County Attorney)
(Address)

Dear Sir:

On (date) I brought my 1973 Pontiac into (name and address of repair shop). I had recently moved into the neighborhood, and they were the closest to me. I heard a funny noise in the motor, and asked them to check it out. They asked me to leave it there overnight, and when I came back the next day, I found practically my entire motor disassembled inside the garage, and I was told that several parts were broken, and that it would cost me $250 to fix it. I decided not to do the work, but when I told them this, they said there was a charge of $150 for checking out the problem, and for disassembling and assembling the motor. I was desperately in need of the car, so I paid them the $250 and got a detailed receipt for the work done and parts replaced.

The funny noise was still there, so the next week I went to a station recommended by a neighbor and he told me that the only thing wrong with my car was a frayed fan belt, a matter of just a few dollars, and that the parts that the first shop had charged me for had never been replaced, but were the ones in place when it came from the factory. I will gladly furnish the name of the second garage shop operator to you, but I would prefer not to reveal it to the first repair shop at this time.

I believe I have been the victim of fraud, and I ask that an investigation be made to correct the situation and to recover my money.

Very truly yours,
Ellen Miller

cc: Attorney General of your state.
    Better Business Bureau (Appendix A)
    Consumers Union (Appendix C)

Consumers Federation of America (Appendix C)
Federal Trade Commission (Appendix B)
Your state consumer agency (Appendix B)
U.S. Office of Consumer Affairs (Appendix B)

TELEVISION SETS AND RADIOS

Another area where complaints are rife is that of television and radio repairs. In fact, the preface to a bill licensing repair shops in New York City states: "The business of servicing television or radio receiving apparatus and audio equipment has become the subject of great abuse."

While the problems in this field dealing with dangerous sets or trouble under a warranty have been covered in earlier chapters, let us discuss the area, as with cars, where there is no longer any warranty coverage and you just want the set repaired at your own expense.

Here are some warnings as to what steps you should take before entrusting the problem to a serviceman, unless you have dealt with him before and are satisfied as to his knowledge and integrity.

Select a repair shop for responsible workmanship rather than price alone. Avoid those who advertise unusually low prices just to get into your home. They then will find "serious trouble," and suddenly the set has to be taken back to the shop. In this field, an unbelievably low price is just that—unbelievable. If still in doubt after checking among your friends and neighbors as to the reputation of the repair establishment, don't hesitate to call your local Better Business Bureau office to see if they have a file on the shop. This little extra effort may save you many dollars and much grief.

Many charges are deemed valid throughout the country. For instance, it is usual to charge a service fee for the TV repairman to come to your home, and this charge may not cover examination of, or work done to, the set. Some people bring the set to the repair shop, but there may still be a "bench charge." By all means, check on the service charge first (the charge for color sets is more than for black and white sets), so that you will not be surprised or overcharged.

If an inspection of the set is made before you give a general go-ahead to repair it, ask for a written, itemized accounting of what needs to be done, which parts are to be replaced, and the cost for same.

Now, let us assume the worst—that is, the set is still not operating properly and the repairer claims there is nothing further that can be done, or you are overcharged or charges are made that are far greater than the original estimate.

Throughout the country, as in New York City, licensing of such shops is now required by many municipalities and the repairers are usually strictly regulated. The first thing to do is to determine whether your locality requires such licensing. Call your local Better Business Bureau, your local Consumer Affairs Agency, or the complaint department of the District Attorney's Office, and they will not only advise you if there is licensing, but will furnish the name and address of the agency responsible. If there is such licensing where you live, write a letter, similar in form to the auto repair complaint letter in this chapter, to the licensing agency, with carbon copies to the repairer, Better Business Bureau (Appendix A), Consumers Union (Appendix C), your local District Attorney, your State Attorney General, and your State Consumer Agency (Appendix B). If licensing is not required, write to the State Consumer Agency, with copies to the others. Remember, keep a copy for yourself. Results should be forthcoming rather rapidly.

AROUND THE HOME

Much trouble developes in renovating, painting, or decorating your apartment or home (although work done on houses is covered in another chapter).

Find out with whom you are dealing before you do so. With regard to decorators, before hiring one, discover if local stores offer free counseling on home furnishing matters, either at the store or in your residence. If you decide to use a private decorator, ascertain from your friends whether they have used a reliable one and what their experience and costs have been. If you still want a private decorator and have not found a reliable one, write to either the National Society of Interior Decorators (Appendix C) or the American Institute of Interior Designers (Appendix C) for the names of reputable members in your area. Once you have such names, call the Better Business Bureau to discover if they have an adverse file on them.

Now you have found your man. Ask him or her for a written estimate. Discuss costs and fees in advance and be sure that all these details are incorporated in a written contract for a given job. Include what services are encompassed (for a decorator also include what furnishings will be part of the agreement), the anticipated date of completion, and the schedule of payments to be made, if you have not agreed to make payment upon completion of the job.

For example, in the case of decorators, the usual charge is one-third of the total agreed-upon price to be paid on signing of the contract, one-third when the furnishings are ordered, and the balance when the job is completed. If you are merely having a consultation, ascertain the price for it in advance, because it has been found that charges per hour vary, from $25 to $2000.

When dealing with decorators, insist on sketches and drawings showing the plan to be followed. With painters, if you want a specially mixed color, give the painter a color sample.

What if things go wrong and there is a refusal to remedy the situation? Most of these artisans are small businessmen, not subject to the authority of federal agencies, and there is usually no question of fraud involved.

First, learn if your community licenses these individuals, as many do with regard to electricians and upholsterers. As with TV repairs, call your Better Business Bureau, your local Consumer Affairs Agency, or the complaint department of your District Attorney's Office, and they will advise you if there is licensing, and if so will supply the name and address of the licensing agency. Send a complaint letter to the agency, with carbon copies to the craftsman, the Better Business Bureau, and your local Affairs Agency.

If there is no licensing, the pattern changes. For decorators, write to the National Society of Interior Decorators (Appendix C), with carbon copies to the American Institute of Interior Designers (Appendix C), the Better Business Bureau (Appendix A), the State Consumer Agency (Appendix B), your local Consumer Agency, if any, and the decorator.

For electricians, upholsterers, painters, and decorators, notify the Better Business Bureau (Appendix A), State Consumer Agency (Appendix B), the local Consumer Agency, and the craftsman.

If you suspect fraud has been involved, also notify your District Attorney and the complaint department of your State Attorney General.

If any activities have taken place interstate (for instance, a decorator from a big city in the next state has handled the work in your home), also notify the U.S. Office of Consumer Affairs (Appendix B).

DRY CLEANERS

Problems with dry cleaners usually fall into two categories: lost clothing and damaged clothing. Most such businesses are quite small, with no fraud involved nor any interstate dealings. This, too, would be a situation to write to the Better Business Bureau (Appendix A) with copies to the cleaner, State Consumer Agency (Appendix B), and local consumer agency.

If the cleaner is a chain operation, however, notify the main office of the chain (the name and address may usually be obtained by phone from the Better Business Bureau or publications that your librarian usually has), the U.S. Office of Consumer Affairs (Appendix B), as well as the others.

EMPLOYMENT AGENCIES

There are fields that deal in other than direct services. Let us examine private employment agencies, for instance. In selecting an agency, use the same guidelines as in selecting any other dealer with whom you trade. Ask your friends and acquaintances who have experience with such agencies in your community, or, if there are none, call the local office of the Better Business Bureau to discover what the file on the agency contains, if anything.

Once you have selected an employment agency, be aware that the person running it must be paid. Sometimes you are expected to pay; sometimes the prospective employer pays. Be sure to ask what the arrangement will be.

In connection with this, certain phrases used in advertisements, or as mentioned to you in conversations, are vital. "Fee paid" means the employer will pay the fee of the agency. However, if you accept a "Fee-paid" job and do not appear for work or if you are fired for a good reason (misrepresentation, moral turpitude), you may be required to pay the fee yourself.

"Fee negotiable" means the prospective employer is willing to pay part of the fee, and you will be expected to pay the balance. Ask questions.

Be sure you iron out the details as to what the maximum fee would be before you accept a job. In addition, if you accept and later change your mind, you may still be liable. If you are to pay the fee, make sure when you are required to pay. All of these details, of course, should be embodied in a written contract. If the agent at the employment center says that special financing will be arranged in your case, those terms should go into the contract, too.

Look for good agencies, for only this kind will deal honorably with you, and only from them will you have a chance to land the job you want. But what is a good agency?

A square-shooting agency should:

1. Interview you with attention to your strengths and weaknesses, and try to match you up to a job suitable to your skills.

2. Inform you of the full details of a prospective job and of the background of the company.

3. Arrange interviews with prospective employers.

4. Give free counseling on the preparation of your resume, if required, and suggestions for your conduct at a particular job interview.

Before signing a contract or agreement with any agency, don't let yourself be given the "rush" act, or be forced to sign without reading the document because of impatience by the interviewer. This is standard procedure to put pressure on you, already nervous, and to tie you up without telling you what you are signing. "It's a standard form" is nonsense. There is no such thing. Read it carefully. Ask questions. Make sure all oral promises or conditions are stated in writing in the document, and make doubly sure you get a copy of the agreement signed by the agent. Be on the alert if any employment agent makes wild promises or claims.

The overwhelming majority of employment agencies are reputable, but the bad apples appear in this, as in any other industry.

If you are sent to an alleged prospective employer and find out that they have not requested any applicants, don't do business with that employment agency again, and immediately notify the Better Business Bureau, so future applicants will be forewarned.

Another ruse that is growing prevalent today is the want-ad describing a wonderful job, without listing the name of any agency. You call and find out that the person on the other end of the phone is not the prospective employer, but someone who wants to be paid in advance to tell you where the job is. Forget it. There is no such job.

Another racket today is the overseas position pitch. You are asked to pay several hundred dollars in advance for some absolutely guaranteed contacts for a glamorous, high-paying overseas job, but all you get after your money is paid over is some slight help in writing a resume and covering letter, and some pre-addressed envelopes to what is represented to you as legitimate employers. The odds are that the envelopes will come back, stamped "Addressee Unknown."

There are employment agencies that fill executive positions, and if this is what you are interested in, first write to the Association of Executive Recruiting Consultants, 30 Rockefeller Plaza, New York, New York 10020, for its membership list, or send $2 to American Management Association, 135 West 50th Street, New York, New York 10020, for *Executive Employment Guide*.

If things work out with an employment agency, all well and

good. If they do not, you will probably discover that you are dealing with a hard-nosed staff that will insist upon its pound of flesh, so there's little to gain in discussing the matter with them.

Most states require such agencies to be licensed. Check with the Better Business Bureau nearest you, or your District Attorney, as to whether such licensing is required, and if so, the name and address of the licensing division.

A typical letter might read as follows:

(Name of Licensing Agency)
(Address)

Gentlemen:
On (date) I went to the (name and address of agency) because of some ads I had seen in (name of paper) for secretarial jobs, a copy of which is attached. As you may notice, all of the jobs were advertised as "fee paid." When I got there, a Mr. Johnson made me sign an agreement with them, telling me it was just standard operating procedure, even though I was to pay no fee.

They sent me to (name and address of employer), Mr. Johnson telling me that this was also a "fee paid" job. I got the job and had worked there for two days when there was a 10 percent cut of the staff of the entire concern, and I was discharged.

Now the agency is dunning me and has threatened suit for what would have been 30 percent of my first year's earnings had I remained there. They now deny that this was a "fee paid" job, but they say that even if it was, I must have done something wrong to be fired after two days, and that I must pay up, or they will get me in trouble. Copies of their letters are attached.

I believe I have become a victim of fraud and false representation, false advertisements, and harassment (they call me late at night to pay up), and I ask that you investigate this matter immediately, as it is affecting my health.

Very truly yours,
Ellen Miller

cc: District Attorney
    Agency

Better Business Bureau (Appendix A)
State Consumer Agency (Appendix B)
State Attorney General
U. S. Office of Consumer Affairs (Appendix B)

APARTMENT LOCATING AGENCIES

Akin to employment agencies, the fraudulent fringe of apartment locating agencies constitutes one of the fastest growing swindles in urban America. This is another "advance fee" scheme, more of which are mentioned later in this chapter.

You see an advertisement in the newspaper offering a large apartment at a low rental. You answer it and find out that you are speaking to an agency which requires you to pay a registration fee in order to find out the details, or that you must pay to become a "member" of the agency that advertises the apartment, or join an "apartment referral service," with fees of about $25 to be paid by you in advance.

Of course, there is no such apartment as advertised, or it was rented years ago (and not by this agency). However, you will receive leads. Unfortunately, you are almost certain to receive obsolete information as to available apartments ("Apartment 3-D? Rented over a year ago!") or ads out of last week's newspaper, or even fictitious addresses. When you complain, a shrug is your only rejoinder, or you are furnished more leads of similar quality.

If you deal with an apartment-locating agency:

1. Find out in advance just what that agency agrees or guarantees to do for you in exchange for your advance payment, *and get it in writing*.

2. What portion, if any, of your money is refundable if the promised or guaranteed service does not work out—*get it in writing*.

3. What qualifies the promisor to deliver the promised information.

Let's assume you have been burned through your contact with such an agency. In most of these cases, you are dealing with outright fraud, compounded by the fact that many of these recently sprung-up agencies are unlicensed, unlike reputable brokers, and in direct violation of the laws of most states.

Write a letter of complaint to the Attorney General of your state with copies to the Secretary of State of your state (who usually handles complaints against those who are acting in the capacity of a realty broker, though unlicensed), the Better Business Bureau (Appendix A), your local or County District Attorney, your State Consumer Agency (Appendix B), and your City Consumer Agency.

OTHER "ADVANCE FEE" SERVICES

Another of the "advance fee" or "future service" businesses that has caused more than its share of trouble for the consumer involves health spas, reducing salons, and karate–judo schools.

The most common type of trouble that the average consumer gets himself into with such an organization is the long-term, iron-clad contract that one is inveigled into, which seems to stand up in a Court of Law, no matter what unforeseen eventualities may intervene—pregnancies, operations, or hospitalizations.

Most of these firms are basically honest, but there is a definite fringe of high-pressure, fast-talking ones that make more of their money out of suing you for broken contracts than out of providing facilities.

The advertisements are glowing, and you may feel lucky to get such a good deal because you were one of the "first fifty" callers. The usual truth is that, whoever calls, that person will be one of the "first fifty" for as long as the organization remains in business. The words "free," "new," "lavish," "full

facilities'' abound, but you are not informed that the fine print
of any agreement will place definite limitations on the facilities
provided and the number of allowable visits, will restrict the use
of certain machines to specified hours, will provide for an extra
charge for a wide variety of facilities, and may even stipulate
that the premises may not be used on certain days.

Before signing an agreement, you *must* inspect the premises.
A refusal to permit you to do so should be the cue for you to
walk out.

Are the equipment and facilities as clean, usable, and new as
claimed? Talk to some patrons there and find out their experi-
ences and ascertain how crowded it gets during popular times.

In reviewing the proposed agreement, ask for a specimen
contract so that you may review it at your leisure. After all, you
are contemplating obligating yourself to spend a substantial sum
of money in the future. Discover if the contract is cancellable,
and under what conditions, and where in the contract does it say
so. What about refunds if you must drop out for a legitimate
reason part-way through the program?

If you are answering an advertisement, make sure the price
and all of the promises in the ad are embodied in the contract.
In some cases, it will be announced that a new health spa is
opening in your community and if you join before it opens, you
are entitled to substantial savings. Find out what happens to
your money if it doesn't open. Is such money being kept separate in an escrow account? What bank? What proof is there of
this?

If you've been a member for a while, and your agreement
provides that you may drop out for medical reasons, ''subject to
review,'' you will probably discover that the doctor working for
the spa has to review the letter from your doctor, and will almost always disagree as to a refund.

The Better Business Bureau is vitally concerned with this problem, so write to them, with copies to the Federal Office of Consumer Affairs (Appendix B) and the Federal Trade Commission (Appendix B), since many of these salons are part of chains operating interstate and their misleading advertising appears across the nation. Send copies to your District Attorney, Attorney General of your state, State Consumer Agency (Appendix B), local consumer agencies, and the Consumers Federation of America (Appendix C).

BASIC UTILITIES

One of the toughest nuts to crack in terms of redressing wrongs done to the consumer is the utility company. In effect, there is no competition to make the utility walk the straight and narrow, and you must confront what is basically an arrogant monopoly.

Some of your most basic needs are filled by utilities. Telephone service, water, gas, electricity, and telegraph are just some of the items falling into this category, although admittedly the most important.

Some of them are government-run, some privately owned. For instance, in 1974, electricity was provided to some 17 million customers by 2,920 publicly owned systems, and some 58 million customers by 275 much larger privately owned facilities.

Typical problems that arise in your dealings with a utility involve whether the readings by the utilities of the meters are "careless," whether a computer (or human) has erred in billing, and quite often, whether someone else is plugged into your meter, or whether someone else's calls are being charged to you.

Before getting into the counter-attack aspect of your fight with the utility company, let us examine that old first line of defense—what you personally can do to (1) avoid a bad situation, and (2) lay the foundation of an attack.

As to electric and gas companies and their bills, assume you have found your bills getting larger and larger, even more so than would be warranted by rate increases. One of the first things that usually crosses the mind is that someone else is hooked into your meter (which, incidentally, is not as far-fetched as it sounds, especially in an apartment house). It is extremely difficult to check this out. Most electric companies claim that, even if someone else is wired into your meter, this is not their responsibility since their only duty is to supply electricity to the meter. Correct or not, this is usually the stand they will take, even in court. To hire an electrician to check on your suspicion is expensive. To check on it yourself, locate your meter; turn off *everything* (repeat, everything) in your apartment, not even forgetting an electric clock, night light, etc., and if the wheel on the meter still moves, there is some other load on it. It would then pay to pester your landlord or superintendent and state that you believe a crime (larceny) is taking place, and that it had better be corrected *fast* before you contact the District Attorney. If the landlord still does not do anything, you may have to hire an electrician to trace the hook-up onto your line and civilly or criminally prosecute that person. You may even find that if a superintendent lived in your apartment before you moved in, the hall lights and other items that require electricity in the general portions of the building are hooked into your line.

Bills based on meter readings or estimates may sometimes be suspicious (incidentally, don't automatically pay any bill without checking it). When humans read meters, there are bound to be human mistakes. As we all know, even computers make a few.

If the meter is inaccessible to the reader, you may have a bill based upon an estimate. The bill should indicate whether it is based on an estimate or actual reading; if not, question the company. Although this evens out the next time the meter is read, you are temporarily faced with a huge bill, or an abnormally low bill followed by a blockbuster the month after. If your bill is based on an estimated reading for two months in a row, demand a meter reading. After all, the succession of estimates may not be because of an inaccessible meter, but because some of the companies are attempting to cut expenses by using costly labor to read meters as rarely as possible, or estimates are based on the amounts used by the people who lived there before you.

You may prevent a claim of inaccessibility and consequently prevent estimated bills by arranging for an appointment with your utility office, and then making sure you are present when the meter reader calls. Always check the meter readings with the utility employee that comes to call, and even more important, check your readings against the bill you finally receive. There is many a slip, etc., and almost never in your favor.

Since utilities have no limitations on back billings, and since a bill for an accumulated period, say, six months, can be a catastrophe, make sure that meter readings take place at least every 30 to 60 days.

If you have any doubt concerning your bill, first request that the utility check it. If the company still maintains its position, insist that the meter be tested for accuracy.

When originally calling the utility, you will probably be asked many silly questions, such as whether you use an iron, or are watching TV excessively. In the light of bills that seem to be overcharges up to and beyond $100 per month, swallow your wrath and keep plugging away.

Keep in mind that many community utilities are switching over to computer operations and billings, and bugs are notorious in such systems. The computer is far from infallible. There was a recent instance where a young couple received an electric bill for a small apartment for one month in the sum of $632. It need not be described what dogfighting ensued and, sure enough, an amended bill came in. For $860! After much argument and fighting the good fight up through higher authority, the bill was again changed, this time to $64.

Telephone bills are also a bane of existence for many consumers. Remember your first line of defense.

If you reach a wrong number, ask the party who answers to tell you at least the first three digits of the phone number you have reached, together with the area code. Then call the operator, give her the information and tell her you want credit. The secret of success in this saving is to keep a record of when and what happens. Keep this record under, or by, your telephone, so that it may easily be found and checked against your bill to see that you actually did receive credit. Another way to avoid charges for wrong numbers if you have a toddler is to put a lock on the phone to prevent playful dialing of a number thousands of miles from home.

If your bills are high, month after month, adopt this program:

1. Keep a log of phone calls (even local ones), the numbers and persons called, and the time on each (use an egg timer) to lay a foundation for your future complaint.

2. On long distance, out of town calls, ask the operator (in advance) to give you "time and charges" when you are through. She should then call you after you have completed your conversation to give you the length of your call and what it costs. Record this on your log.

3. When a bill is received, check the numbers allegedly dialed under the "toll call and telegram" section. Make sure you know the numbers listed as being those you would, or did, call. If any are unfamiliar, ask the business office to advise you as to the names of the parties to whom the calls were made. If these turn out to be strangers, eliminate the possibility of someone in your home having called such a person (a baby sitter, perhaps), and if still sure a mistake has been made, call the business office, tell your story, and demand that you not be billed for such calls. You'll be surprised at how often your demand will be complied with, and usually with courtesy.

4. A seeming overcharge on "additional message units" calls made to your own general vicinity that are above the quota you are permitted per month is much more difficult to trace or adjust. You will be met with the argument that these calls were dialed directly from your home. Ask for the numbers allegedly dialed (quite often there is retrieval possible on such data by the machines the phone company uses), and go through the same process of elimination and demand for adjustment. You will usually run across a stiffer attitude, but you may still prevail if you are persistent enough.

Another saving in money may be effected with regard to an incident that took place when you first had your phone installed. Were you required to pay a deposit at the time to insure that your bill would be paid? Think back as to whether you didn't pay a deposit of $25, $50, or even $100. If so, in many communities today, this is no longer required, for your dealings and length of association with the telephone company entitle you to a refund. Ask the business office. Why should your money rest in the telephone company's pocket?

In each state, there is usually one state agency directly responsible for riding herd on utilities and handling complaints from the public. It is usually called the Public Service Commission, or some variation thereof. For the exact name and address, call the Better Business Bureau, consult your phone book for state agencies, or ask your librarian. There have been many complaints over the years as to the responsiveness of individual public service commissions to consumer needs, and allegations that such agencies are rubber stamps for the utilities, due to politics, etc. However, since individual complaints are at least listened to, and quite often acted upon, the odds are that it pays to carry your fight to the Public Service Commission.

In addition, if enough agencies are advised that the Commission has been placed on notice, and the Commission is aware of this, with the possibility of the harsh glare of publicity hanging over the scene, chances are good that you at least may get fair consideration, and possibly the redress you seek.

You must write to the equivalent of the Public Service Commission in your state, but the recipients of carbon copies will be somewhat changed. Considering the quasi-official nature of the utility, its monopolistic character, the fact that any action detrimental to you has almost certainly not been criminal in nature, a more political, publicity-minded, and consumer-oriented list is desirable. In most states, while the Commission is conducting its investigation, your service will not be shut off. Check with your local or state consumer agency to confirm this.

A sample letter might read as follows:

Public Service Commission
(Address)

Gentlemen:
I reside in Apartment _____ at (address) and have lived there for the past three months. My telephone number is (number). When I first moved in, I called the telephone company office at (address)

and spoke to a Mrs. Simons to arrange for a new telephone number, and possible to replace the phones left in the apartment by the last tenant. She informed me that it would be cheaper to leave the existing phones in place, and retain the same telephone number. I agreed.

After two weeks, I received a bill for an entire month (a copy of this bill being attached) in the sum of $85. Checking with Mrs. Simons, on (date) she looked up the record and found that most of the calls had been placed before I took over the telephone, and told me that my actual bill was $24.92. She said that she would feed the material into the computer and I would receive a corrected bill. I received no such bill.

The next month, I received a bill for the full $85 as arrears, and charges for the new month that included seven long distance calls I had not made (nor did I know the people at these numbers, I later found out). A copy of the bill with the erroneous charges underlined is attached. When I again called Mrs. Simons, she sounded much less helpful, and said she would check it out and call me back. She did not. The next two times I called her, she was "not in."

Now another monthly bill has come in with the same charges as on the last, five more long distance calls I did not make, and threats that my service will be cut off if I do not pay the entire amount immediately. A copy of this last bill is attached, with the five erroneous items underlined. I have a baby in the house, and might have to make emergency and other vital calls to a doctor, and will be severely prejudiced if my service is cut off.

I feel I am being victimized by the telephone company and the mistakes that its personnel and/or computer have made. Please investigate this situation.

Very truly yours,
Ellen Miller

cc: Telephone Company
    The Governor at State Capital
    United States Representative, House of Representatives, Washington, D.C. 20515
    United States Senator, U.S. Senate, Washington, D.C. 20515

The local newspaper editor
The local radio station or TV station
State Attorney General
Consumers Union (Appendix A)
Consumers Federation of America (Appendix C)
U.S. Office of Consumer Affairs (Appendix B)
State Consumer Agency (Appendix B)

INSURANCE CLAIMS

With regard to complaints concerning insurance claims, most involve automobile insurance, especially property damage coverage. The problems fall into two main categories: delay in settling and the amount of settlement.

As to delays in settling, a difference exists if you are making a claim against someone else's company for damage done to your car, or whether you have collision insurance and are trying to get your *own* company to pay for repairs. With regard to your request to have someone else's company pay for your damage, unless it is an open-and-shut case where the evidence is clear that the company is just giving you a run-around, it is difficult to collect, short of suing the negligent party represented by the insurance carrier. After all, the company may have a valid reason for disputing your claim, such as liability (the accident was partly your fault) or that your claim is padded, often based on their own appraiser's report.

The other category—collecting from your own collision carrier—is a different story. You have paid your premiums and are entitled to fairly speedy adjustment. Many companies will still haggle, for if they save $50 per claim and have 10,000 claims per year, the savings amount to some half million dollars.

Insurance companies tend to take a hard-nosed attitude, but most of them, in most states, are frightened of one club you hold over their heads. Unlike some other state regulatory agencies, the Department of Insurance of each state tends to be more consumer-minded and will conduct a piercing examination of complaints, and many companies are afraid of the extent and repercussions of any such investigation.

By all means, write to the Department of Insurance of your state. Check the phone book for the address, under state listings, or address it to the Department of Insurance at the state capital. Send copies to the insurance company, Consumers Union (Appendix C), Consumers Federation of America (Appendix C), and your state consumer agency (Appendix B).

Problems with all other insurance, including life insurance, should be handled in the same way. If you need information in making a complaint as to life and health insurance, write to the Institute of Life Insurance, 277 Park Avenue, New York, New York 10017.

FUNERAL HOMES

Most people prefer to avoid the topic of undertakers and the services they render, but this is a field that is now awash with violations of consumer rights, the fraudulent fringe depriving the loved ones, the next of kin, of substantial sums the decedent expected and desired them to get after death. If you grimace and wish to skip this section, don't. It is the duty of every person to be aware of the pitfalls and how to fight back.

The Federal Trade Commission has recently criticized a substantial minority within the funeral home "industry." Bill padding has reached a point where the average cost of a funeral exceeds $1500, very little of it on necessaries. You might think that it is heartless to begrudge the dear departed the last few niceties, but hidden in the long list of items to be paid for, clouded by the relatives' grief, are items that were not necessary, not provided, or duplications. The casket is only one small item on the list, but even here some undertakers refuse to display less expensive ones.

If misfortune should strike your family, ask a relative or a trusted friend with some experience to help you select a reliable funeral home. It might also help to ask your clergyman for a recommendation. Memorial societies can also help in planning less expensive funerals.

The person who is investigating and making arrangements, if in doubt as to a particular funeral home, would be wise to call the local office of the Better Business Bureau as to whether they have any file of complaints against the home.

Once a funeral home is selected, and there is a decision as to what kind of service is desired, the funeral director should provide an agreement for approval and signature, giving the signer a complete copy. This document should include the price of the service and all it includes, the price of each of the supplemental items of service or merchandise requested, and the amount involved for each of the items which the director will himself advance as an accommodation.

Proposals promulgated by the Federal Trade Commission will take some time to become effective, but future rules will require the 22,500 funeral homes in the United States to prohibit embalming without family permission, will prevent the necessity of embalming before cremation (see below), and will require clear pricing information to be provided, even over the telephone.

Many people, in an attempt to avoid such problems and high costs, have directed that they be cremated, a simple process that recently cost around $75. Some funeral directors, by padding, have run this up to an $800 procedure!

Rules to avoid such unfair business tactics, if simple cremation is desired, are as follows:

1. Don't pay for a casket unless the crematorium actually

requires one.

2. If the crematorium or funeral parlor claims that a casket is required by law, get it in writing, and ask to see the references to the law that the director should have available. State laws do not require caskets for cremation and some specifically prohibit such a requirement.

3. Ask if your state's laws permit private individuals or ambulance service to deliver a body directly (and inexpensively) to the crematorium.

4. Embalming is almost certainly not required, nor costly cemetery space. Put your foot down to these demands.

Another potential money-waster is the pre-paid funeral plan. By the time death occurs, the plan may be out of business or at some different, inconvenient location.

As grief subsides, it begins to penetrate that you have been "taken." What do you do? The great majority of states license funeral directors, and the licensing agency is the organization to write to. Get its name and address from the Better Business Bureau or your librarian.

Outline the details of what happened, attach a copy of the itemized bill, and, point by point, make your complaint. Send copies to the funeral home, attorney general of your state, your District Attorney, the Better Business Bureau (Appendix A), Consumers Union and Consumers Federation of America (Appendix C), U.S. Office of Consumer Affairs (Appendix B), your State Consumer Agency (Appendix B), and the Federal Trade Commission (Appendix B). Remember, attach copies of the bill to each letter, and retain a copy of the letter for yourself.

CHAPTER 10

——— Professional Services ———

Most people think of those engaged in rendering professional services, primarily medical and legal, as imbued with a nobility in their business relations far more than other merchants or mechanics. Truth to tell, the consumer of such professional services is just as likely to be taken advantage of as elsewhere.

MEDICAL SERVICES

Let us examine the medical profession and its shortcomings, deliberate acts, negligence, or callousness. With regard to most (though not all) of the offensive acts, it is admittedly only a fringe group in a profession that is guilty. However, in terms of numbers of patients treated, the total is significant.

Among doctors, there are those who are narcotic addicts, unpredictable in a field that demands full faculties; mental incompetents; professional incompetents; those guilty of malpractice; those who perform unnecessary surgery; doctors who lend themselves to quacks and faddists; those who needlessly prolong treatment for profit; doctors who order an excessive amount of laboratory tests to be performed at labs they secretly own; overcharges; physicians who represent themselves to be of greater competence or training (specialists) than they actually are; those who refer their patients for unneeded treatment, or treatment by a specialist, both medical and surgical, where the motive is splitting the fees paid to the second doctor; and those who arrogantly make false promises of good results or no danger, or go ahead with a course of treatment without even discussing it with the patient. Then there are those doctors who, because they are so busy, simply do not keep up with the flood of new developments in medicine.

What course of conduct can you reasonably expect from a doctor? A privately practicing physician is mostly a free agent, knowing far more than the patient, being unable to fully communicate the problem to a layman patient, and being used to making the sole decision as to what treatment to follow. However, the doctor has the decision and responsibility and cannot delegate this burden to someone else, for instance, a hospital into which he has you admitted. It is a common practice for another doctor, his partner, or a colleague, to substitute for him while he is on vacation or in any emergency, but no ethical doctor may arbitrarily transfer his patient to another doctor's care without the consent and approval of the patient. In obstetrics, a patient is entitled to be properly attended and must not be abandoned. The doctor may not abandon the newborn baby until another doctor takes over. In fact, once the doctor has commenced treatment for any illness, he may not abandon any patient. A doctor must not render treatment in a non-emergency situation without obtaining informed consent (he cannot tell you every medical detail or danger, but he must give you a reasonable idea of what you face and if there are any alternatives).

How may you avoid trouble? In selecting a doctor in a community where you are not familiar with one, use the tried and tested plan, as with any merchant, of checking on his reputation with friends and relatives, or with patients waiting in his outer office when you first visit him. Remember that reputable physicians do not advertise. Does the doctor, before recommending treatment, take a full medical history from you and give you a thorough physical examination? Does he listen to your questions and answer them intelligently, or does he resent his time being wasted and become brusque?

If you are going to see a surgeon, choose one not only to whom you are referred by your general practitioner, but make sure he is a member of the American College of Surgeons or the American Board of Surgery, professional societies that admit only qualified surgeons. This is not a guarantee that you will have a good result from this doctor, but at least you know he is probably qualified. Your local medical society can give you this information before you make an appointment, or your librarian can look it up in one of the professional directories most libraries have. You may also write to the American College of Surgeons (Appendix C).

The question of being qualified is not an idle one. Of some 68,000 doctors in the United States today who act as surgeons, some 57,000 are not certified as members of either society. A representative of the American College of Surgeons has estimated that one-half of the operations performed in this country today are perfomed by doctors untrained or inadequately trained to undertake surgery. An operation on your body should be the subject of as little guesswork as possible.

Is the hospital that the doctor wants to place you in accredited by the American Hospital Association, meeting their standards? One-third of all American hospitals are not. Once again, check with your local medical society or librarian.

If the surgeon tells you flatly that he must operate, have no hesitation in having a consultation with another doctor. The medical profession has found that not only does this procedure cut down on the number of operations actually performed, but it has also estimated that there are two million unnecessary operations per year, with at least 10,000 unnecessary deaths. Besides, no reputable physician minds a consultation for the purpose of confirmation of the need for surgery, and if your surgeon minds, that alone might be a good reason to suspect his judgment or motives.

More pitfalls: If your doctor makes you come back repeatedly, and you see no progress, you might be in the clutches of an overtreater. If suspicious, consult another doctor immediately. Your physician or surgeon may be guilty of malpractice. This might consist of bungled surgical procedures, unexplainably poor medical results, misdiagnosis, performing of an operation without your informed consent, and abandonment, among others. He or his assistants may make errors in medication, or even the administration of it (breaking needles, negligently hitting a nerve with an injection, etc.) "Health clinics" run solely to cash in on Medicaid, may be mistreating you and be totally inadequate to treat your condition. Your doctor may be robbing you with his exorbitant fees. He may not even be licensed to practice in your state (all doctors, in every state, must be licensed).

If you feel that your doctor is guilty of any of the above, what do you do? If the results of any such conduct have caused severe injury to you, don't take it upon yourself to rectify the wrong and collect for your disability. See a lawyer.

If, however, you have merely been a victim without substantial injury (other than to your pocketbook), there are ways of fighting back.

For the doctor who is not licensed (call the Medical Society to check on this, or have the librarian consult a professional register that your library has), notify the District Attorney and the State Attorney General. This is a crime.

For the "Medicaid mill" health clinic, notify the United States Department of Health, Education and Welfare (Appendix B), and your local and state departments of health.

As to fees, there is usually a "going rate" for similar fees within a community, and if you feel that the doctor has been unconscionable in his charges, report this to your state and local medical societies' grievance committees. A discussion of these societies will follow.

There are medical societies primarily on three levels. Nationwide, there is the American Medical Association (Appendix C), state societies, and county societies. For addresses of the state and county societies, consult your telephone directory or ask your librarian. These are private groups, self-policing their profession, and they have no power to remove a doctor's license. The strongest penalty a society or hospital staff can mete out is expulsion from membership. The doctor may still practice, since he is still licensed. However, inability to have patients admitted to a hospital, being ostracized, cut off from the countless benefits of the Society, is regarded by practically every doctor as tragic and much to be avoided.

If you have a complaint, although you should notify the American Medical Association Department of Investigation and your State Medical Society, your complaint should be addressed to the Grievance Committee of your County Medical Society. The complaint should be submitted in writing, and the doctor is usually asked by the society to respond. If there is a conflict, quite often a hearing is ordered at which you may obtain satisfaction. One very large warning, however. If you are a resident of a county with a small population, and consequently a small medical society (it is estimated that three-quarters of this nation's county societies have less than 50 members and nearly half have 15 or less), address your complaint to the state society primarily, so that you will not become a victim of cronyism.

If you feel that the doctor's violation is extremely serious, you should contact not only the medical societies but the State Board that licenses him, which has the power to act against him or withdraw his license. Obtain the name and address of this board from your county medical society, the professional directories in your library, or your state Secretary of State.

Naturally, if you suspect fraud or a criminal act having been committed, notify the District Attorney and the State Attorney General.

A typical letter of complaint might read as follows:

County Medical Society
(Address)

Gentlemen:

I wish to make a complaint about (name) whose office is at (address). In January of this year, I noticed a growth on my left hand. Being new in the community and knowing no doctors, I was recommended to this doctor by the superintendent of my building. I first went to see him on (date) and he examined my hand and told me it was a serious tumor, although he doubted it was cancer. When I asked him if I should see a specialist to get tests, he said it was not necessary, that he was a specialist on this type of tumor, and that he must start treatment immediately. I did not know where else to go, so I started treatment with him.

For the next 25 weeks, I went to him twice a week, and all he did was to have his nurse put some sort of vibrating band on it. He charged me $15 a visit for this "special treatment," a total of $750, for which I have the cancelled checks.

Seeing that the growth was not getting better, and even looked irritated, I went to a dermatologist (name) whose name I obtained by calling your society. He told me that the growth was only a wart, and he removed it in his office.

I feel that I have been defrauded and I request that an investigation be made as to the doctor's fitness to practice.

Very truly yours,
Ellen Miller

cc: State Medical Society
    American Medical Association (Appendix C)
    Medical Licensing Board
    District Attorney
    State Attorney General

Some dentists present a similar problem. There are more than 120,000 dentists in America today, and while, percentagewise, the number of bad apples is small, even a small percentage may amount to a large number.

Assuming you are seeking the services of a dentist, use the reliable guide of asking friends, neighbors, or co-workers to recommend one. Your county dental society (find it through the telephone book or with the help of the librarian) probably has a referral service, but this is no guarantee, however. Ask your family doctor or the county Department of Health. When you get down to a couple of names, make an appointment, but remain on guard. Remember, you are still shopping.

In determining how good a dentist is, keep certain questions in mind at the appointment. Is the doctor prevention-oriented, with advice as to proper care of your teeth? Does he use x-rays in making diagnosis? Is the appearance of the office, the dentist, and his staff clean? Is a preliminary record of your medical and dental history or whether you are allergic to anesthesia or other medication made?

Is he willing to discuss his fee with you before he starts on your teeth? If it sounds high to you, check his charges and estimates with the local dental society, which usually keeps a list of fees generally regarded as reasonable in the area. If his fees are higher than the list, but you would still like to use his services, ask him why the fees are so high. And don't be embarrassed! It is your money.

Ask any friends who know him (and patients in his waiting room) his reputation for responding to an emergency. Above all, back out if the dentist looks like he is going to proceed with a course of treatment without informing you as to what he intends to do, what it will cost, or the possible alternatives or complications.

If you eventually feel you have been taken advantage of by your dentist, use the same procedure as in making a complaint against the doctor; advise the American Dental Association (Appendix C), your State and County Dental Societies (consult your phone book or your librarian), and the licensing board (name and address may be obtained from your County Dental Society, your Librarian, or the Secretary of State of your state). If fraud may be involved, notify the District Attorney and your state's Attorney General as well.

Many Americans undergo treatment by chiropractors, practitioners who adjust the structure of the body primarily by manipulating the spine and using x-rays, but shun drugs and surgery. Over 30 million people have been treated in this country by about 18,000 chiropractors. They are licensed in every state except Louisiana and Mississippi, and in those two states they may practice without state regulation.

There are two major chiropractic associations. The first is the International Chiropractors Association and the second is the larger American Chiropractic Association (Appendix C for both). Although there are state and local societies, it might be wiser to advise both of the national associations, with copies to the state and local groups, of any violation by individual chiropractors. Use the same method and rules as for doctors and dentists in making a complaint, including notifying the licensing board and perhaps the District Attorney and State Attorney General, if fraud is involved. In addition, the Consumers Federation of America (Appendix C) has a continuing interest in this field, so notify them also.

To include veterinarians in the same discussion as doctors or similar medical practitioners might seem improper, but 36 million households have at least one pet, and a broad spectrum of studies has revealed many violations in this field, where every state requires licensing.

How do you avoid risks in choosing a veterinarian? Once again, ask for recommendations from your neighbors and friends. If you can't find one through this means, call your state or local chapter of the American Veterinary Medical Association (use the phone book or librarian), or call the local office of the American Society for the Prevention of Cruelty to Animals or your local Animal Shelter. If you have doubts during any course of treatment, check the veterinarian's credentials with the state Board of Veterinary Examiners.

When you go to the office, trust your first impressions. Is the waiting room clean and free of odors? In the examining room, is the table and equipment clean, the floor clean?

If suspicious of any fraud, check with another vet, and if you catch the suspect in a lie, contact the State Attorney General and the licensing agency. Fees, however, though outrageous, are not subject to state regulation.

Complaints, even with regard to fees, should be made to the American Veterinary Medical Association, 600 South Michigan Avenue, Chicago, Illinois 60605, with copies to the local and state societies, to the state licensing board, the ASPCA, and, if the infraction is severe enough in your opinion, to the District Attorney and State Attorney General.

Hospitals often come in for their share of complaints, including non-treatment of the patient as a human being, carelessness and callousness of some of the personnel, and exorbitant and unwarranted charges.

As to your treatment and handling, the American Hospital Association has recently passed a Patient's Bill of Rights. Some of the most important items deal with your right to considerate and respectful care; complete and understandable information as to the diagnosis, treatment, and what your future condition may be; the explanation of all facts to you so that you may give informed consent or a refusal for any new procedure or treatment; privacy as to the program for your medical care; a reasonable response by hospital personnel to a reasonable request for service; the right to refuse to let your body be used for experimentation; a reasonable continuity of care both during and after your confinement; an explanation of your bill even if the source of payment is insurance or otherwise; and an explanation, in advance, of hospital rules and regulations that you may reasonably be requested to abide by. Not many hospitals have as yet adopted this code, but violation of any such right will serve you in good stead in making a complaint.

If you are interested in obtaining a copy of such a Bill of Rights, write to the American Hospital Association (Appendix C).

As to hospital charges, saving begins even at the beginning. Ask your doctor if he will conduct preadmission tests before you are admitted, which will shorten your hospital confinement.

Once you receive your bill, regardless of the source of payment, ask the hospital for a full explanation of it, and don't be put off by the exasperated air of a clerk or cashier. If tests or x-rays appear more than once on a bill, ask your doctor and a *second* medical authority for an explanation (after all, your doctor has to stay in the hospital's good graces, so as to retain his admitting privileges). Many private hospitals overcharge patients drastically on phone bills. If you believe this to be the case, notify the Attorney General of your state. Several of the states have recently acted on such complaints.

If you have been severely injured as a result of the hospital's negligence, don't try to strike back by yourself. Get a lawyer and learn your rights as soon as possible, especially if the hospital is owned or run by a state or municipality (there may be a time limit on taking action).

In all other cases where you have a complaint about a hospital and its personnel, there are some definite sources of satisfaction.

The first is the American Hospital Association itself (Appendix C). If it is felt that your complaint has merit, this group may intervene to redress the wrong done you. Send them a copy of your letter of complaint. The letter, however, should be addressed to a more powerful organization, one that most hospitals listen to most carefully, a private, non-profit group called the Joint Commission on Accreditation of Hospitals (Appendix C). This group will certify that a particular hospital is living up to certain standards, and accreditation by the organization is eagerly sought by all hospitals for their own professional (and eventual monetary) benefit. Representatives hold an inspection at each hospital every year or two, and also hold local hearings at which those who feel aggrieved may voice criticism or seek answers to questions. No adjudication will be made of your particular complaint, but if the hospital knows that you will bring to the fore certain conditions that will highlight the hospital's shortcomings, which may result in a possible withdrawal of accreditation, you may very well be contacted to adjust your complaint. Write to the Joint Commission to tell them of your complaint, to find out when they will be at your hospital, and when they will hold public hearings. The hospital, too, is obligated to give you the date of the hearing, if it knows.

As a double check on the Joint Commission, you should also write to the Department of Health, Education and Welfare, Office for Consumer Services (Appendix B). If it receives enough complaints, it can undertake its own independent accreditation survey. The Office of Consumer Affairs (Appendix B) should also receive a copy of your letter of complaint.

Many nursing homes have become notorious in this decade, giving the entire industry of some 23,000 homes a black eye. For the purpose of this section, we will refer to nursing homes, although this general classification includes rest homes, convalescent homes, and homes for the aged or retired.

One way to avoid the problems connected with such institutions is to look for an alternative to them. Many areas have a Visiting Nurse Service, therapists, homemakers, home health aides, outpatient care at clinics, and a service for delivering meals to aged and incapacitated people living at home. Investigate and try these alternatives, and if they are sufficient, they're usually preferable to residing at a nursing home.

If such alternative care will not serve your purposes, the next step is to look for a home. At such institutions, different types of care are available, some for personal service, some for medical attention, some for both. If you are leaving a hospital and must have certain care, consult with the hospital's social worker. Actually, if you, or the patient for whom you are assuming responsibility, has been hospitalized for a severe illness, the investigation of nursing home possibilities should begin immediately. Discover what monetary benefits are available to the patient under both federal and state programs. Your family doctor may be able to inform you, but make sure you make a final check with your State Department of Health.

It must be assumed that at this point you know nothing of such homes. Obtain a list of those in your neighborhood that might be suitable from your local Health Department, local medical society, the Hospital or Nursing Home Association in your community, any senior citizen or social work group you may be familiar with, the district office of Social Security, clergymen, relatives, and friends. Your doctor is also a source of names, but when you obtain a name from him, ask him how many of his patients have been in that home, how many have been transferred, and why.

You can certainly eliminate many possibilities on your list by merely making calls to the homes to find out if they provide the certain type of care that your individual case requires, and whether they participate in the Medicare or Medicaid programs, assuming that such type of assistance is obtainable.

Your best bet for adequate care is usually a non-profit home, but that generally will have a long waiting list. It will not hurt, however, to visit the home anyway to serve as a comparison with other prospects, or even to place the name of the patient on the list.

Visit as many of the institutions on the list as conveniently can be done—large ones, small ones. Try to arrange to stay on each visit for at least an hour. A refusal of this long a visit usually shows that the home has something to hide. Short tours, offered by many homes, reveal nothing.

All states require licensing of nursing homes, and most places display such licenses openly. If you don't see it, ask to see it. Check that it is current. If they have no license or won't show it to you, walk out—fast!

Visits should take place in the late morning or at mid-day, so you may see what type of lunch is being served. Insist on seeing every floor of the home, including the kitchen, bathrooms, therapy facilities, bedrooms, and dining area.

While inspecting the premises, keep in mind its location (nearness to the family doctor, relatives, etc.); fire safety (are the exits marked, not blocked, etc.); whether all bedrooms exit into a corridor and have windows; and the general cleanliness and condition of all areas and the grounds.

You must ascertain whether the home has a doctor available in an emergency, if only on call; whether a thorough physical examination is given promptly upon admission; if there is an arrangement with a nearby hospital if acute illness strikes; ask to see menus, and find out about eating rules and dieticians, and whether the institution provides the specific diet or therapy the patient requires; and inquire whether a patient's private doctor is allowed to attend the patient at the home. With regard to money, ascertain what is the basic monthly charge, exactly what is received for it, what is extra, and whether each extra is a monthly charge or a one-time payment. There is a big savings, also, if the home permits medicines for the patient to be bought on the outside.

Now you have narrowed your choice down to two or three homes. Contact the state Health Department and ask to see (as is your legal right) the latest Medicare and Medicaid inspection reports or resumes. The department will advise you where such reports may be seen.

You have decided—but remain wary. If the home wants you to sign a "life" contract, be advised that the contract usually may not be cancelled and there is a good possibility that the home will not supply intensive care, if needed later on. Be wary also if a large deposit or payment of a "finder's fee" is required. This ties you hand and foot by taking away resources in advance. Find out if the deposit may be made in monthly payments instead of your being forced to liquidate assets.

Assuming that the patient is in the home, the problems that usually crop up involve bad food, overcrowding of rooms, blind or disabled patients being placed on an upper floor with no elevator, unworkable call-bell systems, poor toilet and medical facilities, forcing patients to work without pay, and social security checks and other funds addressed to the patient being intercepted by the home. Under federal law, each patient is entitled to $30 per month allowance for personal use, but many institutions intercept even that. Certainly, all of the above are grave violations and cry out for complaints.

What are the realities, however? The patient, or the loved ones of the patient, who would ordinarily make a complaint to the authorities, are afraid to do so because of the fear that any complaint will be met by the home operator and staff with retaliation against the patient.

There is really only one solution, aside from transferring the patient. A mild complaint may very well be met by spiteful retaliation on the "hostage," but IF A BIG ENOUGH AND LOUD ENOUGH COMPLAINT IS MADE, AND IS BROUGHT BEFORE AS MANY AGENCIES AS POSSIBLE, retaliation becomes risky and will usually not be contemplated. After all, the operator of the home cannot indulge in personal spite or permit his staff to do so if it will endanger his entire operation. It may even be wise to retain a lawyer to pursue the complaint, if the problem is acute enough and finances can stand the expense.

A typical form of complaint letter follows. It is addressed to the local Social Security Office (whose address may be found in your telephone directory under "United States Government") which functions as a clearing house for complaints about *all* nursing homes, whether or not they receive government funds.

The list at the end of the letter of those who will receive carbon copies (thus letting the home know who has been advised) is the most important thing, even if some of the organizations have no jurisdiction over the home (that is, the institution may not be a member of the group, etc.).

District Social Security Office
(Address)

Gentlemen:

On November 4, 1974, I arranged for my mother (name) to be admitted to the (name of the nursing home), located at (address), for medical care and personal service, as per the copy of the contract attached to this letter, and she has remained there since then. Copies of the other documents and bills with respect to her stay are also attached. She is 81 years old, in frail health, confined to a wheelchair, but is clear of mind.

From the beginning, she had complained about her food. She is supposed to be on a restricted diet, but she has been given the same food as the other patients, and the home does not even have a dietician, although I had been informed they had one. She is in a room with five other women, although there is room for only three people. The toilets are constantly breaking down and her call-bell system has been broken for four months (list your other complaints but avoid petty ones). I have complained to the administrator on numerous occasions, but nothing has been done to correct the situation.

I ask that an investigation be made as to the conditions in the home and that its license be reviewed in light of the investigation.

Very truly yours,
Ellen Miller

cc: Administrator of the nursing home
(If on Welfare) patient's caseworker or county welfare office
State Medicaid agency (check the phone book or ask your librarian)
State Health Department (same sources)

State Licensing Authority (same sources)
State Board responsible for licensing nursing home administration (same sources)
United States Senators, U.S. Senate, Washington, D.C. 20510
U.S. Representative, House of Representatives, Washington, D.C. 20515
State and Local elected representatives (call your Board of Elections for information)
Joint Commission on Accreditation of Hospitals (Appendix C)
American Nursing Home Association (Appendix C)
American Association of Homes for the Aging, 529 14th Street, N.W., Washington, D.C. 20004
American College of Nursing Home Administrators, the Eig Building, 8641 Colesville Road, Silver Springs, Maryland 20910.
Better Business Bureau (Appendix A)
Local Chamber of Commerce (telephone book)

LEGAL SERVICES

Most complaints about lawyers revolve around fee disputes or the fact that the lawyer is not resolving the matter fast enough. Very few complaints involve actual fraud or theft. The legal profession is primarily self-regulated through the American Bar Association (Appendix C) nationally, and through state and local bar associations (consult your telephone book) in conjunction with the courts. In the past, such bar associations have been exceedingly stern and demanding with regard to lawyers' professional conduct, and most lawyers fear the slightest complaint to such groups because of the heavy penalties—including suspension or disbarment—administered for relatively light infractions or carelessness in the relationships with clients.

If you have a problem with a lawyer, usually just a mention of your intention to complain to the bar association will result in an easing of his position. Should he remain adamant, advise the bar association in writing of your complaint, and the lawyer will be required to respond in writing. A hearing may be held, or, if your position is obviously correct, action will be taken against him. Results are swift and often gratifying.

Of course, if criminal conduct on his part is involved, you should also write to the District Attorney and State Attorney General.

Don't be afraid to fight a professional. You will quite often obtain better redress of the wrong done to you than with a businessman.

CHAPTER 11

Moving, Travel, and Transportation

Keeping on the go seems to be our national pastime. Moving to a new residence, travelling on business or for pleasure, the carriage of our goods and ourselves is big business—always a happy hunting ground for those who would take advantage of the consumers.

The movers who transport furniture and other goods may cause you much grief unless you know the rules and how to protect yourself.

As in the selection of all other merchants, how you go about picking one is important. As usual, check with your friends, neighbors, or even the superintendent of your building, should you live in an apartment house, as to who they would recommend. Ask them why they recommend a particular mover, and if the answer is that they've heard of the mover through advertising, forget the recommendation. In this field especially, advertising guarantees nothing. While shopping around is advisable, the firm that quotes the lowest price may not be the best (it probably will not be). Forget it if you are offered a "guaranteed" flat rate. Reputation is what counts. Call your Better Business Bureau as to whether they have any complaints about your contemplated mover. Contact the Transportation Department of your state (consult the telephone book or your librarian) and find out if your state is one that licenses movers. If so, find out whether your prospective mover is licensed.

Once you have selected your mover, your rights and liabilities are basically determined by whether your move will be interstate, passing from one state to at least one other, or will take place entirely within the state where you now live. Interstate moving is much more strictly regulated.

The federal agency that controls interstate movers is the Interstate Commerce Commission (ICC), and they are strict. In fact, their regulations provide that the mover must give you a booklet as to your rights, prepared by the ICC, at least 24 hours before contracting with you for your move. Read it carefully. Most legal terms are avoided, and it makes sense to most average people.

At the same time, the mover must hand you a "report card," showing the past accuracy of the company in estimating charges, the frequency of loss or damage claims, promptness in pickup and delivery and time taken to settle claims against it. By obtaining several estimates, the track record of the companies may be compared, and a more informed decision may be made.

All such movers must file a tariff with the ICC, a copy of which may be examined at the movers' office. A tariff is merely a chart of rates and charges.

When you get down to brass tacks—the writing of the actual contract, called the "order for service"—it must contain many things, first of which is the name, address, and phone number of you as the shipper; the person to whom it is going (referred to as the consignee), even though it is yourself at your new address; and the carrier's delivering agent.

There must be a statement of the agreed pickup date and delivery date, or the time within which this will be accomplished. If the carrier cannot pick up your goods on the date stated on the order for service, it must notify you by phone, telegram, etc., of the fact, the reason for the delay, and a time when the furniture will be picked up. As to delivery, the moving company is not limited to the exact date specified, but to a reasonable time thereafter. Of course, you may arrange to receive the shipment on a certain day, the so-called "expedited service," but there is an additional charge for this. Incidentally, if you only order the regular delivery service and the date for delivery as stated in the order for service has passed, hound the moving company at least once a day about it no matter how annoyed they get, because there have been cases of companies that claim they tried to get you but couldn't, and then stick you for a healthy storage charge.

The order for service must also include the shipper's contacts en route, if any, and at the destination; a complete description of any special services ordered; and any identification or registration number assigned to the shipment by the carrier.

Another portion of the order for service states the amount of *estimated* charges and the method of payment. You may obtain a written estimate or approximation of the cost beforehand, but it is not binding on either you or the carrier. The *exact* cost of your move cannot be determined until your goods are weighed after loading into the van. The entire van rides onto a huge scale, the weight of the truck is deducted from the total weight registered on the scale, and you are charged for the balance. Incidentally, the location of the scale to be used in weighing the shipment must also be stated in the order. At your request, the carrier must notify you of the weight and charges on your shipment. If you are suspicious, you may request before delivery that it be reweighed on another scale at the destination (although at your expense).

As to method of payment mentioned above, the order will state the maximum amount to be paid in cash, certified check, or money order to induce the carrier to give you your possessions at the destination. You may usually forget credit in interstate moving.

However, if the total exceeds the estimated amount plus ten percent, this additional sum may be paid within 15 working days.

Now comes the time for the pickup. Whether you pack or the packer does, there are certain things that only you, or someone hired by you, will do. The refrigerator and washing machine must be disconnected, and anything tacked down or nailed up, such as drapes or carpeting, must be freed.

When the pickup man comes, he will make an inventory. BE THERE! He will, quite often, mark the inventory slip with notations showing that certain items are "gouged," "marked," etc. Make sure a proper description is entered before signing the inventory, and note on it, by item number, which descriptions you disagree with. Don't let him tell you that you can't write on it. Nonsense! Tell him to get his boss on the phone and he will change his tune. You will also get a bill of lading. Hold on to it. It is your receipt and represents the contract of carriage of your possessions.

It must be noted at this point that the interstate mover is not liable for the full value of lost or damaged goods unless you pay extra for such protection. The formula is complicated, but if you are interested in such full protection, read your ICC booklet and ask the man who is filling out your "order for service" at the time it is filled out.

Time passes and the move is over. When the unloading starts BE THERE and take out your inventory sheet immediately. Check off each item as it is brought in. If anything is missing or damaged, point it out to the delivery man and mark it on your own copy of the inventory. After the dropoff is completed, the truck man will ask you to sign a delivery receipt, or his inventory, or both. Don't sign it unless one or the other of these documents states that there is a claim for such damaged or lost articles. If he won't mark it on the papers, you insist on doing so before signing. Just telling the driver, without writing it down as stated above, is not enough. Also, don't sign any delivery papers until the delivery is complete.

If you find out at a later time that something you overlooked was lost or damaged, you have nine months to make a claim (of course the longer you wait, the more your claim will be regarded with suspicion). Once a claim is filed with a mover (send a copy to the ICC—Appendix B) it must be acknowledged in writing by the mover within thirty days after receipt, and the carrier must pay or refuse to pay within 120 days after receipt, or let you know every thirty days thereafter what the delay is all about. Of course, to make a claim on goods that you noticed were missing or damaged at time of delivery, you should have some proof of your claim, the best being the written notations made at the time of delivery on the shipping papers.

Copies of everything, including all correspondence, should be sent to the ICC. It cannot determine if the carrier should pay, but it can help "expedite" matters. If you wish to deal directly with the carrier's insurance company, you may write for the information to the Director, Bureau of Operations, Interstate Commerce Commission, 12th and Constitution Avenues N.W.,

Washington D.C. 20423.

When the move does not cross state lines, the ICC is not involved. Rules are much more fluid, and usually are much more severely limited on the amount of liability on the part of the carrier, about half of what a carrier might owe on a loss involved in an interstate move. Arrange for additional insurance with your insurance broker before such a move, and you will find that the slight additional cost by way of premium is worth it.

Incidentally, in selecting a "local" mover, beware of estimates, as you may be given a very low estimate and it will then work out to some three times this amount after the furniture is in the mover's possession. Shop around and see what the usual price is. Go for reputation, not the rock-bottom estimate. Because of these abuses, many states have now set limits on far over the original estimate the eventual charge may go, but there are too many ways of getting around this.

As to local moving damage, most reliable movers have an unwritten rule that if a damage is reported one or two days after delivery, the mover will assume responsibility, even if you have signed a release. Don't forget to make and check off an inventory even in these local moves, however.

If your problem involves an interstate move, and you can't wait for the relatively slow process of letter writing, the Interstate Commerce Commission has a "hot line" (see Appendix B). Get the name of the person you speak with, tell him your problem in as few words as possible, and stress the urgency of the matter ("they didn't deliver my furniture, and I have no crib in which to put the baby"). Quite often, the resolution of your problem will be expedited.

Your problem, however, will usually not be of such urgency (damaged furniture) and it is better to have your complaint in writing. Formal written complaints may not be as easily pigeonholed as a phone call may be. Basically the same organization in both interstate and intrastate moves should receive carbon copies of the letters of complaint, and it is advisable to notify the ICC even in a move taking place wholly within one state. After all, the same firm may also be licensed for interstate moves, and it would not want to get a bad reputation with the ICC.

Interstate move complaint letters should be addressed to the Interstate Commerce Commission, but "local move" complaint letters should be addressed to the Attorney General of your state (in some states, the local moving industry is controlled by some regulatory agency, and the Attorney General will refer your letter).

A typical letter of complaint in an interstate move might read as follows:

Interstate Commerce Commission
Washington D.C. 20423

Gentlemen:
    I made an agreement with (name and address of moving firm) on (date) to move my furniture from my old apartment to my present residence. I am attaching a copy of the agreement. I understand I was supposed to receive a booklet from them as to my rights before I signed, but I received nothing.

    They were supposed to pick up my furniture on (date), but they picked it up two days later without calling or advising me of the delay, and when I called them in the meantime, no one seemed to know anything about it. On the inventory, the movers marked everything as gouged or damaged, but I only signed it after he let me write on it my disagreement with these statements. I am attaching a copy of my copy of the inventory, as well as the bill of lading.

    When it was delivered, the entire back of the sofa was ripped and I have been informed by an upholsterer that it would cost me more to repair it than it cost me. It was only two months old, and I am enclosing a copy of the bill of sale to show its price.

I called the company immediately, but they would not let me talk to anyone in authority. I sent them a letter of complaint and a copy to you (although I am enclosing another copy), and they wrote to me three weeks later, a copy of their letter being attached, that they are investigating my claim.

It is now six months since my furniture was moved, and I have just received a letter from them, a copy of which is attached, telling me that they will not pay anything for the couch.

I respectfully request that you investigate their actions. I have no more money to buy a new couch, and I am humiliated when anyone sees it in my home.

Very truly yours,
Ellen Miller

cc: Moving Company
    State Consumer Agencies in new and old states (Appendix B)
    Federal Office of Consumer Affairs (Appendix B)
    Attorney General of the old state
    Attorny General of the new state
    Consumers Union (Appendix C)
    Council of Better Business Bureaus (Main Headquarters, Appendix A)
    Consumers Federation of America (Appendix C)

We have considered the moving of your personal effects. When it comes to ourselves, millions of Americans arrange for their plans and reservations through travel agencies. Here, one is liable to meet trouble also.

As should be your procedure in dealing with any firm that provides goods or services, look for the most reliable agency by checking with your friends or neighbors as to whether they can recommend an organization they dealt with that proved trustworthy. In addition, the local Better Business Bureau may be of particular help concerning the reputation of any particular agency.

When visiting such a firm, be aware that anyone may call himself a travel agent, legally or illegally. Is the agency bonded? Look at the walls for a posted license.

Most worthwhile travel agents hold approved sales agency status from one or more conferences of passenger carriers, including the Air Traffic Conference (ATC), the International Air Transport Association (IATA), and the International Passenger Ship Association (IPSA). Ask if your agency has such a status. Look at the walls and literature for any certificates or representations to this effect.

For proven reliability, choose an agency that bears a certificate or insignia as a member of the American Society of Travel Agents. Its standards of membership are strict, requiring that the agent shall have been in business for at least three years and shall have held at least two carrier conference authorizations for two years each. Furthermore, it is required that the firm be financially sound and of good character.

How do you deal with a travel agent? Inform him of just what your needs are, and how much you have budgeted for your trip. Ask him which of his services does he charge a fee for, and which he does not. In most cases, his fee comes from the hotel, airline, etc., with whom he makes arrangements on your behalf. If he arranges a tour or itinerary for you, there may be a modest fee which you would have to pay. Most railroads pay no commission, so the agent might have to charge you a nominal fee for making such arrangements.

When you receive your vouchers or tickets, make sure they match the itinerary for which you are being charged.

Charter flights present a substantial problem today. Ask what your rights are to a refund in the event of a cancellation by you or the charter. Ask about any time limit to notify the charter people of your cancellation and still collect the refund. Find out which airline has been scheduled to carry you, and confirm this through a separate call to the airline. If they won't tell you which airline, something is wrong and a graceful change of agencies might be in order. If you are told some airline about which you have never heard, for your life's sake it is advisable to call the local civil aeronautics office (consult your telephone directory) and ask if that particular airline is certified for charter flights. They're not? Don't go! In entering into any written agreement with an agent, have it spell out your rights, if you cancel, to get back all, part, or none of your money. It is better to know where you stand immediately.

Most legitimate complaints against travel agencies involve the wrongful loss of deposits; prepayment of services to an agency that becomes insolvent, and your money disappears; and tours that advertise first-class travel, but you wind up with economy flights, dingy hotels, or second-class rail accommodations.

Package tours represent an especially troublesome subdivision of these problems. Many agents will claim that they are not responsible for non-delivery of what was promised, because such tours are bought from a wholesale tour operator who has made all the arrangements. To reinforce their position, such agents put similar disclaimers of liability in all their brochures and contracts. Don't let yourself be talked out of pursuing a complaint because such disclaimers are flashed at you, and you are triumphantly told that you signed the documents subject to them. Most states today ignore the disclaimers and, if you can prove your complaint, the agent will be deemed responsible.

What remedies are available to you if you have a legitimate complaint? Many consumer pamphlets will tell you to sue in your local small claims court, and you may be forced to do so, but there have been numerous articles over the past few years debunking the efficacy of small claims courts, to the extent that even if you recover a judgment, the odds are you will never collect a dime. No, the agencies are more worried about bad publicity or possible criminal prosecution than they are over a small, possibly uncollectable, money judgment.

On any of these complaints, write to the Attorney General of your state (phone book or librarian) with copies to the agency, the Better Business Bureau (Appendix A), your state's consumer agency (Appendix B), and the U.S. Office of Consumer Affairs (Appendix B), as well as your local District Attorney (phone book).

Being actually on the move today usually means going by air. Many airlines have been guilty of violations of your consumer rights. Your rights, basically, are to certain minimum standards of service en route, and receiving your baggage in proper shape at the other end.

You are also entitled to know what service may be expected; what is the cheapest available fare; what restrictions and conditions are applicable; what additional charges may be made for TV or radio entertainment, and for drinks; what the carrier's limit of liability is for damaged or lost luggage, and any alternative plans or payments that would protect you beyond these limits; and, perhaps most importantly, what your rights are if the flight is oversold.

Most of this section will deal with legitimate airlines that may be guilty of treating you or your luggage improperly, but there are still a few, very few airlines, which must be watched for criminal activities. Some of them attempt to cash in on illegal (and unsafe) charter flights. You can usually spot them by their ads, which never include details of when cancellation may be made, or how much time must be spent on the trip; a fancy name of a promoting organization is given, but not the name of an actual airline; etc. Some advertisements prominently display a time period and a price, but a reading of the small print reveals that the price doesn't apply to the time period. No more will be written about such airlines and promoters, because the advice is simple: avoid them. If defrauded, notify the District Attorney and State Attorney General immediately, but don't get defrauded. Avoid them like the plague.

Most airlines are subject to the rules and regulations of the Civil Aeronautics Board (CAB), even foreign airlines that extend their operations to this country. The CAB has certain limitations, however. For instance, the board has no authority over airlines under its jurisdiction to try claims for damages for forced refunds, but the airlines fear complaints, for the CAB may act if a breach of regulations is found. In addition, the CAB has no say-so over intrastate carriers (airlines that operate completely within one state), air taxis with a maximum of thirty seats, or commuter plane carriers.

With regular airlines, many disputes arise as to the fare charged. All airlines answerable to the CAB must file a tariff (list) of rates and rules at every location where tickets are sold, and you have an absolute right not only to see it, but if you don't understand it, to have it explained to you. The fare that you must pay is the one in effect on the day you fly, even though you purchased tickets before the fare went up. Also, it would pay to find out if you are eligible for a special fare, such as an excursion rate, but heed the warning that you must comply *exactly* with the terms and conditions of the offer.

One of the complaints that has aroused the most public indignation refers to delay in departure and arrival, and being "bumped"—that is, being denied a seat on the plane.

Since there are usually cancellations by prospective passengers, an airline might sell 65 places for only 60 seats, so that the plane will take off with a full load despite cancellations. The

CAB has ruled that a carrier must offer a certain amount of compensation to any passenger holding a confirmed (usually properly validated or stamped) reservation for a particular flight who is not permitted to board a plane because the seats have been oversold.

This rule of compensation does not apply to foreign airlines, flights completely within one state, or air taxis. Another exception is if the passenger who is being "bumped" has not complied with check-in requirements (time when to check in, board the plane, etc.). Again, if the reason for denial of a seat is due to the substitution of a smaller plane for the original larger plane, due to operational or safety reasons, the rule does not apply. If the carrier is able to book you on a flight scheduled to land at your destination within two hours of the original arrival time on a domestic flight, or four hours on an international flight, once again the carrier need not pay. Lastly, for reasons of security, all carry-on luggage may be searched, and although you have a right to refuse the search of your person, the carrier may deny you boarding, without penalty on its part.

However, if there is a denial of boarding due to any reason, the carrier must furnish you with a written explanation of the rules of "denied boarding compensation."

Assuming that none of the exceptions apply, and that you should be compensated, you must receive the price of the ticket as payment, not less than $25 nor more than $200, which must be paid to you within 24 hours. If the payment is not made within the 24 hour period, you have 90 days to make your claim and complaint in writing.

Now you've been bumped and the money is not that immediately important, but getting to your destination is. Don't leave the check-in area, walk away, and try to make your own arrangements. Retain the flight coupon—the carrier is required to honor it as soon as space becomes available. This advice also refers to flights that have been cancelled.

If the flight has been cancelled, the airline personnel must assist you in reaching your destination (or refund your money, if that is your wish). They must provide you with certain complimentary services if there is a delay of more than four hours. Limited communication facilities must be furnished, meals will be provided during normal mealtimes, hotel accommodations will be provided if the delay stretches into normal sleep time, and transportation to and from the hotel will be arranged for.

Lost or damaged baggage is another thorn in the side of the traveller. If all baggage has been offloaded and you are still waiting for yours, notify the airline personnel immediately and the plane will be searched again. Each airline has a special form for reporting lost or damaged luggage, and the personnel there will fill out the form for you. If they can't find the baggage within three days, you will receive a claim form, and you have 45 days to fill it in and return it.

Hold on to the baggage claim check and don't surrender it until you have received your luggage. Settlements are usually made within four to six weeks, except in periods of peak travel, when it takes a little longer.

What is the airline's liability for luggage? First, it is not required to pay for fragile items packed inside the baggage. On domestic flights, the carrier's liability is usually limited to a top amount of $500 per fare-paying passenger. On international flights, recompense is based on a formula involving baggage weight, not value. On domestic flights, if your baggage is worth more than $500, you may obtain extra coverage by declaring the excess when checking in and paying a fee for such additional coverage. Incidentally, the CAB cannot tell the airline what to pay you for your lost or damaged baggage, but the airline hates to have a bad record with this agency, so be sure to notify this governmental body.

Claims of all kinds are supposed to be reported first to the airline, and if you have not received a satisfactory response in a "reasonable time," to the CAB Office of Consumer Affairs, Washington, D.C. 20428. The CAB also has a "hot line" (Appendix B) where you may call on matters of urgency. You should also notify the United States Office of Consumer Affairs (Appendix B) by carbon copy of the complaint letter and attachments, and, with regard to overcharges, to the Civil Aeronautics Board Bureau of Enforcement (Appendix B) and the Consumers Union (Appendix C).

By the very nature of things, there are less complaints about trains and buses than about airplanes. Most rates are standardized and regulated, no one is "bumped," and delays are usually minuscule compared with airlines. The handling of baggage is not so fraught with peril of loss or damage. However, inevitably, there are complaints.

With regard to long distance trains and buses that cross state lines, the controlling federal agency is the Interstate Commerce Commission. Its stated duties are to seek reasonable transportation charges and adequate and efficient service. It requires such carriers to keep schedules open to public view that show rates, fares, and other transportation charges.

It cannot adjudicate your claim for loss or damage, but it can revoke a carrier's certificate or permit, suspend a carrier's rates, and impose fines for violation of economic regulations. In short, notification to the ICC, in combination with notification to consumer and political elements (which tends to place the ICC on its mettle), often results in sufficient pressure on a carrier to effect resolution of your claim or problem.

For instance, the Commission has detailed rules respecting a nationwide reservation system for trains, whereby (similar to airplanes) you may be entitled to free meals and a hotel room if your connection between trains is missed as a result of a late train. Another regulation states that complaint forms should be readily available on all trains and in all stations. If they are not, this is another cause of complaint and pressure, isn't it?

Commuter trains are not covered in the regulations, and may not be subject to the jurisdiction of the Interstate Commerce Commission. Most local and commuter buses are not covered, either. However, each state has a regulatory agency that covers such type of transportation. Usually it is called the Public Service Commission, but a consultation with your state Attorney General, local consumer group, or your librarian will yield the information as to the name and address of the state agency that enfranchises and regulates such lines.

Address all letters of complaint to the regulatory agency involved. That is, if the train or bus is long-line, crossing state lines, travelling substantial distances, write to the Interstate Commerce Commission (Appendix B). If local transit is involved, write to your state regulatory agency. In both cases, send copies to the carrier, your senator, congressman, State Consumer Agency (Appendix B), Consumers Union (Appendix C), United States Office of Consumer Affairs (Appendix B) and your local newspaper or consumer reporter at your local TV station.

Don't be surprised if you have trouble with some car rental firms. The large organizations usually supply late-model cars, well-maintained and adequately insured. The problem usually arises when you seek (rightfully) to save money, and fall victim to the lures of the fringe operators, the ones who make wild promises, advertise impossibly low prices. "Five dollars per day, no mileage charge," sounds wonderful, but only after you have swallowed the bait will you find out that weekend rates are higher, no gas at all is included, and the tiniest and least comfortable of foreign cars are available at such rates. Quite often you will also find out, too late, that "per day" means 9 A.M. to 5 P.M., not 24 hours.

Check out the true costs before renting a car by finding each and every item you will be charged for. Different sized cars fall in different price categories, so find out in advance which cars are in which categories. For instance, a Dodge Dart is a compact car, although admittedly one of the largest of the compacts. Many rental agencies, however, charge for it as an intermediate car at an intermediate price. Also find out in advance which categories include in the price such options as power steering and air conditioning.

Try to get the agency to guarantee you the category you request, which will insure you the lower rate (assuming you have requested a lower category car) if they are out of such class of cars when you are ready to pick it up, and have to give you a larger car. The reason for this is that the gimmick most often used by a shady operator is to promise you the smaller car, and then, when you are desperately in a hurry to pick up the car and commence your journey, to say they only have a larger car at a higher price; take it or leave it. You must take it, and so you lose money.

When the agreement or contract is placed before you for a "hurry up" signature, don't hurry or be intimidated by all the small print. Read it carefully, especially with regard to limitations. May the car be taken out of state? Are there any types of damages or lawsuits not covered by the over-all policy? Ask for *full* coverage, which may cost you $1.50 or $2.00 more per day, but it's worth it. If you have previously received a quoted rate from the main office, check the rates carefully. Sometimes local offices charge different rates than that charged by the main office. In addition, several of the companies have franchised local offices (a different owner than the main firm, but entitled to use the company name), and such franchises will quite often set their own rates, higher than the main office sets as a charge.

Once the car is produced, inspect it for body damage. If you find any, make sure it is stated on the face of the contract, so that no claim may be made against you when you turn the car in.

Complaints are mostly from defective cars, overcharges, failure to receive a refund of your deposit, and misrepresentation of services. There are no federal laws covering the business of such firms, but practically every state and locality has its own consumer-protection laws on the subject. You must write to your state and local consumer agency (Appendix B), the Consumers Union (Appendix C), Better Business Bureau (Appendix A), and, if fraud is suspected, the State Attorney General and your local District Attorney.

A typical complaint letter might read as follows:

Your State Consumer Agency
(Address—Appendix B)

Gentlemen:
    I recently had need of a car to drive to a neighboring state on a matter of emergency. I saw an advertisement in a newspaper by (name of rental firm), a copy of which is attached, offering rentals of cars at a price I could afford, with no limitations stated in it, as you can see. I called the local agency, located at (address), and spoke with Mr. (name). He said he had a small car available at such a price and he asked when I would need it. I told him I needed it the next day, and he said to come in.
    I went to the office the next day, but the clerk said that they had no more cars at such a price, only a larger one at a higher price,

and that I had better take it before they ran out of those also. I did so, and signed a contract, a copy of which is attached. There was some damage to the left rear, and I pointed it out to the clerk, Mr. (name), but he said he knew about it and not to worry.

I drove the car some one hundred miles and it broke down. It cost me $150 to have it repaired. A copy of the bill is attached.

When I turned the car in, there was another clerk on duty who refused to permit me to speak to either the manager or anyone else. He claimed I would have to pay for the damage to the car, and would not return my deposit, which he claimed was being applied to the damage. He also refused to consider my bill for the car repairs, stating that I must have done something wrong to the car to cause the breakdown. He also demanded another day's rental because I turned the car in at 6 P.M., and the "day's rental" in their advertisement only extended to 5 P.M. I called their office for the next three days, but was not allowed to speak to anyone in charge.

I ask that an investigation be made of this firm and of my complaint, because I feel I have been defrauded.

Very truly yours,
Ellen Miller

cc: Rental Agency
    State Attorney General
    District Attorney
    Consumers Union (Appendix C)
    Better Business Bureau (Appendix A)

While you may undergo much aggravation with hotels and motels, especially out-of-state, there are not too many areas of complaint that arise regularly. By and large, they have more rights than you do, although an attempt is made by management to satisfy you, so as to keep your patronage in the future.

The decision as to which room to assign you usually rests with management, although a specific accommodation has already been promised to you. This is true, however, only as long as there is no fundamental difference between rooms.

In addition, you may be refused a room because of your dress, uncleanliness, or actions. Lacking these excuses, however, a hotel or motel must accept all others for whom it has room, and properly care for such guests. The rub, of course, is your inability to prove that rooms are available. If you have a reservation confirmed in writing by the hotel, however, you have a good complaint.

Once you have been accepted as a guest, no further contract is required. Even the need for registration varies from state to state, some requiring registration, and only some of those requiring that you register in your true name.

Should you decide not to pay for your accommodations, most states still retain the rule whereby the innkeeper has a lien on your baggage and may hold on to it till he is paid. New York is one of the few states that has a different rule.

Still, no matter how fine a hotel or motel you are in, problems do arise where you have a good complaint.

Before paying your bill, check the rates posted in the room, and then compare it with the bill. If there is a difference, raise the roof with the manager. In reading the bill, take time to go over the extra itemized services to be sure you are the one who used them. It is quite common for charge slips to be put into the wrong file, or even mistakes to be made by human operators in punching the information into a billing computer.

Some of the biggest hotels have been guilty of petty practices. Many of them were caught charging two to three percent over the legal rate, and charging the excess off to initials on the bill, such as MS (miscellaneous) or next to the tax item, TAX-IMS, or some other unintelligible letters. Have you ever found SUND (sundries) on your bill, or INTMS (for internal message service, meaning incoming phone calls and messages within the hotel itself)?

Most of these items are not posted on the notice in your room and are illegal. Though it may be small change to you, it has been estimated that one large chain cleared 5.4 million dollars in one year by using this system.

Another very big name in hotels and motels was caught advertising its overseas accommodations at a certain price, but failing to reveal that this amount would not be accepted in American currency, unless an increased amount was paid because of the trouble the dollar was in overseas at the time.

An extremely common problem that guests have with hotels and motels involves damage to the guest's car. If the car is stolen or damaged, the first thing that will be pointed out to you is the fine print on the parking garage claim check saying that the management is not responsible. The overwhelming majority of states have held that this does not bind you, if the car was left with the host's representative or doorman. If you have parked it yourself, however, though it is in a parking lot provided by the management, you are not usually entitled to any relief.

There is no specific regulatory agency on either the nationwide or state level that controls motels and hotels (except as to sanitary conditions, as previously discussed), but most complaints achieve some results if addressed to the Attorney General of the state in which the inn is located. Since there is a good chance that you are not a resident in that state, you may worry about home-town favoritism. To take care of this, send copies of the complaint to Consumers Union (Appendix C); the Federal Trade Commission (Appendix B), if a complaint involves fraud or rates or advertising; the consumer agency in the state in which the hotel or motel is located (Appendix B); and National Headquarters of the Better Business Bureau (Appendix A), thus letting the local BBB office know that their central Big Brother is keeping an eye on what they're doing when central

BBB refers the complaint to the local BBB office.

In moving, travel, and transportation, you will be met by adversaries who have faced such complaints before, and who will maintain a hard position, but you must keep complaining, again and again, until you achieve satisfaction. Most such opponents fold their defense, like a losing hand of cards, if enough pressure is applied.

CHAPTER 12

When They Attack Your Credit, —— Credit Cards, and Earnings ——

One of the biggest boosts for business—as well as one of the most mixed bag of blessings and curses called down upon a consumer—has been the unbelievable growth of credit extension. An early slogan, "buy now–pay later," describes it perfectly. As with any aspect of consumer dollars, there have been abuses. People, unleashed from the buying restraint of only spending cash on hand, have bought everything imaginable, from furniture to clothes, from gambling chips in Nevada to funerals, with much less regard for the price or the bargain, and even less regard for how much extra they were paying over the long pull of repaying the credit extension or loan.

After decades of abuse and robbery of the consumer, the federal government passed a bill that sought "truth in lending." While admittedly weak and not all-comprehensive, the law is a vast improvement over the wasteland it replaced.

The law covers all persons and institutions that regularly extend or arrange for credit. Not only are loan companies, department stores, and credit card organizations regulated in their dealings with consumers, but the law even covers such others as doctors, dentists, and hospitals. Of course, no law would ever abolish your payment of interest and charges on the credit extended to you—no credit would ever be extended under such circumstances—but the federal Truth In Lending law does not even fix the amount of rates and charges. Most states, however, have enacted such limitations, and these apply to your credit transactions.

Truth In Lending (let us call it TIL) starts with advertisement. If a business mentions one feature of credit in an advertisement, for instance, the amount of down payment, it must mention all other terms, such as the number of payments, the amount of each, and over how long a time repayment continues.

With regard to loans obtained from banks, finance companies, and the like, or installment contracts to buy goods or services, you must be informed, in writing, of many important things.

First, there is the total finance charge. A finance charge is in the nature of a service charge, the amount of money it costs to obtain credit, the right to buy an item before we can afford it. The total finance charge is made up of such items, over and above the cost of the purchase, as interest on the money borrowed; the charge for obtaining a credit report on your ability to repay (the report is prepared by an investigative firm, called a credit bureau, and their charge may be passed along to you); loan fees; appraisal costs; and premiums for credit insurance (to insure the lender that he will not lose by your default or death, with you, of course, paying the premiums). Taxes are not included in the total, but you must be advised of them by an itemized statement.

You must be further informed of the number of payments, the

amount of each, and over what period of time the loan must be repaid; any amount to be charged for late payments; and a description of any security the creditor holds on your property.

Furthermore, with credit sales, the seller must advise you in writing of the cash price, the amount you are being credited with by reason of a down payment or trade-in allowance, the amount you are financing, the finance charge (as above), and all other fees.

A second form of "loan" regulated by the TIL involves purchases made through charge accounts or similar plans. Information is given to you in two stages.

When you open an account, you must be told what the service charge is (sometimes called a periodic rate), and this may be expressed in terms, for instance, of 1 percent per month for amounts of $500 or more, and 1½ percent for amounts under $500. You must be further advised of the number of days you have to make payments on any future outstanding balances so as to avoid a finance charge, the minimum payment required at any one time, and whether the seller retains a security interest, a lien, or a right to repossession, in the goods you will buy.

After buying items under such a charge account, your actual billing statement must inform you of the finance charge in actual dollars and cents plus the balance of any unpaid debt to which the charge is being applied; the annual percentage rate; how they figured out the balance still due; and an itemized account of all transactions since your last billing, such as purchases, returns, payments, and rebates. Most department stores today now list the charge in terms of "per month," say, 1½ percent, and annually, say, 18 percent.

Thus, the two important figures that you must keep in mind are (1) the finance charge or service charge (the amount of money over and above the cost of purchases) paid to obtain credit, and (2) the annual percentage rate. This latter item is the best measure of comparing credit costs no matter how much money is owed, or over how long a period there is to repay it.

The TIL law makes special provisions for credit transactions in which a home is used as collateral to guarantee the repayment of the debt, usually involving a situation where a contractor will work on your house. You have three business days from the time you enter into such an agreement to think it over and cancel the entire deal. The contractor is not allowed to start work until these three days are up. Such a creditor must give you written notice of your right to cancel, and your cancellation must be in writing. The best way of sending such written notice of cancellation to the creditor is by certified or registered mail, return receipt requested.

Warning: The three day waiting period is waived, thus depriving you of your right to cancel, if you sign a paper for the contractor or creditor stating that you need the credit immediately to finance repairs that are necessary to avoid danger to you, your family, or property (the roof is falling in and a storm is due). To avoid this waiver of your right, read any papers you sign very carefully, and don't let the contractor rush you by saying, "It's just the usual form, etc."

Getting back to the annual percentage rate, it becomes most important when you are shopping for credit, for example, before buying a new car. The car may be financed through the dealer, a finance company, a bank, a credit union, a savings and loan association, or borrowing from an insurance company on your life insurance policy. There are wild variations each of them charges by way of an annual percentage rate (one may charge 6 percent, while the other charges 18) and the difference, during the time you are paying out the loan, may amount to hundreds of dollars. It pays to shop around before you accept the first line of credit extended.

If there is a provision when you buy on credit (most notably through the use of credit cards) giving you a certain number of days after billing during which you may make payments so as to avoid finance charges, there exists a situation where no finance charges are due where you defer payment for about seven weeks following the purchase. Let us assume that you have 25 days after the date on the bill in which to make payment without any finance charge penalty, and further assume that you have observed, from past bills, that the date the bill is prepared is always on the tenth of the month. You should then buy an item one day *after* the bill is prepared, that is, on the eleventh of the month (in our sample case). You will then not be billed for it until the tenth of the *next* month, and will then have 25 days after that to make payment without penalty. Thus, if your billing date would be July 10, you could buy a radio on July 11. You would then be billed on the August 10 bill, and payment could be made without penalty up until September 4. You then will have used credit from July 11 to September 4, or some 55 days, without it costing you a dime in interest. If you had taken out a loan when you first bought the item, you would have paid interest from the first day.

Warning: Don't forget to pay in person by the last day, or by mail well in advance of the last day, or else the finance charge will become due.

If you don't get your bills till long after the billing date, thus cutting down on the time to pay without interest, complain to the Federal Trade Commission (Appendix B) and the banking department of your state (obtain the address from your librarian).

Some people, if they pay a regular loan ahead of time, expect to receive a substantial rebate. You will not. You will have no valid complaint if the rebate is a small percentage of the interest you would have paid for the full loan period. This is standard business practice in the loan papers and in the accounting, and all you will really help is your credit standing.

Another problem that sometimes dictates not buying on credit is the fact that if you buy from a store on the installment plan and something is wrong with the merchandise, quite often you will be forced to make the balance of the payments and may not use the defense of faulty merchandise as an excuse for stopping such payments. This is because of a very old doctrine known as "holder in due course." The store sells your installment contract to a third party, usually a financing company, and it is the financing company that is receiving your payments. It has not sold you the goods, and you may not use such a defense against it. Recognizing the inequity in such a situation, the federal government, in interstate transactions, and some states have recently permitted you to assert claims and defenses against a creditor as you had against the seller, if the seller arranged for the loan with a bank or credit company, or referred you to them (as in car sales). In most states, however, you must pay the creditor, but may make complaint to organizations as in any other purchase of faulty products.

Nine federal agencies handle enforcement for industries under their supervision, and only four of these are important to the consumer. These agencies may not interfere to obtain redress for you where your rights have been violated in loan or extension of credit situations. They are limited to attempting to impose criminal penalties on the offenders, and you are permitted to sue in the courts. Still, if you make the offender aware that you seek to invoke criminal penalties against him, there is strong pressure to adjust your differences.

Federal credit unions are regulated by the Office of Supervision and Examination of the National Credit Union Administration, 1325 "K" Street N.W., Washington, D.C. 20456.

Retail department stores, consumer finance companies, and other types of consumer credit establishments are regulated by the Division of Consumer Credit of the Federal Trade Commission, Washington, D.C. 20580.

Airlines and other creditors subject to the regulations of the Civil Aeronautics Board must answer to the Bureau of Enforcement, Civil Aeronautics Board, 1825 Connecticut Avenue N.W., Washington, D.C. 20428.

Finally, all creditors subject to the Interstate Commerce Commission (movers, etc.) are regulated by the Office of Proceedings, Interstate Commerce Commission, Washington, D.C. 20523.

Naturally, all other interested governmental and private agencies should be notified by copies of any complaint letter. A sample of such a letter might read as follows:

Division of Consumer Credit
Federal Trade Commission
Washington, D.C. 20580

Gentlemen:
I wish to make a complaint about certain problems that I have had with (name) department store, located at (address), with regard to my charge account (number).

When I first applied for such an account, some three months ago, I was required to sign an agreement. When I asked for a copy, I was told it would have to be countersigned by a store official first, and they would then mail me a copy, together with an explanation of all finance charges and interest I might be subject to, and my card. Two days later, I received my card, but no other papers. I did not press the matter, thinking they would send it to me in time.

I made a number of purchases and kept copies of the receipts. I then began to receive bills, the first being received some twenty days after the date on the bill. I am attaching a copy of the bill and the envelope it came in to show the late date it was sent to me. The bill permitted a fifteen day grace period from the date of the bill for payment without interest being assessed and so I was already being charged interest when I got my bill. Furthermore, three items listed on it had not been purchased by me. I have circled these items on the attached bill.

I called the store and spoke to the credit manager (name) and she said it must be the fault of the computer, and matters would be straightened out. I made prompt payment for the items I had bought.

The next month I received the bill, once again late, with the same items I did not buy listed thereon, and interest at 18 percent per year on the full first bill, not even giving me credit for the payment I had made as soon as I received the bill. A copy of this second bill is attached.

I called the store again, and on three occasions attempted to speak to (name) but she was always "too busy."

My credit and health are being ruined by this aggravation, and I ask that you investigate this matter.

Very truly yours,
Ellen Miller

cc: Better Business Bureau (Appendix A)
    State Attorney General
    State Consumer Agency (Appendix B)
    Office of Consumer Affairs (Appendix B)
    Consumers Union (Appendix C)
    Consumers Federation of America (Appendix C)
    International Consumer Credit Association
      (Appendix C)

Another phase of credit that has been in the limelight lately involves the use of credit cards and what the consumer's remedy is if the cards are stolen or lost, or if there are errors in billing.

In the last decade, credit cards have become the substitute for the small personal loan. Half of all American families now have at least one credit card, and the losses due to theft and wrongful use of the cards are now estimated at some 150 to 300 million dollars per year.

The Truth in Lending law has now been extended to partially cover the consumer who has such a card or cards. First, it requires a statement to be made to the applicant of the interest or finance charge he will pay if payment is not made within the stated time, usually an astronomical 18 percent per year.

Second, no credit card may be mailed except in response to a request or application for one. If you receive an unsolicited one, report this immediately to the nearest Federal Trade Commission office (Appendix B).

If your card is lost or stolen, you now have no liability at all if the issuer of the card has failed to inform you of your potential liability, and if it has not provided you with a self-addressed, pre-stamped notice to use to notify the issuer that the card is lost or stolen. Incidentally, keep this notice in a place you can't forget, perhaps with important papers, so you will not have to start hunting around for it in an emergency.

There is also no liability if the card does not have your photograph or some other means of identification (such as a signature) on it to show that the user is the one authorized to use it, although you are still required to notify the issuer promptly of its disappearance. Furthermore, you are not liable if you report the loss before the card thief uses it.

One of the most important safeguards is the fact that you are only liable for $50 per card, even if all the prerequisites have been fulfilled by the issuer, and even if you fail to notify the issuer promptly. The catch, of course, is that most people carry more than one card—an American Express card or something similar; a card good at certain gas stations, such as Mobil (where, you must remember, hundreds of dollars may be charged for tires, etc.); charge account cards for individual department stores; and various óther types of credit cards. Let us assume the average person has four cards—the liability is not $50, but four times $50, or $200. This alone dictates prompt notification to the issuer so as to cut down on your liability as much as possible.

It is interesting to note that persons who use credit cards for business purposes are entitled to the same liability protection as those who use it for individual needs alone.

Be alert for a scheme much in use lately by thieves. You have lost your cards and some kindly gentleman calls you to tell you he has found them and is mailing them back to you immediately. Of course, to avoid all the aggravation involved in cancelling the cards, and then being issued new ones, you wait for the mail—and wait—and wait—while the thief goes on a charging spree, confident that you will not have reported the loss to the company.

What should you do right this minute to avoid problems with future card losses?

Take all of your credit cards out of your wallet or purse and lay them on the table. Yes, that special one, too; take it out. Don't fool yourself. Be tough, now, and remove only those that are indispensable. The rest—destroy them by cutting them at least into halves. Make a list of those you keep, with the name and address of the issuers, and the account number of each card. Keep the list in a safe place, but definitely not in your wallet or purse. Perhaps you could keep it in the same place you are holding the self-addressed envelope to notify the issuer of the disappearance of a card.

Another good habit is to sign your card as soon as you receive it, to avoid theft and an easy forgery.

Recheck all your cards every couple of weeks. One could have disappeared without your even realizing it. If a card is missing at this periodic check, phone the issuer and follow up with a letter or telegram, referring to the call. The truth-in-lending envelope is all very well, but you want to speed notification to save even that $50 per card.

If you move, notify the issuers of your new address immediately. If you delay, this could result in the renewal card being sent to the old, incorrect address where the card might be lost or stolen, unsigned and subject to forgery, without your even knowing anything about it. If you realize that your credit card is due for a renewal replacement and you don't get it within a reasonable time, notify the credit card issuer promptly.

Be careful of your card when you are making a purchase. Don't present or mention it until the transaction is completed. You are inviting fraudulent extras by the running off of a series of blanks if the clerk has the card for too long a time before the sale is over. If the clerk asks, "Is this a charge?" before you've even made a decision, you're in trouble if you deal further with that clerk.

If there is an error on a sales slip stamped with your card, or signed by you, make sure you actually see the old slip destroyed before you sign a new one.

Save your receipts and check them against your monthly statement. This is your best defense against computer error and human error or fraud. When you pay the bill, pay by check or money order and write the account number on the check, thus preventing mixups. Compare the slips you receive at the end of the month with the receipts handed to you at the time of purchase, and see if they match, or if there has been fraudulent alteration.

While in many state transactions (although not in interstate commerce) a lender is not responsible if the goods you bought with the loan are faulty, there has recently been enacted a Fair Credit Billing Act, dealing with credit card transactions, which permits you to refuse to pay a credit card charge for an item that was found to be defective. However, the consumer must have made a good faith effort to solve the problem with the dealer and the transaction must have taken place in the same state or within fifty miles of the address given by the consumer to obtain the card.

That old bugaboo, computer error, has been responsible for many credit card billing errors. If you suspect one, tear the billing card or statement in half, accompanied by a letter to the president or top official of the credit card company. You should even call the store or bank to get his correct name. Send a copy of the letter to the secretary, Federal Trade Commission, Washington, D.C. 20580, as well as copies to all of the other agencies and organizations who received copies of the last sample letter set forth in this chapter.

A regulation now in effect requires the creditor to acknowledge and resolve any problems on a claimed billing error within 90 days, upon proper notification by a customer to the creditor.

There is a fraud involving credit cards that is now prevalent. Firms will advertise merchandise that sounds like a bargain, and all you have to do is give them your name, address, and credit card number and the product will be sent to you by mail. They then file any number of bills or fictitious orders, charged to your account, get paid, and skip town. The simple rule is that you should not use your credit card for mail order purchases.

For any complaints involving your credit card, follow the general trend of the last sample letter, with copies to the same organizations.

As a final word about credit cards, if you must carry a large amount of cards and thus subject yourself to substantial liability at $50 a card, ask your insurance broker about credit card insurance as an endorsement, or rider, on your home owner's policy. The premium will run just a few dollars for $500 coverage, and proportionately thereafter. Do not pay any money to join any credit card service that notifies the company when the cards are lost. This is not insurance, and you are still responsible for up to $50 per card.

We have been assuming that you have had no problem with obtaining loans or credit cards. Before any such line of credit is extended, however, most often there is an investigation in some form as to your ability to repay, items that would make you a bad risk for credit, insurance or employment, and kindred details of your private life. This investigative procedure has turned into Big Business, and examples of error and fraud abound which directly affect you, but which, until recently, you either knew nothing about or were unable to correct. It is the same situation as attempting to still malicious rumors when you don't even know who is spreading them—but in this case it affects your pocket directly. An estimated hundred million Americans are spied upon in one form or another each year.

These credit investigations are clearly a danger to your privacy, but the right of privacy today seems all but lost. The only recourse you therefore have, speaking practically, is to clear up the record as to any harmful misinformation.

Most of the actual digging being done on behalf of the creditors, insurance companies, and prospective employers is accomplished by about 2100 independent credit bureaus. Most are allied with a trade association called the Associated Credit Bureaus of America. They tap any number of sources of information, including other credit sellers, lenders, public records, newspaper clippings, other credit bureaus in the association, field investigations, and inquiries that are made by telephone and letter. It is fairly safe to state that there is a file on you somewhere.

In this field, there are usually two types of investigations. The first is often described as an "investigative credit report," mostly relied upon by life insurance companies and prospective employers, which goes beyond the usual known facts of a person's life history, and includes subjective judgments by the investigating bureau as to a person's character, quirks, and mode of living.

The second type, known as a "consumer report," destined for credit rating service, is much more limited and objective, but nonetheless still capable of damaging error. This report usually covers the individual's credit background, history of repayment of bills, tax liens or other judgments, bankruptcies, and some personal facts, such as one's employment record, arrests, indictments, and convictions.

Both types of reports are subject to abuses in research. A man may have "slow pay" or "delinquency" chalked up against him when he refused to pay because he had an argument with a seller of merchandise. There may be inaccuracies by mistake in computer input, such as reporting a man as divorced instead of married. Irrelevant items may creep in, such as domestic problems, that do not involve financial status. Information, once acquired, may be leaked to unauthorized persons. The consumer may be denied credit without being told that it was on the basis of such a report, and so he would still have no knowledge of the problem. The records might not be updated, so that there would be, for instance, no showing of an acquittal after an indictment. If errors are discovered, there might be tardiness in correcting them. The record might include much malicious hearsay, without the consumer's version on the record.

"Medical information," as contained in the records, often includes sex aberrations, drinking habits, drug abuse, the birth of children out of wedlock, whether the subject races, or flies, and whether two martinis are taken before dinner. While some of the items may be important to an analysis of the individual, many are erroneous or just plain inventions, and the fact that they are considered as medical information is not only silly but unfair, as will be seen later in this chapter, in the discussion of your rights with regard to discovering the medical information section of your file.

Further abuses involve credit bureaus that use the telephone and claim they had personal interviews with sources of information, the habit of some of the bureaus to force their investigators to dig up derogatory material (one such large-scale scandal was uncovered in 1974), and attempts at evading consumers' rights in discovering what their files contain.

The federal government has now set guidelines to protect your rights through the Fair Credit Reporting Act (FCRA). The law attempts to protect you against false or obsolete information being circulated about you, and to permit you to take necessary steps to correct any such situation (as well as to make the credit bureaus somewhat more responsible).

Of course, you could be denied credit for many reasons other than on the basis of a report. The people to whom you have applied for credit may, for instance, call your references directly, or make a decision based upon something else. If you are denied credit because of such a reason, you must be informed at the time of the rejection that you may make a request in writing within sixty days for the nature of the information which caused the rejection. Although the nature of it must be disclosed, the source of the information need not be, and you are entitled to enough facts to challenge or refute its accuracy.

Should your application have been denied because of an adverse consumer report prepared by a credit bureau, however, the firm to which you have applied for credit or otherwise must not only advise you of its decision and the fact that it was based in part on the credit report, but must supply the name and address of the credit bureau that supplied the report. Now the fun begins.

Although you may arrange a telephone interview with the credit bureau or agency, don't do it unless you are prohibitively far from its place of business. You are better off arranging for an appointment at the agency, during normal business hours.

When you appear at the bureau, you will have to present proper identification. You cannot be charged for the interview if you have been denied credit within the last thirty days, or for certain other narrow reasons, but a moderate charge is usually made if you have not been denied credit within the stated time or received a collection notice from the collection department affiliated with the bureau.

During a personal interview, you may bring another person of your choice, in addition to your spouse. Do it. You may be too excited to listen to what is told to you, or to write everything down.

"Listen" is what you will do. You are not entitled to see the file itself or its contents. The representative of the bureau will disclose all information (except medical) in your file and will tell you who or what is the source of such information, unless such information was discovered by field investigation. You will be told the names of those who have received employment reports about you within the last two years and all others who obtained credit reports about you in the last six months.

Now, what information are you looking for; what might prejudice you?

The first point is, who has been receiving this information? Consider those who received it in this light. Was it being used to consider you for credit, to review or collect on your account, to consider you for employment, or to consider you for insurance? If not one of these, was the information given pursuant to your written instructions or an order of a court, or was it for a legitimate business need, such as a potential business arrangement? All of these are legal. Neighbors or relatives, inquiring out of curiosity, are not entitled to receive a report, and if they lie about it, there is a substantial criminal penalty.

Not even a branch of any government (Internal Revenue Service or Federal Bureau of Investigation) may obtain such a report unless the governmental agency, be it federal, state, or city, is on the point of extending credit to you, collecting or reviewing your account, employing or insuring you, or if it is considering you for some benefit, such as a license or security check for a position. Fishing expeditions are out. In any other situation beside the above permissible ones, the credit bureau may only reveal name, address (both present and past), and place of employment (both present and past.)

What may you do or demand, after hearing what is in your file? If you claim the information is incomplete or incorrect, and unless your request is frivolous, you may demand that the item be re-investigated, and if it is found to be inaccurate or cannot be proven, the information must be removed from your file. Whoever received this incorrect or incomplete information in an employment report within the last two years, or a regular credit report within the last six months, must be informed of the deletion or amendment of the information in your file. This must be done at no cost to you.

You may demand, and the credit bureau must so act even

without your demand, that a report of a regular bankruptcy must be removed from your file after fourteen years, or certain suits and judgments after various periods of years. Since the time period is tied to certain concepts of the law, you should bluster and demand that the item be removed, and you will be informed quickly enough what that time period is in your state. Various liens, outstanding taxes, and accounts, arrests, indictments, and convictions may be reported up to seven years. None of these limitations apply if the transaction in which you are now involved deals with credit or life insurance applications of at least $50,000, or an employment report for a job that pays at least $20,000.

What happens if there is an investigation, or the agency goes through a halfhearted attempt to uncover the truth, but the dispute still remains between yourself and what is stated in your file?

You then have the right to place a short statement of about 100 words in your file as to your side of the story, and this, or its summary, must be included in any future report containing the disputed item. You also have the right, for a moderate fee to be paid to the credit bureau, to have your statement sent to certain businesses.

The key here to correcting your record is follow-up. Follow up to determine the results of re-investigation. Check if those named as companies receiving the report have recently received the corrected version, or your version.

You have the right to sue the reporting agency for damages, attorney's fees, and court costs if it willfully or negligently violates this law. If you feel you must take this step, see an attorney.

Of course, there are loopholes. What if the representative of the credit bureau is not telling you everything that is in your file? Suppose you haven't been turned down for credit as yet, but merely have a suspicion that you will be; what credit bureau do you interrogate? Furthermore, the organization entrusted to administer the law—the Bureau of Consumer Protection of the Federal Trade Commission—is barred from acting on behalf of an individual consumer. The "medical information" that need not be revealed to you may cover a multitude of sins that are listed as "medical" for the sole purpose of hiding them.

Still, aside from the remedies listed above, there are means of redress available to you. The major means, as usual, is the blockbuster letter to put the pressure on certain organizations as well as the credit bureau, with the knowledge of all concerned that the others are watching them.

In connection with this, the United States Senate has an active "sub-committee on consumer credit" that is dealing directly with the faults of the law, and a copy of any complaint letter should go to it in care of the United States Senate, Washington, D.C. 20515.

A sample letter of complaint might read as follows:

Bureau of Consumer Protection
Federal Trade Commission
Washington, D.C. 20580

Gentlemen:

I believe I have been victimized by the actions of a credit bureau, whereby I have been greatly damaged, and I ask that you investigate this matter to set it right, without a long and expensive lawsuit.

I applied for a credit card at (name and address of department store) on (date), and was informed a week later that I had been rejected. When I asked why, I was informed it was because of a credit report issued by (name and address of the credit bureau). I had to call the bureau six times before I could even get an appointment to see them.

When I appeared there on (date) I had a conference with (name), a representative of the bureau. He read what he claimed was the entire file to me, but aside from a few small errors, such as my marital status, there was nothing derogatory in my record, although he would not read me the medical portion of the record. He promised to send corrections of the small mistakes to the department store immediately so I could get a card.

When I went to the department store some ten days later, I was amazed to find that not only had the credit bureau not sent along the promised corrections, but I was told in confidence that the reason I had been rejected was because I was allegedly arrested once on a morals charge, and that I had not found out about this allegation because it was in the medical portion of my record.

I called the bureau representative immediately, but he refused to discuss the matter any further, nor would he make another appointment.

I have never been arrested for any reason, much less on a morals charge, nor have I ever been indicted or convicted, not even for a traffic ticket. I intend seeking a government job shortly, and if this is the report that will be furnished about me in the future, I will be irreparably harmed. I cannot wait for a lawsuit to come to trial, because during the years this would take, I would be deprived of my credit, reputation, and future. I ask that action be taken immediately.

Very truly yours,
Ellen Miller

cc: Credit Bureau
    Sub-committee on consumer credit, United States Senate, Washington, D.C. 20515
    State Attorney General
    District Attorney
    State Consumer Agency (Appendix B)
    Better Business Bureau (Appendix A)
    Consumers Union (Appendix C)
    U.S. Office of Consumer Affairs (Appendix B)
    International Consumer Credit Association (Appendix C)
    Industry Relations Director, Associated Credit Bureaus, Inc., 6767 Southwest Freeway, Houston, Texas 77036

Women have a special problem, which the government is trying to correct under the Federal Equal Credit Opportunity Act and similar legislation. The problem is twofold: to obtain recognition as a person for the sake of establishing oneself as an acceptable credit risk, and to fight discrimination by creditors because one is a woman.

For years, creditors have been treating women as non-persons. The singles rarely used credit and the marrieds only had their husbands' credit evaluated. In this modern political climate, now is the time to take steps to establish your ability to repay—the cornerstone of your attempt to obtain personal credit.

Consider (all in your own name) opening a checking account and asking the bank, if it issues charge cards to checking account patrons, to issue one to you personally; apply for retail credit for yourself, for which you will pay with your own checks; taking out a small loan in your own name and making *prompt* payments (remember, the purpose is to establish you as a good credit risk), or buy something on the instalment plan but, once again, pay on time.

The second phase of the problem is how to fight discrimination. If there is a question about your income, and you are divorced, lenders must now consider alimony and child support payments as part of your income with regard to your ability to repay. A creditor now may ask if you are married, unmarried, or widowed, but not if you are divorced. Some states have laws that are even stronger than the Federal statute, whereby if you are seeking personal credit, no question may be asked as to your marital status. If denied credit, you must be told why. Send a written request for an explanation as soon as possible after the turndown; you must be answered in writing within a reasonable period of time.

If you believe you have been discriminated against because of your sex or marital status, notify your state consumer agency and the Office of Saver and Consumer, Federal Reserve Board, Washington, D.C. 20551. You should also consult with an attorney, since the law grants a right to sue the creditor.

There comes a time in some consumers' lives when the question is no longer one of credit, but how to get out from under a crushing burden of debt, and what rights you still have against creditors' questionable collection practices.

You would be surprised at how many lenders are understanding about temporary financial reverses and willing to help you arrange things so payment will be easier.

Sit down and talk to the counseling or credit service at the store or other place of business where you have run up a bill. Quite often an easier repayment schedule may be worked out. Sometimes this involves cutting up your remaining credit cards, as alcohol may be gently removed from the grip of an alcoholic. The arrangement is often subject to your living up to your part of the bargain—no more buying sprees, etc. For your own protection, however, if the seller agrees to an extension of the loan or debt, or refinancing of it, ask for it in writing. Don't be fearful that the whole deal will fall through because you have such temerity. It will show to the businessman or woman that you are developing financial maturity and responsibility.

There is also an organization, with offices across the country, called Consumer Credit Counseling Service, that serves the same function as the store advisor, that is, it goes over your debts and shows you the way out of the wilderness by budgeting and sometimes speaking to your creditors to obtain their consent to the plan. This organization provides its services free, or for a modest fee, so if you run into some organization that is similarly named but wants a good deal of money in advance, forget it. You may find this organization by consulting your telephone directory, your librarian, or even one of your creditors.

Whatever you do, don't think that you may get out of your debt-ridden situation by becoming involved in a debt consolidation plan, fraudulent or not. This is the sort of transaction where you take out one huge loan to pay off all of your outstanding debts and then just make one payment a month.

If the plan is honest, it is still bad economics. Most of your outstanding debts include a good deal of interest, and if you pay all of them off, and then have to pay interest on the new loan, you are paying interest on interest, which is not the route to recovery. Worse, there are dishonest debt consolidation firms. Thinking that you only have to make one payment a month, you blithely send your payments to these frauds. However, they never did pay off your old creditors, just stalled them, or they applied your first few payments to a "credit fee," and never made payments on the old debts. Your first knowledge of this will be when you are sued or your property is repossessed. Stay clear of such a situation, but if you become burned, notify the postal authorities, the State Attorney General, and the District Attorney.

Debtors have been clay pigeons for years, subject to every known form of false and improper collection practice.

Many consumers who could not keep up payments after buying items thought that they could just clear up the debt by returning the purchase, only to find that there was repossession of the item, garnishment (or seizing) of part of your salary, AND a judgment for some exorbitant amount claimed to be still owed, called a deficiency judgment.

Repossession laws backing up such voracious tactics were, and still are, widespread throughout the United States. About three-fourths of the states permit installment contracts to include a wage assignment clause which voluntarily tells your boss to pay over part of your earnings without even a court order or a judgment, merely a default in one payment.

Almost all states permit garnishment—which is involuntary and pursuant to a court order or judgment—of a portion of your salary that varies from state to state. Almost worse than garnishment is the threat of it, for most people think that their bosses will be so annoyed with the paper work and court involvement that the debtor will be fired. Many people also get trapped into garnishment because they co-signed notes for friends and relatives who thereafter defaulted, leaving the burden on the "good guy."

Some consumers fool themselves by assuming that they will have their day in court to tell their stories, and that the champion of "the people," the judge, will get them out of the hole. Nonsense. Many never have their say in court because a judgment is obtained against them without their ever knowing a lawsuit has been started. Some phony process server will sign an equally phony affidavit that he served a summons on you. By failing to answer the summons you never received, presto, there is a judgment. Default judgments have been described as the number one consumer credit trap today.

Just as bad are the numerous transactions in which people unknowingly sign "confessions of judgment" that provide for the amount of the judgment, court costs, attorneys' fees, even waiver of the service of a summons and of trial by jury, and, most amazing of all, waiver of any and all errors—which excuses a confession signed in blank—and this is then filled in with all of the numbers afterwards. Once again, a huge judgment will be entered against you without your ever appearing in court.

It has been found that the real swindlers only deal with bad risk applicants, never those whose credit is good. Most users of such tactics are stores specializing in installment sales, door-to-door credit sellers (still, despite the new laws), shady used car dealers, "small loan" companies, and a large number of collection agencies.

Incidentally, most of the laws covering such "creditors' rights" provide that notice (if any is even sent out) be sent to the last known address. Notify the post office of your change of address if you move. Don't think that they will never find you if you move without leaving an address; they will—whether it is through a sub rosa contact in a utility company that can find out where you moved, or by some other sneaky means.

The federal government has finally done something about at least part of this entire problem, in the Federal Wage Garnishment Law (FWGL). This law limits the amount of what may be taken out of a person's salary in any one week, or from being discharged for any one garnishment. It doesn't affect the underlying debt, the state procedures for garnishment, or wage assignments.

The law provides that, after taking out withholding taxes and social security, only about 25 percent of the balance may be garnisheed in any one week ("about," because there is a complicated formula that may be used instead, and the amount that may be reached is the lesser of the two figures). It must be realized that, when we speak of what amounts may be reached by garnishment, we are not speaking of court orders for support or alimony, bankruptcy court orders, or debts due for state or federal taxes. It should also be noticed that no garnishment is allowed where after-tax earning is $48 per week or less.

As to loss of employment, your boss may have been served with any number of legal papers, garnishments, levies, or what have you, but if they all refer to one indebtedness, he is not allowed to fire you. More than one indebtedness—well, you're on your own. Incidentally, if the employer illegally fires you, he may be fined up to $1000 or a year in prison or both, so this provision has some teeth.

The FWGL also provides that if a state law contains better protection for the debtor (for instance, you may not be fired for two debts), the state law takes precedence.

This Federal Wage Garnishment Law is enforced by the Wage and Hour Division of the United States Department of Labor. All inquiries to this division, made by mail, phone, or personal interview, are answered. Find the local office nearest you in your telephone directory under "United States—Department of Labor—Wage and Hour Division."

Certain basically improper collection tactics are fought through different agencies.

Long-arm collection tactics involve contracts whereby the defaulting debtor may be sued in a court thousands of miles from his home. While this is not really illegal, the Federal Trade Commission (Appendix B) is exerting pressure on the practitioners of such ploys. Notify it at once, as soon as you are advised that you are in such a situation.

If a debt collector makes harassing phone calls, notify the Federal Communications Commission (Appendix B) and your telephone company. It is a violation under the rules of both to make repeated phone calls merely to harass, and there have been many cases where recording equipment is installed to get the evidence. The collector is then advised his phone service will be discontinued unless he can prove he has stopped such practices. That usually is effective. If you receive harassing letters for payment of phony or non-existent claims, notify your postal inspector at the United States Postal Service (Appendix B).

There are collectors who will threaten all sorts of things unless you pay up, including physical violence. Contact your District Attorney after the very first call.

If you find that you are being victimized by any of these practices where you are a debtor, write a letter setting forth all of the facts to the Federal Trade Commission (Appendix B), the Better Business Bureau (Appendix A), your union, your State Consumer Agency (Appendix B), and your State Attorney General. You may also be in dire need of legal advice, so go immediately to your local Legal Aid Society, in addition to the letters to the above agencies.

When they attack your credit, your earnings, your pocket, don't despair. Fight back until you win.

CHAPTER
13

——————— Where You Live ———————

You are not safe from victimization even in your own residence, whether it be a private home or a rented apartment.

HOME IMPROVEMENTS AND REPAIRS

Almost forty million Americans own their own homes, which represent some 63 percent of all residential units. Naturally, from time to time, repairs or alterations are required.

As in dealing with any contractor or mechanic, your twin guides must be the reliability of the contractor and wariness in all stages of your business with him.

Though none are foolproof, there are many clues to the reliability and reputability of the man who will work on your home. Ask him for the names of previous customers and make sure you contact them before you enter into any contract. Question the merchants in town who would be best informed of the contractor's reputation, such as the local lumberyard and hardware store. Call your local Better Business Bureau office as to whether they have had any complaints about him.

Call the local office of the Federal Housing Agency (your

telephone directory or librarian will tell you where it is). Each local office usually maintains a "precautionary list" of contractors who have been reported or complained about for unsatisfactory work, at least on FHA-financed improvement work.

Call your town hall. Are home improvement contractors required to be licensed in your community? Licensing not only partially weeds out the fly-by-nights, but provides a readily available tool for fighting back, should you be taken advantage of by the contractor. If licensing is required where you live, is the firm you are contemplating licensed? If the answer is readily available from town hall, fine; if not, ask the contractor to exhibit his license. No reputable businessman, hoping to get your business, would refuse.

Obtain a number of estimates, not only for the purpose of getting a suitable price, but to compare what various workmen think needs to be done so you will have some understanding of what is necessary to avoid being taken. Never pay for an estimate. Reliable contractors do not charge for them.

Don't make a decision based solely on the lowest price. Many newspapers carry advertisements for the type of work you require at a price much lower than the estimate you received, but more often than not, these are just fraudulent come-ons till the advertiser can talk you into something else.

Watch out for contractors who quote a flat rate to you without ever having seen what must be done. Most jobs, such as siding, remodeling, resurfacing driveways, and the like, vary in size and scope from one house to another. These "flat-rate" contractors plan to take advantage of you some other way, once the job is theirs.

Once you have decided on the man who will do your work, make sure all promises are put into a written contract, and get a copy of it signed by the contractor. Double check before you sign it that some very important items are included, such as work to be done; amount to be charged; the work completion schedule; brand names of important items of material; and coverage by the contractor for injury caused to anyone during the course of the work. If the contractor is arranging the financing of the job (not a good idea at all), see that the full financing cost of the loan is included in the contract price, as well as the payment schedule you must meet. There is a certain type of procedure designed to avoid expensive and delaying lawsuits, called arbitration, so request that an automatic arbitration clause be included. Have included a clause that the contractor will clean up any mess when the job is finished. Make sure there are no blank spaces in the contract. If there are, write "void" in them, or draw a line from one corner of the blank space to the diagonal corner.

In obtaining guarantees, in the contract or as a separate document, keep in mind that there are two different types that you are entitled to. The first is a guarantee or warranty by the manufacturer against defects in the material, and the other is that of the contractor covering proper installation of the materials, and of work actually performed.

As to the financing, many people try to arrange for it in advance, or just on their own, by consulting with banks or savings and loan associations. This will not only save you money (as you know, not all loans carry the same interest and charges), but it will make you independent of the salesman and his promises to obtain the financing for you, and you are then able to shop around for the best contractor to meet your needs.

You should also remember that if you sign a contract for a loan for an improvement to your home in which you put up your house as security, you have the three business-day cooling-off period in which to reconsider. If you do change your mind, send a letter out immediately, certified or registered mail, return receipt requested. The contractor is not legally permitted to start work until the end of the period, except under certain unlikely conditions.

Now the job is completed, but there is still much for you to protect. Liens against your home may be filed by any supplier or subcontractor unpaid by the general contractor, although you personally have never dealt with such supplier or subcontractor. Before you make payment, or sign any papers permitting payment by the financing bank, get a sworn statement from the contractor of all persons who actually did furnish material and labor on your job, and the amounts still due each. Get a waiver of the lien, or mechanic's lien, from the contractor, and have him obtain waivers from everyone listed on the sworn statement. It may sound tedious and complicated, but many a homeowner has thereafter spent thousands trying to remove a lien when he could easily have avoided the entire problem (the contractor will be at his most pliable when he is trying to get payment) by asking for two papers.

Needless to say, make no payment in cash, and do not make any payment or sign a "completion certificate" so the contractor may receive payment from the bank, unless the work is finished to your satisfaction.

Before getting into the problem of specific home improvements, there are a few general schemes that you should be aware of.

In the "model home" swindle, a salesman appears at your door and points out work that needs doing which he observed while driving by. In a confidential tone, he lets you in on the secret that his nationally famous firm is expanding its operations into your area and would like to use your place as a "model home," to show what his firm can do by way of improvements.

After your home is repaired by his firm (for the usual charge), your neighbors will be invited to drop in and see for themselves. For each neighbor who orders improvements, you will receive a commission. A little greedy calculation tells you that you may recoup your entire cost from the commissions, so that you, in effect, will be receiving the repairs for a net cost of zero. Forget it. First, all of your neighbors will be asked to sign contracts for repairs to their houses, so that *they* will be the firm's model home, and there will be no other prospects for whom you may receive commissions. Second, you will be charged well in excess of what a local contractor would charge, so you are not "just as well off as before."

The old "bait-and-switch" pokes up its head in home improvements, as well. You are all set to accept an offer of work or materials at a wonderful price, until a chilling word is dropped into the proceedings. "Of course, if the above ground pool model in our special offer springs a leak (at this price, what can you expect?) the water would run downhill onto your neighbor's property, so you have nothing to worry about." The salesman is there. He has impressed you. You really want a pool, so you permit him to tout you into something at a much higher price, which he intended to sell to you in the first place.

Two other general frauds to watch out for in this field are deals with unrealistic guarantees, and prices that you later find out don't include the cost of both labor *and* material.

Let us review certain home improvement dangers in detail, though keeping in mind the other warnings made earlier in this chapter.

In-ground pools are a hot item these last few years. You're satisfied with the contractor, but is he a member of the National Swimming Pool Institute? This is not an absolute guarantee of reliability, but, because of the screening processes used by the

Institute, it is some indication that the firm is on the up-and-up. A legitimate contract for a pool lists everything, including swimming area dimensions, depth, and type of filtration system. Check if a permit to build the pool or a fence around the pool is needed. If it is, the cost of this, including a fence and gate, should be integral parts of the overall cost. Find out what the warranty will cover and over what period, but find this out before you sign the contract. In addition, a reliable contractor will instruct you in its operation, including the filtration system, chemicals, and the like. Make sure he does. Before the contractor works on your premises, demand proof that he is covered for property damage and liability insurance. You are demanding nothing difficult or out of the ordinary, because the man's insurance agent has forms which are typed up and given to the contractor attesting to such coverage, a copy of which you should receive.

Incidentally, don't be fooled by the media ads that advertise pools at a substantially lower price, but, in tiny letters use "O.D." after the size of the pool. This means "Outer Dimensions," and includes the concrete portion around the pool. Your "50 feet pool O.D." may turn out to be 30 feet of swimming area or less.

The purchase of flowers, trees, shrubs, and other nursery stock presents more specific problems. If a door-to-door salesman claims to be a representative of a local or well-known nursery, check his credentials carefully, since the odds are that he is not. It is also quite risky to order nursery stock by mail, from advertisements, unless you know for a fact you are dealing with a reputable firm. Each neighborhood has an Association of Nurserymen, whose address you may ascertain in the local telephone directory, or from your Chamber of Commerce. If you're going to put in your money, perspiration, and care on nursery stock, and you plan to deal with a new source, check first with the Nurserymen's Association.

Just one word will suffice for lumber, if you plan to do a job yourself or want to check on the supplies used by the contractor. Only dry wood (where the sap has dried up) is to be used, to prevent warpage and shrinkage. Lumber is graded 1 through 4, with 1 being the best.

Many tears have been shed by home-owning consumers over lawn sprinkler systems that they had installed. Most complaints involve defective parts, inferior workmanship, and incomplete jobs.

There is no sprinkler system that you can reasonably expect to work forever. A decent warranty usually is for one year for material used, performance, maintenance, and against defective workmanship. If you are offered a "lifetime" guarantee, you are probably dealing with a crook.

When arranging for such work, ask the contractor for a scale drawing of your property, showing the sprinkler locations, valves, pipe layouts, etc. Include the drawing of the proposed layout in the contract, and make sure it is referred to in the contract, stapled to it, and initialed by all parties. Of course, the contract must also cover a description of the work to be done, the price of the job, how and when it is to be paid, any allowance for deletions agreed upon while the work is in progress, the specifications of materials, and the extent of the guarantee and maintenance.

You must never pay money in advance of completion unless you are sure the company is reliable. A request for advance payment often shows that the company is inadequately financed (no matter if the request is couched in terms of "good faith" on your part).

All of the general rules set forth in the beginning of this

chapter about dealing with contractors should be kept in mind in any home improvement transaction.

Three things should be especially remembered if you are considering termite control. First, there are very few reliable firms that price a job by the quantity or number of gallons of poisons or chemicals used, but this is often the price method employed by swindlers. Second, if you are given a "free check-up" for termites by a company that you don't know very well, be prepared to find a few dead bugs spread around as "proof," with such bugs placed there by the "free" investigators. Ask for further proof, such as termite tracks, or, better still, call in another company to confirm the findings. Third, if you are informed you have termites, and your roof is about to fall into your cellar, take an awl or ice pick and stick it into some wooden parts of the house at the point where they meet earth. If the instruments penetrate easily, you do indeed have termites.

As a short warning, specifically about work to be done on driveways, make sure the contract contains adequate specifications, such as the kind and depth of the base, the thickness of the surface that the contractor will apply, the exact dimensions of the finished driveway, the completion date, and the extent of the guarantee.

Many sellers of storm and screen doors and windows are notorious for "bait-and-switch" tactics, so don't be fooled. Here, especially, check in advance with previous customers and your local Better Business Bureau. This type of installation is ready-made for fraud. For instance, if the advertisement that attracts you promises "stainless steel," find out if what is to be sold to you has only a stainless steel face. In other words, beware.

Use the usual rules of careful shopping and negotiating with regard to water softeners, including calling the Better Business Bureau in advance, checking the credentials of door-to-door salesmen, shopping around, and recognizing the ridiculously low prices as an invitation to fraud. Get a receipt for any deposit, and remember that a legitimate firm will not ask for payment in full before delivery.

There is no basement waterproofing system that is 100 percent effective, so if the salesman offers such a guarantee or makes such a representation, walk away. Since the procedures are so complicated, choose reliability over any other attractive come-ons, including price. Check the guarantee.

Big rackets have recently been uncovered in the sale of home fire safety equipment. Your first line of defense must be to deal only with a reputable firm, and to make sure that the equipment and components all have the seal of the Underwriters' Laboratories ("UL") attached. Obtain competitive bids, even if only to compare the type of safety coverage and quality of systems offered by the various companies in the field. If a representation is made by the salesman that the installation of *his* system will result in a reduction of your fire insurance premium, verify this first with your insurance agent.

Furnace repairs and replacement seem also to be a home for the purveyors of fraud and scare tactics. Beware of the firm that gives you a ridiculously low price on a "clean and repair" deal, then finds the unit is irreparable and attempts to sell you a new one. A variation of this is the workman who appears at your door, just having finished a similar job in your neighborhood, and asks if he may inspect the unit with no obligation to you. He then dismantles it so that it cannot be put together again, warns that the condition is dangerous, and wants you to buy a new one on the spot. Scare tactics; don't buy the unit or the tactics. Shop around, if you feel you may be in the market for a new unit, but under no circumstances let the man at the door in to make his "free" survey.

There are innumerable other items of repair or improvement to a house that may cause trouble to the home owner, such as additions to the house itself, the building of terraces and patios, repair or replacement of the roof (there are organized groups of itinerant and fraudulent roof repairers, as you may have read in the newspapers), house painting, and home insulation. Most of your questions and worries are answered by following the general rules of this chapter, and maintaining the twin safeguards of obtaining a reliable contractor, and practicing wariness thereafter.

What should you do in the event of a genuine dispute, however, or if you find you have been cheated?

If you have been lured into a phony deal by a misleading advertisement, notify the local office of your Federal Trade Commission (Appendix B). There is no question, should you suspect fraud, that you should notify the Attorney General of your state, as well as the District Attorney of your region. If anything has transpired by mail, notify your local Postal Inspector (ask your local post office how to contact him) or write directly to the United States Postal Service (Appendix B).

Under any circumstances, notify your state consumer agency (Appendix B), and other consumer organizations (Appendix C), especially the Better Business Bureau (Appendix A).

If you have financed the work through a lending institution, you must be aware that you are, in most cases, legally required to continue to make payments, despite the fact that the contractor may not have fulfilled his obligations. However, you should definitely inform the bank or finance company acting as a collection agent, in writing, if you have a justified dispute with the home improvement contractor, and wish to suspend your payments pending a resolution of the argument. In some areas of the country, there are actual laws making the lending institution subject to any defenses you have against the contractor, suspending the rule of "holder in due course," and, in effect, making the bank responsible for the contractor they financed. In many other areas of the country where such laws have not been passed, the bank is interested in pleasing the depositor, and so, though it may not help, it cannot hurt to notify the bank also.

A sample letter of complaint might read as follows:

Attorney General of Your State
(Address)

Dear Sir:

I am writing to ask you to investigate a situation where work is being done on my home by (name and address of contractor). I received an advertisement in the mail, a copy of which is attached, offering what appears to be an acceptable deal to install a complete sprinkler system in my lawn. When I called the company, a Mr. King appeared as its representative. I told him I would want a diagram of what was to be done added to the contract, and he agreed. He presented the drawing and the contract to me, and it was signed. He asked me for a thousand dollars on account, saying this was to show my good faith. I paid him this amount by check. I'm enclosing copies of the contract, drawing, and both sides of the cancelled check.

He told me, although it was not included in the contract, that work would begin in one week, as soon as my check cleared the bank, but the company didn't start till three weeks later. My entire front lawn was ripped up, and then I saw the pipes that were being laid were not in the same design as on the diagram. When I called Mr. King on (date), he said prices of labor and material had risen, and I would either have to pay more money, which was to be paid in advance, or that fewer sprinkler heads would have to be installed, despite the contract.

I refused and told Mr. King that I thought he should live up to the contract, or replace my lawn and give me back my thousand dollars. He refused, removed his workmen and machinery, and left my lawn all torn up. He said it would remain that way until I agreed to his terms.

I respectfully submit that I have been the victim of a fraud and I ask you to take action.

Very truly yours,
Ellen Miller

cc: District Attorney
Better Business Bureau (Appendix A)
State Consumer Agency (Appendix B)
United States Postal Service (Appendix B)
Federal Trade Commission (Appendix B)
United States Office of Consumer Affairs (Appendix B)
Consumers Union (Appendix C)
Chamber of Commerce (telephone book)
(If licensing is required for home improvement contractors in your community, send a copy of the letter to such an agency. Get the name and address from the Chamber of Commerce of your librarian)

There are any number of problems that may arise to beset the home-owning consumer. Taxes and problems with neighboring parcels of real estate are foremost in this category, but most of these problems do not fall within the scope of this book since they are best met by consultation with an attorney. There are a few helpful hints that will be stated, to possibly avoid the necessity of such involvement.

As to tax assessments on your property, there are two vital points to keep in mind. First, by the time you receive notice that your tax has jumped to a substantially higher amount, it is too late to do anything about it or to consult with an attorney to file a legally acceptable protest. Find out two things from City Hall: when the new assessments and tax rates are listed, and what is the last date to file a protest or appeal. Then you can check the amount of any increase in the books of the city or town and make a rational, timely decision whether it pays you to go through the expense of hiring an attorney for a protest.

Concerning the second point, those in the know with regard to tax reappraisals are aware of the fact that tax assessors are entirely too busy to reappraise each house, each year. They look for two occurrences which are dead give-aways to an increase in the value of a house. Most alterations to houses require the filing of plans, requests for permits, etc. These houses are reassessed almost automatically. Second, in driving through a neighborhood, if the appraiser notes a house that has had an obvious alteration or addition made to its exterior since his last tour, that house is due for a reappraisal.

Nuisances committed by neighbors are often a problem of the home owner, whether it be an encroachment on your property by a fence, or something similar. These problems, too, must be brought to an attorney's attention, but there is one thing you should do that may avoid future arguments. Check with the lawyer you used when you bought the property as to whether a "survey" was included. This is a drawing showing exactly where your property begins and where it ends. If not, he can put you in touch with a surveyor who, for a modest fee, will prepare a diagram of your property. In this manner, many arguments as to who may build or grow where will be avoided, with a consequent savings in attorney's fees.

IF YOU RENT

Those who live in rented premises have their own set of problems. Aside from certain helpful hints set forth, your best bet is to see an attorney with *any* major problem that arises with regard to your tenancy. If a legal paper is served upon you by the landlord, don't ever ignore it or try to handle it yourself. Don't take a chance that the paper served upon you is meaningless. It may safely be said that you will lose. A further recommendation is to find an attorney who knows landlord–tenant law in your neighborhood. A general practitioner will usually be ignorant of the fine touches that in your case may mean the difference between winning and losing. Find out who is known to handle such cases from your tenants' association, other tenants' associations in the city, the union you belong to, or the Legal Aid Society in your town.

For those who live in rented premises, mostly apartments in apartment houses, the trouble begins with the lease. Most are form leases, drawn up by real estate associations, overwhelmingly weighted against the tenant, but which most people are forced to accept, glad to get a decent apartment in this residence-short society.

For instance, most written leases provide that whatever the landlord does or does not do, though expressly promised, your duty to pay rent continues, independent of his actions.

Major problems arise with regard to services, including heat and hot water, painting, defective boilers, flooring, and radiators, plumbing leaks, loose and cracked windows, vermin, cracked walls, peeling paint and plaster (which children may eat), and sporadic superintendent service.

The first step in fighting against the landlord is to find out who the landlord (owner) is. Neither an agent nor a superintendent is the owner, usually. Although you may have a lease, and an owner is listed on it, this listed owner may no longer own the property at the time you wish to do something about a condition in the building. Some communities require the filing by an owner of its name and address with some branch of the community government, and some even require a plate bearing this information to be posted in the building lobby. Assuming that things are not made this easy for you, it will be necessary to dig out the information.

Record systems are maintained in different manners in each community. Go to the Office of the Tax Assessor, Building Department, or Hall of Records in your town and start asking how to find out who owns your building. You will need the address, and, from this, most communities have an index that will eventually lead you to the records indicating the "last owner." Don't be afraid to keep asking questions of the clerks in the various departments. Though some arrogant or lazy ones may try to brush you off, ask to speak to their supervisors, and watch how attitudes change.

When you finally do come up with the name of the owner, it may be a dummy corporation—that is, a corporation formed specifically to shield the identities of the true owners. However, for your purposes, this will suffice.

Now, for the attack. The first step, utterly useless but necessary as a foundation for succeeding steps, is to write a letter to the owner, as short as possible, outlining the deficiencies in service and send it *registered* mail, return receipt requested. The reason for sending the letter registered, instead of certified, which is cheaper, is that many leases and local laws require any notice to the landlord to be sent in this manner, and it is better to comply with a possibly non-existent rule and spend a few extra pennies than it is to fail because you didn't give notice in the proper manner. The reason why the letter, in and of itself, will be useless, is that no landlord will jump just because a tenant sends him a registered letter.

You have a choice of directions for your next step. Should your locality have some form of rent control, and should your apartment be rent-controlled, the odds are that you will be able to make application to the agency for a reduction in rent because of the reduction in services. However, the average tenant will be more desirous of getting services restored, rather than obtaining a rent cut.

Most housing in most communities is governed by housing codes, prescribing what conditions of a building are legal and which are not. Notify the Building Department in writing, certified mail, of what is wrong and ask them to make an inspection. Many departments are slow to act, so keep bombarding them. The end result may be violations of the Housing Code being slapped on the building. No landlord likes this for a number of technical, legal, and financial reasons.

In the same manner you found out who the owner was, you should be able to find out which is the bank that has a mortgage on the property. There is almost no apartment house that doesn't have a mortgage on it. When you find out who the mortgagee (the holder of the mortgage) is, write to it and let it know in what manner the property is being allowed to become rundown. Most banks have no interest whatsoever in helping a tenant, but the purpose of your letter to them is to make somebody in charge worry about the loss in value of the property serving as the security for the mortgage and to force the landlord to make the necessary repairs.

Finally, if any of your complaints are a violation of the law, a menace to health, or a public nuisance, you may want to go to court. In this regard, you should consult with an attorney or, if you feel you actually want to do it yourself, find out if there is a Housing Court in your community (check with the Legal Aid Society or your neighborhood police station). If there is, go there, explain your problem, and follow the procedure as laid out by the Clerk of the Court. If there is no Housing Court, explain your problem at the police station and go to the Court they refer you to.

Aside from the problems with housing referred to above,

there are other health hazards and nuisances connected with rental facilities. Rat infestation, elevators that get stuck and broken, and littered passageways and steps are common. Indeed, some of the horrible conditions and vandalism are deliberately caused by the landlord, to create vacancies in the building for the purpose of selling it, changing it to a condominium, or replacing the building with something more profitable. After the heat stops or the windows are boarded up, letters come from the landlord, offering to help with "relocation," and perhaps offering a bonus for moving. These health hazards and landlord harassment may be grounds for lawsuits, but since each locality has different laws, do yourself a favor and consult with an attorney first.

In addition to the remedies suggested above, there are three others that sometimes help, dealing with the landlord's insurance and liability, the secret area where a landlord may be badly hurt.

Try to find out from the mortgagee bank, or have a tenant-oriented lawyer find out, who the insurance company is that insures the property for accidents or fire (sometimes a helpful superintendent will give you the information). Write to the insurance company, listing all of the conditions that may lead to a fire or an accident. As in the case of the bank, the insurance company may force a correction of the conditions as the price of maintaining insurance on the premises, or threaten to raise the premiums (which the landlord will do anything to avoid).

With regard to the registered letter that you originally sent to the landlord, if you have included a condition which is dangerous, such as a badly broken step or no lights in the hall, and someone later gets hurt because of this condition he has had actual notice of, his position in a lawsuit will be badly hurt, and his insurance company may take reprisals against him for failure to act, thus costing them money. Landlords know this, so when they receive letters describing such conditions and using the magic words "You now have *actual notice* of the condition," many smart landlords will immediately remedy the situation. Lastly, if you are the person actually hurt by such a condition, consult an attorney immediately, not only to recover for your injuries, but to see that appropriate action is taken immediately so that the particular condition cannot continue to exist, to someone else's peril, or even your own.

A further problem that arises with rented premises is your right to sublet your apartment to someone else, should you wish to move out of it before your lease expires. It is clear that, in the absence of extraordinary circumstances, if you sign a lease for two years, you are stuck with paying rent on that apartment for two years. Situations arise, however, where you have to move out before that time. The question then becomes: what are your rights under the lease? Have a lawyer or a person knowledgeable in the subject look at the lease before you sign. If nothing is said in the lease about subletting (where the person taking over the apartment pays you, but you remain directly liable for the entire period of the lease to the landlord), or about assignment of the lease (much rarer where the new tenant takes over your obligations completely, and you are off the hook), you may sublet the apartment or assign the lease. The catch is that there is practically no printed standard form of lease in the country today that does not have some provision limiting this right.

The usual limitation is the statement to the effect that there shall be no subletting or assignment by the tenant without the landlord's written consent. If you push a landlord at the time of execution of the lease, he may add a phrase to the effect that consent will not be unreasonably withheld, which is much better and gives you practically a free hand.

If you see the landlord is out to give you a tough time in subletting the apartment, keep a written record of your efforts to rent the apartment, with names and addresses of those who came, those the landlord turned down, with dates, conversations, etc. If the landlord thereafter sues you for the balance of the rent due under the entire term of the lease, you will be in a position to show that the apartment was not re-rented because of the landlord's own doing. You will find that re-renting sets the approximate time upon which your liability on your lease ceases, so you can see that such a defense will be important.

Let's be perfectly honest. Most leases are drawn up by the best legal minds that owners can hire to prevent the leases from being broken. Once you have signed a lease, you are supposed to be in an iron straitjacket—the lease—with no way to wriggle out.

Still, there are ways. Many state and city laws modify leases to the extent that they may be broken under certain conditions. You will only find out how if you consult an attorney, for the means are different everywhere. However, it pays to know some of the grounds for lease breaking so that you may make an informed decision as to whether it even pays to spend money for a legal consultation.

Of course, we are talking about written leases. There are oral leases, agreed upon by an exchange of words, which should not be too difficult to back out of, and month-to-month tenancies. If there is an oral agreement or a month-to-month tenancy, you should give written notice to the landlord of your vacating of the apartment at least 30 days before you vacate, or at least a full rent period (should rent be due, say, every two weeks).

With written leases, the terms of the lease govern. If you are promised quiet enjoyment of the premises, and nuisances exist, you may be able to back out of the lease. Again, check with an attorney. When you compare his fee with what you would have to pay during the balance of the tenancy, the investment pays.

If you are evicted, actually or constructively (which means, in effect, that such conditions exist in the building that you are already forced on your way out), your obligation to pay rent under the lease ceases. If fire renders your apartment uninhabitable, your lease is, in effect, broken. In some parts of the country, actual partial eviction constitutes grounds for avoiding a lease. For instance, if a ceiling is coming down, and it is dangerous to live in one or more rooms of the apartment, the law may permit you to break the lease unless the landlord makes immediate repairs. Once again, the law must be checked through counsel.

One thought must be kept in mind. Assuming that you are unable to break the lease, no one can arrest you for moving out anyway, or abandoning the apartment. Further assume that the landlord can find you—a reasonable assumption in light of today's means of discovering the present location of citizens—you will then be responsibile for any period of your lease that the apartment remains unoccupied; if the apartment is rented for a lesser amount than you were paying, the difference in rental between the present rent and what you were paying, for the balance of the lease; the costs necessary to prepare the apartment for the new tenant, such as painting; and, possibly, attorney's fees and costs. This may run to a good deal of money in the initial calculations, especially when you add in the cost of your own attorney to defend the action, but what the practicalities are constitutes an entirely different situation. In this landlord's market, no apartment will go unrented for more than a month or two, and it probably will bring a higher rental than you paid. All other elements are subject to proof at an extended trial whose outcome is not that certain, and so your lawyer should be able to reach a compromise settlement whose burden upon you will not be onerous.

Being practical, once again, in view of this landlord's market in apartments, a direct approach to the super or landlord may reach the desired result at a very low cost, possibly one month's rent.

Keep in mind, however, that no termination of a lease is valid unless it is signed to that effect by the landlord (not the superintendent). The mere acceptance of keys by a superintendent or agent may be later construed as an act which was to help in subletting, a situation which does not release you from the terms of the lease.

In the same vein, writing "paid in full" on the back of a rent check will have no meaning or effect in releasing you.

A sore point with most tenants involves "security." In most instances, at the beginning of a lease, the landlord requires the tenant to put up one or two months' rent in advance to be held by the landlord during the term of the lease to insure that the tenant will live up to the lease, and that the apartment will be turned back to the landlord in the same condition it was, except for normal wear and tear, as at the commencement of the lease.

When signing a lease, don't be afraid to ask whether the local laws provide for the security money to be placed in an escrow account (where the landlord cannot spend the money for his own purposes). An interest-bearing account? What bank? What interest? Keep this information to turn over to the attorney general of your state should your escrow money be wrongfully withheld from you at the end of the lease.

The refusal of landlords to return security funds at the end of a tenancy on the grounds that the apartment has been damaged or it would cost that sum to return it to its old condition (remove wallpaper, replace fixtures, etc.) has become so notorious and widespread that tenants must take precautions from the earliest moments of occupancy. When you move into the apartment, take color photographs of the condition of the apartment and do the same thing when moving out. This will be invaluable evidence if you have to sue the landlord to get your security back. At the end of your lease, request an inspection of the apartment by the owner, agent, or superintendent, to see if anything is found amiss. Arrange to be there at the time of the inspection, preferably with witnesses.

Although it is against the terms of lease, and cannot be recommended to the reader, if the security is for one month, many people have been living the last month in the apartment without paying rent, known as "living out the security." The landlord, of course, may start an action for eviction, but it surely will not be decided in one month, and if he thereafter sues you for damage to the apartment, he has to get his money from you, not the other way around.

There are usually two reasons for eviction proceedings instituted by the landlord. The first, one that we are not particularly concerned with in this book, is the fact that the tenant does not have the money to pay the rent, is occupying the apartment for the purpose of maintaining a nuisance (such as for gambling or prostitution), or just won't pay the rent because he is a deadbeat. For such persons, no help will be found here.

The second category of tenant that the landlord seeks to evict is the one who has been victimized by the landlord's maintenance of the building and won't pay rent until he gets what he is supposed to get. Under any circumstances, if an eviction suit is started against the tenant and the tenant decides to pay, the rent should be sent by certified mail, return receipt requested. If the landlord accepts it, many states will call the eviction action dead at that point, but many other states will permit the landlord to continue with his proceedings. Check with a local lawyer as to what your state and community permit. If the landlord refuses the envelope containing the rent, keep the envelope unopened when you get it back, until you get to court, and show it to the judge in that condition. It will help you on the question of good faith, and the judge may well order the landlord to accept the rent right then and there, and will dismiss the eviction proceeding.

If you decide to withhold rent because of the condition of the premises, be aware of some of the various grounds that different states permit such action on and consult with an attorney as to whether such grounds are applicable in your state.

You owe no rent on a lease if you have been actually evicted. For instance, if the house has been condemned and you have moved out, there is no further liability on your part. Indeed, eviction consists of any act which deprives the tenant of the use of the premises, or so substantially affects the use that the tenant is not getting what he bargained for in the lease.

No rent is owed if there is actual partial eviction, that is, if it is so dangerous to use certain rooms in your apartment (ceiling collapsing, etc.) that you have been, in effect, actually evicted from part of your apartment.

A defense is available to a suit for nonpayment in some states if there is constructive eviction. The water is completely shut off, the house is dying, or a similar condition exists, and you are, in actuality, already evicted.

A few states today permit a defense of a warranty of habitability of the apartment to be interposed to an eviction proceeding for non-payment. As you receive a warranty or guarantee when you buy a new item that it will work properly, the warranty of habitability holds that when a landlord rents an apartment to you, he warrants or guarantees that the place is fit to live in.

There are other defenses permitted to non-payment in other states, but once again, consult with an attorney first.

Some states permit the withholding of rent, such sums to be used to repair the building, and some states go further and say that the withheld rent should be paid into court and the court will order the repairs. Even among those states that have such laws, the laws differ, so get legal advice. The same is true for a claim of rent abatement (or no need to pay rent) because there are certain violations on the building.

In any event, at any stage of your tenancy when you see trouble developing, keep a log or record of any conversations had with the landlord, anyone from his office, any agent or superintendent, as to the date, time, place, and substance of the conversation. Many lawsuits, whether instituted by you or the landlord, demand specific information as proof, and you will have it, if the need arises. Don't be self-conscious; it is your first line of defense.

If you are a tenant, no form letters will be of much avail to you. There will be legal forms and lawyer's letters aplenty, but your best attack is to know your rights and when to pursue them Do so without hesitation. The landlord has no time to retaliate for the sheer sake of it, and he would have no hesitancy to attack you were he in the right.

CHAPTER 14

—————— **False Advertisements** ——————

Advertising quite often consists of perfectly legal but deceptive types, not directly fraudulent, but possibly leading up to fraud once the ad draws you into the seller's clutches. Let's face it, the men who practice commerce in this manner are past masters at the art of preying on your alleged gullibility and avarice, while staying that hair-breadth away from provable fraud.

How many times have you heard the phrases "Fantastic Price Reductions," "Unbelievable Savings," "All Items at Wholesale Price," "Formerly," "Regularly," "Nationally Advertised," "List," "Value," "Up to __% Off," "Outlet," and "Warehouse"? Believe them at your own risk.

Watch for ads that proclaim "$__ and Up!" How high is up? What is the full range of price? What is a top price? This is another come-on.

There isn't a claim that can be disproved, that can't be weaseled out of. No one can do a thing for you except yourself, and that's by disbelief and non-purchase.

Admittedly, not all such ads are false. Many stores, especially supermarkets, advertise loss leaders (merchandise offered at a loss on a select few items in order to entice you into the store), and we all recognize this as a legitimate buyer–seller ploy.

Half-truths in pricing are often contained in ads. A ridiculously low price, known in the industry as a "low ball," is just that—ridiculous.

How many ads have you seen that advertise a "free" offer? Keep reading, and you will probably find, in tiny print, limitations, conditions, or modifications that render the word "free" a mockery.

Many ads fail to disclose extra charges for installation, delivery, etc. Most ethical stores and the Better Business Bureau feel that an advertised price should include all costs to the consumer, with the exception of sales tax. But it is not illegal to keep mum about these extra sums. Use your common sense and ask what additional charges will be made.

Quite a number of ads have layouts (aluminum siding for a house, for instance) that tell you in no uncertain terms that the quoted price is for a certain number of square feet. The house, as illustrated in the ad, however, is a huge residence. Don't let your eye overrule your common sense. Question, always question.

It has been found that many companies advertise their product or service for a certain price for a "limited time only." Check to see, or ask, if this price constitutes a specially reduced price, or if the price quoted is their usual price, with only the words being used to stir you to action.

Certain ads, especially on watches, state a very good price, indeed, but also set forth, in small print, that not all parts are guaranteed. Don't buy, unless you are sure that only the guaranteed parts will fail.

Another set of ads that are half-truths involves implied low cost for life insurance because you are dealing directly with a company. Incidentally, most often these ads are sent to parents of college students (the college being the source of the mailing list). The way to test this is to contact your local savings bank (savings banks have some of the lowest rates for insurance, since they, too, sell directly to the customer). Compare prices and quite often you will find you are not being offered any bargains. If the proposition still looks good, but the name of the insurance company is not familiar, call or write your State Department of Insurance, or go to your local library and ask to see Best's Ratings on the Company. Unless the named organization gets a "most substantial" or "very substantial" margin listed for contingencies, don't buy the insurance, because you are then possibly dealing with a fly-by-night, hit and run company that may wind up bankrupt and your premiums will be lost.

The subject of ads with regard to quacks dealing in food fads, health devices, and miraculous drugs has been previously discussed.

Now, let's suppose that you have bitten at the bait anyway and have been fooled. Let us further suppose you suspect that the seller has gone that one fatal step beyond the bounds separating a seller's normal exaggeration of half-truth from actual deception and fraud.

If you still have the paper, magazine, flyer, or other writing that contained the advertisement, or can get hold of a copy, or can photostat the ad from the copy of the periodical to be found in your local library, do so as soon as you can and as soon as you smell trickery. You will need this in order to make a claim to the proper parties.

There is not much to be gained by making your claim initially to the seller. It set out to fool you, has done so, and will usually not voluntarily return your money. A letter addressed to the proper authorities with carbon copies to the seller may sometimes instill sufficient fear of governmental or organizational action against the seller to cause a hasty attempt to settle your claim.

One of the major authorities that deals with misleading advertising is the Federal Trade Commission (Appendix B). Since February 1974, they have committed their investigative facilities to monitor advertising at the local level. They have recently cracked down on questionable advertising for, among other things, companies that will "sell" your song lyrics, hair replacement firms, and business schools that make beautiful promises about the earnings of their graduates. A report to the FTC in writing will ordinarily be kept confidential and the FTC will proceed in its own name.

Now, for the catch. The Federal Trade Commission will not get involved in a private controversy, and will not seek to get your money back or other satisfaction. However, if the seller is aware that you are getting the FTC on its trail, the indirect effect of notification to this agency may result in satisfaction to you.

Primarily, you should notify three types of organizations: your state and local criminal agencies (Attorney General of your state, your District or County Attorney) your state or local consumer agency (Appendix B) and your private consumer rights organizations (Better Business Bureau, etc.—Appendices A and C). You should also advise the paper that carried the ad, as well as the Federal Trade Commission.

Some of the governmental criminal agencies have even arranged, recently, for victims to be recompensed.

A sample letter might read as follows:

Attorney General of your State
Consumer Frauds and Protection Bureau
(Address)

Gentlemen:

I'm enclosing herewith a clipping of an advertisement from the (newspaper or periodical) taken from its issue of (date), with regard to some ski boots that were being sold at (name and address of firm) for $10, starting the next day. I was there early the next morning, when the store opened, but I was told that these "special" ski boots had already been sold out. They tried to sell me much more expensive pairs, and became abusive when I wanted to walk out. To avoid a scene, I bought another pair for $30.

I'm enclosing another clipping from the same paper, dated two days later, that shows the same ski boot still on sale. When I called the store after the second ad, they wouldn't even talk to me.

I feel that I have been victimized and I respectfully request an investigation be made as to such practices, and, of course, I would like to return the boots I was forced to buy, and get my money back. Thank you.

Very truly yours,
Ellen Miller

cc: (Store)
    (Newspaper or periodical)
    Federal Trade Commission (Appendix B)
    District Attorney (telephone book)
    State Consumer Agency (Appendix B)
    Better Business Bureau (Appendix A)
    Consumer's Union (Appendix C)
    (Whatever other consumer groups from Appendix C you wish
       to advise)

Remember, keep a copy of your letter and include, with each of the carbon copies you send out, photostats of the clippings or other enclosures.

Don't drop it. Don't rationalize doing nothing about it. Do it this very day!

CHAPTER
15

— How to Avoid and Fight Fraud —

We dealt previously with false advertisements, usually composed of half truths by over-eager businessmen who are quite often legitimate. Many offers, however, made by mail, advertisement, on the phone, and in person are meant, by and large, to defraud you.

Public losses have been estimated by mail fraud alone at over one hundred million dollars per year. The smooth operators who deal in these types of swindles prey on the elderly, retired, poor and uneducated, but quite often the rest of us are also bedazzled into losing money to their practiced wiles.

There is no end to the number of schemes that are being used today—diet pills, aphrodisiacs, bust developers, anti-smoking devices; cures for arthritis, cancer, diabetes, obesity, impotence, headaches, baldness; get-rich-quick schemes; phony educational and real estate ploys.

The fraud merchants are difficult to find after they have struck, and it is much more difficult to stop them or recover your money. They rarely use one "front" corporation for more than a year at a time, and as soon as the authorities crack down on that corporation, the hidden operators open up under another name. "Money back" guarantees are valueless under these circumstances, and even a "good address" (such as on Fifth Avenue in New York, for instance) means nothing since this may be just a rented desk. Of course, a request to send money to a post office box is often a dead giveaway of fraudulent intent. Any limitations on the word "free" as used in an advertisement is another tip-off, such as "Free! Send only $9.98 for (item) and you get free (another item)."

In this type of a situation, your best position is, as usual, your first line of defense. (1) Check if the organization is legitimate, and (2) know the swindles prevalent today and avoid them.

As to the reliability of the seller, write to or call the Direct Mail Advertising Association (Appendix C), your local or national Better Business Bureau (Appendix A), or your local Chamber of Commerce (check with the phone book or your librarian).

Most fraudulent schemes fall into certain patterns, readily identifiable.

The "bait and switch" fraud has been called the biggest retailing gyp in the country today. A fabulous offer is advertised for a certain product, such as a vacuum cleaner, and once you fall for it and fall into the clutches of a salesman at your home or at a selling location he shows you that the item is not very good, but he just happens to have a better one (at an inflated price) ready for immediate delivery. Since the customer usually needs it anyway, and the item is available, the higher price is wangled out of the customer.

Another variety is the fake contest. You receive a phone call that "you've won" a new sewing machine, and may pick it up as soon as you come to the selling location to select and pay for a cabinet whose cost, you later discover, is more than the total worth of the machine and cabinet together.

The "Mary Kelly Estate" swindle is another prevalent scheme. A common name is selected, whether it be Kelly, Smith, or whatever, and all persons bearing such names, as printed in phone books across the country, receive dignified letters stating that a person of the same last name has died and the writer can provide you with information to enable you to claim the estate of $50,000 or some other large amount, if you will only send ten dollars for such information. It sounds silly, doesn't it? Millions have been made on this "missing heir" scheme alone.

Once again, parents of children are notified that they have been chosen to be part of a "pilot educational program," but the catch is that you must buy a set of encyclopedias. A variation on this is that you are given the set free, but you have to pay ten dollars a month for three years to get the supplements, and this total cost is far above the actual value of the entire set.

COD parcels are sent to unsuspecting people, of items not ordered, and when you pay the charge, you open the package and find an item inside that is valueless. A variation of this, and one of the meanest frauds known, involves sending COD packages to a person who has just died (names are obtained from obituary columns), and the bereaved relatives, thinking that the package contains something the deceased wanted, pay the large COD charges and discover the same junk inside.

People have been induced to invest in "large earning cattle deals," and the post office has found that, even if there are such herds, the promoter of the scheme usually does not even own them. The best advice in this, as in most of these offers, is if the deal promises a very high rate of return or involves exotic collateral, forget it.

You are promised work at home if you send fifteen dollars for a kit or information. When you do, you then receive a letter stating that the fee is not refundable, the company cannot be reached by phone, and it only uses a box number for correspondence. The topic of "work at home" will be discussed in greater detail later in the chapter.

Chain letters come to you, and you are in effect paying for a chance of winning a large prize. Skip it.

A scheme that was formerly used much more often when people were less informed (although it is still practiced among the poor) is to offer you merchandise "on approval," if you will sign a "receipt." The receipt turns out to be a contract, and you are stuck with paying, for instance, seventy-five dollars for a fifteen dollar watch. Furthermore, the contract included a wage assignment, and the promoter goes directly to your boss for payment.

Another swindle is to send you a check, payable as a "discount" if you buy a certain item at "full price," the "discount" price being far and away higher than the value of the goods. A variation of this is persuading you to pick up the "unpaid balance of payments" on a "repossessed" item. A bargain, correct? You will find that the unpaid balance is much more than the total worth of the item.

Although most book and record clubs are honest, many have made it almost impossible to refuse these items by the use of the "negative option" method. In other words, unless you notify the company well in advance of the mailing date, you will receive the announced selection and must pay·for it. The trouble is, you never know how, when, or where to so notify the company. Now the Federal Trade Commission has taken a hand and issued regulations that all promotional material must state "clearly and conspicuously" how to notify the supplier NOT to send the item, whether there are any requirements that a certain number of selections must be bought within a given year, and what rights there are to cancel the agreement to participate. Furthermore, the subscriber must be given at least ten days before the shipping date in which to notify the seller not to ship the merchandise.

If you are going to respond to such offers anyway, make sure you keep a record of your order and a copy of the catalog or advertisement on the basis of which you made your order.

If you have dealt with a firm whose location is only listed as a box number, and have inevitably been burnt, there is a postal regulation that permits you to obtain the name of the post office box holder, and its actual business address, if you can show that the box is being used commercially and that there is some evidence of fraud or receipt of faulty merchandise. Write to the Postmaster, in care of the Central Post Office, in the city in which the mail order company is located, requesting the above information, enclosing a copy of the advertisement to show that a business is involved, and a very short tale of how you have been defrauded or harmed. You will receive the information in fairly rapid order.

However, the speed of your reaction to being defrauded may be vital to enable the authorities to catch up with the fraud merchants, so advise all pertinent agencies at once.

Write to the Consumer Protection Office of the United States Postal Service (Appendix B), with copies to the local United States Attorney (check with your librarian), your state Attorney General, the Attorney General in the state of the promoter, your state Consumer Agency and those in the state of the promoter (Appendix B), the Better Business Bureau (Appendix A), Consumers Union (Appendix C), and the District Attorney of the area in which the promoter is located, if such area is close enough to you to enable you to physically cooperate with the

District Attorney. Do it fast! It is not only a question of punishing the cheats, but there have been many instances whereby pressure from one of the above agencies has resulted in restitution.

While many of the above frauds are widespread, there are certain areas in which scheming has affected millions of investors, and for goodly sums from each of them. They are special problems that require additional explanation and solution.

One such area involves fraudulent land sales, with the real estate usually located far from the purchaser. In effect, this scheme cashes in on most men's dreams of retirement and the good life.

You have certainly seen the advertisements, shown everywhere, of new developments springing up in the south, the west, and other places, where you can get in on the ground floor. Many are honorable offers of honorable developers. Many are not.

Some tip-offs to the fast hustle become apparent with offers of free vacations and trips to the "general" site, free dinners and films to acquaint you with this golden opportunity, and similar high pressure tactics.

Of course, the illusion presented is far from reality, when misrepresentations go unchecked. Oral promises by the salesman to repurchase the land after a certain time prove valueless, because they were not included in the contract. A good defense you may have to a suit brought by the developer goes a-glimmering, because of a legal switch of your obligation and promise of payment to a financing company, against whom the defense is doubtful because the financer is a "holder in due course." The land you have bought may be in a desert, hundreds of miles from anywhere, with no transportation available, no hope of any basic utilities, water, or recreational facilities. With shady operators, the lot you have been told you own may "shrink" upon being described in the legal papers, and you, still blissfully thinking you own up to "that tree," may build a house partly on another man's land and wind up in hot water, both in court and out. (*Tip:* Get your own surveyor.)

As your first line of defense, awareness and cynicism, don't take the salesman's word about local plans, nearby zoning for industry, tax assessments or highway plans. Check it out with town hall in the area.

Find out, if you can, how the developer has done at his present site and elsewhere. Don't check with the developer's references, so eagerly offered. Check through your own bank. Ask your banker what financial arrangement he would offer you if you bought such a lot. His reactions are quite liable to provide you with an informed insight. Also check with people who have dealt with the developer before.

Incidentally, one of the most vicious ploys that have been used, ruining countless people, is the deal whereby your lot is bought on an installment contract. People who get a legal-looking paper think that they have actual title to the property—but they don't. While the installments are being paid, perhaps for years, if one installment is missed, such contracts provide for forfeiture of all the money you have already paid in, *plus* the land. As a variation, even if you don't miss a payment, there may be a lawsuit against the developer and your land, still in his name, is taken away to satisfy someone else's judgment against the developer.

What do you do if you find the proposition interesting? If advertising is taking place across state lines, lots being sold to residents of states other than that where the land is located, this represents an interstate land sale, and as such is regulated by the Office of Interstate Land Sales Registration (OILSR) of the

United States Department of Housing and Urban Development (HUD). The first thing you should do is write to OILSR, Washington, D.C. 20410 (Appendix B) to find out whether the developer is registered. If not, forget it, because you are undoubtedly about to be fleeced.

This agency has now made certain rules applicable to all developers of interstate land promotions, the first of which is that they must register with the agency. The rest of the rules are for your protection.

The most important of the protective rules is that the promoter must furnish you with a property report, containing much you had better know before you invest your hard-earned money. There are two warnings with regard to this report. First, you may overlook it because the promoter has sent you a huge batch of promotional material, and has buried the report in the middle of it, hoping you will not read it. Find it and read it! Second, some promoters deliberately put too much information in the report, winding up with a document of many pages, scarifying in its legalities, once again hoping that such a document will cause the reader to avoid reading it and hope that all will turn out well, and who's going to get bogged down in all those legal terms, anyway? You will, if you don't want to lose thousands of dollars. Skip the "whereases" and "wherefores" and look for the following information.

The report must include distances to nearby communities over paved or unpaved roads; any liens on the property; arrangements for placing your contract payments in special funds (escrow), so that the developer can't fiddle around with the money before you get the property; nearness of recreational facilities; availability of sewer and water facilities or septic tanks and wells; current and proposed utility services and charges; the number of homes currently occupied; problems with the soil and foundations that could cause trouble in construction or with regard to septic tanks; and the type of title you will receive to the land. The first page must state in large red letters, "purchaser should read this document before signing anything." There must be a disclosure of the record of any lawsuits against the developer, or any health department or other disciplinary action taken against him, any violations or bankruptcies, together with any other revealing factors about the land and the developer.

The other literature provided by the developer must reflect the true character and condition of the property (underwater, in a desert, etc.), and inform you that HUD has not passed any judgment on the value of the property. If the advertisements state that the land may be subdivided, they must also state the cost and method of doing this.

So far, we have been talking about interstate land sales only, but not all of these are covered. The rules only apply to those sales in which large tracts of land are broken up into many small home sites, but, after all, that is the area in which fraud most often occurs.

As to those promotions that are covered by these rules, if a prospective buyer has not been furnished with a copy of the report, before or at the time of signing of a purchase contract, he may elect to cancel the contract and obtain a refund. If the buyer has not received the report at least 48 hours before signing the contract, he has 48 hours in which to cancel the contract after signing, and must receive a refund. One warning goes with this: If you are taken out to the land to see it, and then asked to sign a contract, don't do it unless you have read it thoroughly. Viewing of the land may be a waiver of the 48 hour cooling-off period.

As to complaints, if the matter involves an interstate land sale, write to OILSR as listed above, with carbon copies to the real estate commissions in the states where the dealer is head-quartered and the land located (see your librarian who has directories with this information), the Attorney General in each of those states and in your own state, the Governmental Consumer Agency in those states and your own (Appendix B), the Better Business Bureau (Appendix A) and Consumers Union (Appendix C), and, if you suspect fraudulent ads, the Federal Trade Commission (Appendix B). If you, the promoter, and the land are all within the same state, write to the Attorney General of your state, and send copies to all of the above (after all, the deal may still be interstate as to other buyers). It might also be wise to discuss the terms of the contract, if a substantial amount is involved, with a lawyer.

A sample complaint letter might read as follows:

Office of Interstate Land Sales Registration
U.S. Department of Housing and Urban Development
Washington, D.C. 20410

Gentlemen:

I wish to make a complaint against (name of company), with headquarters at (address).

I read an advertisement for the sale of a retirement home site, a copy of which is attached hereto, and I sent my name to the company as being interested. I was invited to a dinner, which was held at (place) on (date), at which time movies were shown of a wonderful area, all built up and with happy residents walking around. A salesman then spoke to me and told me that there were only a few lots left, and I had better buy one that night or lose my chance. I gave him $250 in cash, for which I received a receipt, and signed a paper that was just supposed to be a binder, but which I later learned was a contract. I was not given a copy of the contract. The salesman told me that I could back out at any time.

I thereafter had second thoughts about the property because I knew nothing about it. I did not receive any report about the land, only some shiny brochures telling of the possibilities of living there.

The next day, I sent a letter, certified mail, return receipt requested, to the developer telling him I did not want to buy the land and asking him for my money back. A copy of the letter and the return receipt is attached.

I then received a letter from the company stating that I had bought the property, and that I would be sued unless I paid the balance. A copy of this letter is attached.

I believe I have been the victim of fraud, and I ask that you investigate the matter and do all that is necessary to get my money back.

Very truly yours,
Ellen Miller

cc: Real Estate Commission of the state where the seller is headquartered (see your librarian)
Real Estate Commission of the state where the land is located (same source)
Attorney General of the state where the seller is headquartered (same source)
Attorney General of the state where the land is located (same source)
Attorney General of your state
Government Consumer Agency in the state where seller is headquartered (Appendix B)
Government Consumer Agency in the state where the land is located (Appendix B)
Government Consumer Agency in your state (Appendix B)
National Better Business Bureau (Appendix A)
Consumers Union (Appendix C)

Dealing with real estate problems on a different level, you may have trouble with cemeteries. Many do not live up to their maintenance care agreements, and recently there has been a wave of occurrences in which tombstones are knocked over and buried by the management as "unsafe," and then an attempt is made to sell you a new tombstone at an average cost of $500. Write to the Secretary of State and the Attorney General of the state where the cemetery is located.

Another special area of fraud involves "pyramid" sales and the selling of franchises. Pyramid sales involve a drawing in of prospects with respect to a line of merchandise or services, where the bulk of any profit turns out to be the ability of the first line of prospects to talk their friends and acquaintances into investing money so that *they* may sell such goods and services, and they find that there is no money in the proposition unless they can talk *their* friends and neighbors into investing, and so forth. Naturally, there are just so many prospects in any community, and the result is that, in effect, you are asked to swindle your friends or lose practically all the money you have invested. The sale of franchises is similar, but is characterized by glowing promises of easy profits in return for your designation as the "exclusive" distributor of goods or services that are unmarketable.

Telltale signs of smooth swindles in such deals are found in the advertisements, which include exaggerated promises of profit for little work, endorsements by individuals and manufacturers who are not named, promise of free samples (for which you must send money) and undue pressure to invest. This will include trips to "headquarters," and your being confidentially informed that several people are bidding for the opportunity being offered you, and you had better fork over your investment immediately so as not to lose a golden opportunity. Incidentally, if you go to one of these meetings, leave your checkbook at home and sign nothing. There is no such urgency as described by these smooth-tongued swindlers. They will even tell you, if you have no money, how to lie to a bank and get a loan to cover the down payment.

There are a few preliminary tips on awareness as your first line of defense. Get the details by phone, if you can, and if such details are vague and indefinite, forget it right there. If your interest is first aroused by an advertisement, be immediately suspicious of any help-wanted ad that does not state that a wage or salary will be paid, does not disclose that selling will be required, or that an investment is required. You are being lured into a pyramid deal, or a purchase of a franchise.

Once you get the details, steer clear of any setups that promise big profits for little work, or where the franchiser seems more interested in lining up more franchisees or distributors than he is in selling a product or service. Insist on detailed financial statements (after all, if you are going to be a businessman, act like one), a full description of your responsibilities, and the names of the board members of the franchise firm. What training is offered? Check everything. If a celebrity's name is used, ask yourself if you would be interested in the deal without hearing his name. If not, forget it.

Ask questions of yourself. Realistically, would the product be acceptable to the public? Who will pay for promoting it? How does the product compare with its competition? How long has the company been in business, and what is its growth potential, assets, and liabilities (if some of these questions confuse you, it at least shows you what you should be familiar with before you risk your money). How much time and how much money will you have to invest? Is high position and pay being promised for no experience, and if so, why? What ''management position'' requires no experience?

If, after all this, you still like the set-up, verify the claims made to you. Whatever the item is, talk to dealers of similar items and find out if there is a market for it. Check on endorsements from manufacturers referred to in any literature. Has the operator been in business for at least one year? Ask the promoter for the name of a person at the manufacturer's office you can discuss your questions with, even as to how much they have made under average market conditions. Refusal to refer you to such a person usually spells out fraud. But, you say, you have been promised a full refund if not satisfied, even in writing. If the company is shady, out to make a quick dollar and then disappear, what good is the promise worth?

Although pyramid sale and franchise sale swindles seem to sell almost every product or service (including food delivery service, gas additives, selling memberships in a discount service, soap and cosmetics), let us examine two examples that are the current "glamour stock" of this fraud in the street.

Cashing in on the leisure activities boom, franchises are now being sold in the travel agency field. An exclusive area is promised (without explaining how other travel agencies are to be prevented from operating in the same area), you are told that no experience is necessary (in this big, incredibly complex field), and the "training programs" turn out to be a couple of short lectures.

As a first line of defense, how do you protect yourself? Call the Better Business Bureau as to whether there have been any complaints against the company behind the promotion. Ask information from the American Society of Travel Agents, 360 Lexington Avenue, New York, New York 10017, and also ask for any literature on the subject of what is required to go into such a business. Read books about the subject and take a short course in it. In other words, with an "opportunity" like this, it will still be available at a later time and you should not let yourself be rushed into it until you know on what you are risking your money. Let's face it, even when you bet on something as risky as a horse race, you know how your horse did the last few times out. See if any of your friends know a travel agent, and arrange to have a short talk with him on prospects in the industry.

Ask the promoter for substantiation of his claims. For instance, you will almost certainly have been promised a "successful ad campaign" to help your business get off the ground. Tell the promoter you want to study the advertising campaign that will be available to you to see if it suits your purpose. Since it is a "successful" campaign, ask when and where the advertisements will appear. On television? On radio? In which magazines?

The second example involves investment in a vending machine franchise. Tip-offs to fraud are phrases in the advertisements, such as "lab-tested," "location-tested" and "non-competitive." There is a promise of huge earnings, but in the vending machine business, where are they to come from? Another tip-off is an advertisement used as bait that seeks men to service such machines on a part time basis, and when you respond to the advertisement, the pitch is made to sell you the machines, the route, etc. Another clue is that verbal promises are made at an interview, such as a promise to buy the franchise back if you are not satisfied, or help with covering your territory, but you are told that these promises may not be included in the contract, because, "the others would find out, and there'd be trouble, etc." Walk away.

Most times, if you do invest in a questionable operation, you will find out that the machines promised are just no good, or the quality of the goods sold to you by the company (at exorbitant prices) for distribution through the machines is sub-par, or, when the machines break down (as they will) the company will not respond to your request for service calls.

Assuming that you have been caught in the toils of these swindlers, remember that many of these promoters are of the hit-and-run variety, and you had better alert those who may help you just as soon as what has happened to you strikes home.

In August 1974, the Federal Trade Commission declared pyramid schemes illegal, but they will continue to flourish during years of legal maneuvers and quibbling as to whether each individual enterprise that is attacked is a pyramid. You must not expect such schemes to disappear just because of one adverse ruling, so remain on your guard.

Write to the Attorney General of your state, with copies to the Federal Trade Commission (Appendix B); the Postal Inspector at the United States Postal Service (Appendix B); the Securities and Exchange Commission, Washington, D.C. 20549, if this seems to be a national scheme; the District Attorney of your community; your state Governmental Consumer Agency (Appendix B); the national and local Better Business Bureau (Appendix A); Consumers Union (Appendix C); and the Consumer Federation of America (Appendix C). Do it fast! As in the sample letter regarding fraudulent land sales, enclose copies of all literature, contracts, correspondence, and other pertinent papers.

Another field of fraudulent endeavor is the "spare time earnings" or "envelope stuffers" swindle. This appeals to the poor who need a second income, the unemployed, those desperate for work, and the shut-ins. Advertisements are found in the mail, local newspapers, national women's magazines, comic books, and science, mechanic, hunting, and fishing periodicals.

Tip-offs to the larcenous nature of the propositions involve statements that "no experience is necessary"; or offers of materials, kits, etc., at a high price which you must pay before you can create anything to start earning money yourself; advanced payments are requested from you to show your "good faith"; glowing testimonials in the advertisements bear the initials of the persons only, so that you may never check with anyone; there is a blanket offer to buy your entire output of whatever the kit you buy is supposed to make (but then the promoter rejects everything you have made as "not up to standard"); wild claims are made for how much you may earn; and advertisements, though placed in the help-wanted section, turn out to be jobs where only commissions may be earned.

There are many variations of such propositions. Familiarity with the more common types will serve as your first line of defense, alerting you to the modus operandi of such swindlers.

In responding to an advertisement to earn extra money stuffing envelopes, you find that you must pay a fee in advance to show your sincerity, sometimes as little as one dollar. You receive a packet of "direct mail ads" which promises the same thing you fell for. You mail them out and pay one-third of any money received to the promoter, keeping two-thirds for yourself. Thus, this variation on the chain letter type deal can only make money by drawing others into the web.

Then there is the set-up where you pay a small fee in advance to get a sure-fire resume and they list the firms that desperately need home workers. What you actually get is, at best, a few blank resumes in which you are required to fill in the spaces, and a list of companies that will never need any home workers. Of course, you will never obtain a job by this method, but you will obtain an offer from the promoter to become his agent and pull others into the scheme, the old chain letter swindle again.

Advertised "inside secrets" on how to make money, for instance, in the mail order business, draw many people into the net. In return for your money, you receive literature touting a book, pamphlet, or plan that lets you in on business secrets, such as, "work hard," "save your money," and the like. Some of these books that cost consumers ten dollars have been produced for fifty cents. It is the promoter who is saving his money.

A variation on the ''inside secrets'' routine is the ''career training'' pitch. Here, instead of one book, you receive a series of training courses that are worthless, such as burglar alarm installation and worm raising (this was actually advertised)!

The prospect of selling small items that one may make is exciting to many people looking for an opportunity, but first you must buy the equipment and supplies from the promoter. Since these are highly overpriced, you will never be able to sell the items you make.

A sophisticated fraud, involving no opening fee, is one where you buy into a program as an ''official distributor.'' You get mats for newspaper advertisements or catalogs for cheap junk. This material shows your name and address and it is up to you to pay for it all—the cost of running the ads and periodicals and mailing of the catalogs. If orders come in, you deduct your commission and send the balance to the promoter who, *you hope,* will ''drop ship'' the merchandise to the sucker. Think of what is happening. You are paying for the dealer's advertising. He makes money both on what you sell and the supplies you buy from him. If he doesn't deliver the merchandise to the one who sent money to you, only you will receive the complaints. Neat, huh?

Before falling for any scheme, ask yourself these questions. How much is the plan, book, or secret really going to cost me? What will be purchased and what will be sold? Can a living be made at it? Is the product to be sold what people will actually spend money for? Is there a request to send money to a box number (a danger signal at any time)?

Let us assume the worst, that you have been victimized. Before getting into the how-to's of complaining, a common, but crude, squeeze should be de-bunked. Countless children have clipped out coupons from comic books to obtain greeting cards to sell, and the first thing the parents know of it is when they receive a bill for the cards, and threats of lawsuits. Forget it. Unless the parents have agreed to the purchase, or deal, or whatever it may be called, it is not legal, and you should let the promoters go whistle for their money, and inform the authorities about the threats.

In these type of fraudulent transactions, that is, the "spare time earnings-envelope stuffers" swindles, write to the Attorney General of your state, the Postal Inspector at the United States Postal Service (Appendix B); the Federal Trade Commission (Appendix B), if the matter involves a false claim of earnings; the District Attorney of your community; your state Governmental Consumer Agency (Appendix B); your local Better Business Bureau (Appendix A); Consumers Union (Appendix C); and Consumers Federation of America (Appendix C).

Another facet of fraud conducted primarily by mail is the easy mail order degree. There are "degree mills" scattered across the country, which provide great difficulty to anyone attempting to crack down on them. First, only about eighteen of our states have retained control over degree-granting privileges of "colleges," and many of the other states have gone so far as to issue state charters to many of the fraudulent ones. The Federal Trade Commission, which ordinarily would have control over advertisements published interstate by "educational" institutions, is thus robbed of any say, inasmuch as the FTC may not impose any sanctions on state-chartered schools. Second, some of them open and close so fast the postal authorities have no chance to catch them using the mails to defraud.

So, once again, you must use your common sense as your first line of defense. As an easy beginner, run if someone offers to "sell" you a diploma. Be aware that there are no lists of bad schools, those to be avoided. If you are interested in finding a correspondence school that offers a valid degree, either under-graduate or graduate, check with your public or college librar-ian, and the *Higher Education Directory* published by the U.S. Office of Education.

Characteristics of fraudulent schools run the gamut of high pressure tactics; so-called "talent tests," where you will cer-tainly receive a high grade and where no one fails; willingness to sign you up for a course regardless of your background, prep-aration, or abilities; and a salesman telling you, "This is your last chance to sign up."

Other indications of fraud arise if the salesman informs you that the Better Business Bureau or a Public Educational Agency has endorsed the school (these groups never endorse an individ-ual school), or if a school that allegedly prepares you for a ca-reer in civil service tells you it has a connection with the gov-ernment (none of them do). Furthermore, don't believe any school that "guarantees" you a job. It may have an effective placement bureau, but no legitimate school ever guarantees any job.

If, after hearing the details, you are still undecided, take fur-ther steps, including calling the Better Business Bureau as to whether there have been any unfavorable reports on the school; write for information to the school, for its brochures and cata-logs; write to your state's Department of Education; and ascer-tain from the school or your librarian whether the school has received accreditation from the National Home Study Council. This is the only group that is authorized by the United States Office of Education to accredit correspondence schools that meet certain criteria. Accreditation has not meant, over the years, that a certified school is good, but merely that a school that has not been accredited should be regarded warily.

Check certain other things, on your own. How long has the

school been in operation? What do its students and graduates think of it? From what you hear, are its business dealings on the up and up? Are the instructors competent and qualified? Are its rates reasonable? Are the courses effective and practical?

Assume you're happy with what you found out. Examine any "application" you may be asked to sign, because a usual gimmick of such mills is to have you sign a contract under the guise of an application, and you are stuck for a full course, though you may drop out of the course in a few weeks. Check the cancellation clause of any contract, since, if you are permitted to cancel, there may be a "fee" payable, which is almost as much as the full course would be.

Complaints should be addressed to the Bureau of Higher Education of the United States Office of Education, Department of Health, Education and Welfare, Washington, D.C. 20202. Carbon copies should be sent to your state Attorney General, your state Department of Education (obtain the address from your librarian), and your state Governmental Consumer Agency (Appendix B). On the off chance that the school is one that has been silly enough not to obtain a state charter anyplace, notify the Federal Trade Commission (Appendix B) of the school's fraudulent advertisements. By all means, notify the United States Postal Service (Appendix B).

Trade schools are another phase of the problem. While much of what has been written about home study courses applies to this field as well, there are certain special considerations.

Before you invest your time and money in any course, you must find out if this training will help you get a good job. Some schools lie about guaranteed job opportunities, government approval, and a phenomenal average of earnings of their graduates. Presume these are lies, and start where the truth is.

Get up the nerve and contact several prospective employers.

They know what they want in an employee. Call or visit the personnel offices and explain your problem. Get information primarily as to whether such an organization would hire anyone from the prospective school, whether any have been hired and if it was because of the school training, and whether such training would make any difference in a starting salary.

Another important point is whether there are any jobs available in the field in which you are interested. Check this out with your State Employment Agency and the Union, if any, that would be applicable.

As to the school, check the dropout rate. If it is too low, the school and its courses are too easy and will do you no good in your chosen work.

For complaints, complain to the same organizations as you would for home study schools. Veterans have certain additional rights (cooling-off periods, special refunds), and problems should be taken up with the local VA office first.

While there is no law to prevent junk mail, we all know how annoying it is, and there are ways of attempting to get yourself off the "sucker" mailing list.

Some help will be provided if you write to the Direct Mail Advertising Association (Appendix C) and the Direct Mail Marketing Association (Appendix C) and request an application (which will be sent to you free of charge) to be removed from "junk" mailing lists. When received, fill it out and return it. Some relief may be expected.

Another solution presents itself when the envelope says "address correction requested." Return the piece of mail, unopened, with word "refused" scrawled on it. After all, it costs the sender money to have the piece of mail returned. Some people even write "moved" on the envelope, but that doesn't solve anything.

Packages are a slightly different story. Postal regulations forbid the mailing of unordered merchandise by insured or C.O.D. mail, so if you receive an unordered parcel C.O.D., refuse it, refuse to pay for it, and notify your local postmaster immediately. If you receive a package (non-C.O.D.) with unordered merchandise, such as key chains, good luck pieces, etc., you are not obligated to either keep it or pay for it. If the package has not been opened, write "return to sender" on it and put it back into the mail. If you have opened it, put it aside for a reasonable time, and then do what you will with it. Most states treat such merchandise as unconditional gifts, so check with your Better Business Bureau to see if yours is one of those states. Of course, if the sender comes around within a reasonable time and asks for his merchandise back, give it to him (but demand reasonable storage charges before releasing the goods).

The nastiest attack is sexually oriented material and advertisements, This can be stopped by law. Get a form PS2201, an "application for listing," at any post office and fill it out. If you are still getting such material after thirty days, report it to the postal authorities, an investigation will be made, and the postal service will institute criminal or civil action.

Door-to-door salesmen, though the butt of many jokes, have caused innumerable heartaches among housewives by their swindles and fast-talking frauds.

However, there are certain behavioral clues that should give you fair warning. Watch out for the salesman who doesn't state immediately that he has something to sell, but instead "is making a survey" or is working his way through college. If goods are offered to you on approval just as long as you sign a receipt, don't be surprised if the "receipt" turns out to be a binding contract. Notorious frauds involve door-to-door sellers of books and encyclopedias. Don't do business with any door-to-door salesman unless he is willing to come back in a few days, after you've had time to shop around, and think things over ("I won't be around this neighborhood then," is the usual reply to your request, but if he wants to make a sale, he'll be around).

Don't even bother listening to the man at the door if he offers you a free encyclopedia or anything else for your "testimonial," or a list of your friends, or says you have been "specially selected."

Speaking of this latter ruse, those who push magazines and book subscriptions use similar tactics, informing you that you have a "lucky phone number"; that your subscription is free, just so that circulation may be increased, but just sign on this line (then read the contract to see how much the "free" subscription will cost); that your subscription may be cancelled by you at any time (don't believe it unless you see it written in the contract); or that you are receiving a special price, which later turns out to be the regular price.

When such a salesman comes to your door, make sure he has written identification and that all of his promises are in writing. One safeguard is to ask if the company is a member of, and the salesman has proof of such membership in, the Direct Selling Association, a trade group that is the only one that prescribes a code of ethics for its members.

Since June 1974, the Federal Trade Commission has come to the aid of the consumer and has prescribed rules for such sales, primarily a "cooling-off" period after the sale when you may change your mind.

The seller must give you a copy of a contract in the same language as the sales pitch (if he spoke Spanish to the purchaser, the contract must be in Spanish). He must explain to you your right to cancel the contract you have just signed, and must furnish you with two copies of a completed form entitled "Notice of Cancellation'' at the time you agree to buy the goods or services, or when you sign any contract. These copies must be attached to the contract or receipt and must be in large type. This notice must advise you of your right to cancel the contract or purchase without penalty or obligation within three business days of the deal, and that any down payment made, or goods traded in, or any checks, notes, or other negotiable instruments, must be returned to you within ten business days after your notice of cancellation.

Of course, you have obligations, too. You must have the goods you received ready for pickup at your home in basically the same condition as when you received them. If the seller doesn't pick them up within two days after your notice is received, you may keep the goods or do what you will with them, with no obligation on your part You will still be liable, however, if you don't have the goods available for the pickup within the specified time, or if you don't return the goods after promising to do so.

There are other important safeguards in the new rules, but you had better beware of the limitations, too. The goods must have a purchase price of $25 or more, the seller must be engaged in interstate commerce, and the law doesn't apply to sales made after a prior negotiation at the seller's place of business, or if the entire transaction took place by phone or mail.

In the event of fraud or violation of the rules, a sample letter of complaint might read as follows:

Federal Trade Commission
(Field office address nearest you—Appendix B)

Gentlemen:
    On (date) a salesman came to my door and told me he was selling vacuum cleaners at what seemed to be a good price. He had a dem-

onstration model with him, with all the attachments, and he showed me how well it worked. I signed a sales agreement without bothering to read it, a copy of which is attached hereto. I paid him in cash and he brought in a sealed carton and left rather hastily. I think his name was Mr. Houston.

When I opened the sealed carton, there was a much smaller unit than what was demonstrated to me, and it had no attachments. I then read the contract and saw two copies of a notice of cancellation on it. I sent one in the very same day, and kept the other, a photostatic copy of which is attached to this letter. I did not hear from the company so I called them on (date) and spoke to (name). He said the company had never received the notice of cancellation, and that they would not return the money.

Since it was the company that addressed the notice of cancellation, I believe there is no chance that they did not receive my notice, but that I am a victim of fraud, I ask you to investigate this matter and do what is necessary to get my money back.

Very truly yours,
Ellen Miller

cc: Direct Selling Association (Appendix C)
　　U.S. Office of Consumer Affairs (Appendix B)
　　State Attorney General
　　District Attorney
　　State Consumer Organization (Appendix B)
　　Better Business Bureau (Appendix A)
　　Consumers Union (Appendix C)
　　Consumers Federation of America (Appendix C)

How often have you heard stories about fraudulent charities? Many charities are worthwhile; many are fakes and do a huge business. Individual giving accounted for 86 percent of 22 billion dollars given to charity in 1972. One of the biggest names in charities, a Veterans' group, took in 21 million dollars in 1971 and spent 45 percent of that amount on fund raising. Incidentally, be especially wary of Veterans' groups, since the worst experience has been had with them.

Another example is the Asthmatic Children's Foundation, where a representative recently admitted that during its ten years of operation, the charity had collected 9.9 million dollars and had spent 86 percent of it on executive salaries, direct mail costs, and other overhead.

The charities, both real and false, range from starving children to the sick, diseased, blind, and refugees, the underprivileged, Veterans, and any other needy pocket of our civilization.

Once again, the first line of defense is wariness. Avoid doorbell ringers, especially around Christmas time, and scrutinize names of organizations carefully, because many phonies have designed their names to sound like legitimate charities. If you are tempted to give to a "cannister lady," ask for her credentials and permit. Don't be embarrassed. If she is on the level, she will not object. Never send money in response to a phone call from a stranger, especially if he represents himself to be a priest, rabbi, minister, or judge. If you are touched by his appeal, ask him to send a written or printed report on his organization, but don't hold your breath waiting for it.

Who has not received unsolicited items through the mail, contained in literature asking for a donation? Do not feel guilty if you do not send a donation, for this is the very sort of group that turns practically nothing over to the charity itself. Furthermore, the item need not be returned or paid for.

If you are contemplating aiding charity, the Charity Funds Bureau of the New York Attorney General's Office has a list of all tax-exempt charities in the United States. Send a self-addressed, stamped envelope to this organization at 2 World Trade Center, New York, New York 10047, ask them about the specific charity you have in mind, and the Bureau will advise you if your charity is on the list.

As an alternative, you might check with your local United or Community Fund (contact the Chamber of Commerce for the address and phone number), or write to the National Better Business Bureau (Appendix A), who will send you factual information on the charity.

Complaints should be registered with the Attorney General of your state, your District Attorney, your Chamber of Commerce (telephone book or librarian), and, if any part of the transaction took place by mail, the Postal Inspector of the United States Postal Service (Appendix B).

One of the last of the big frauds involves mail order insurance. The appeal here is made to working and limited-income families. It is mostly sold by mail, and primarily deals with accident and health insurance, and life insurance policies. The names used are similar to reputable companies, usually including the word "Equitable" as part of the title. The mails are basically used to invade states in which the company is not licensed. The fraud lies in the fact that these companies pay little or no benefits, based on technicalities, and, no matter what is promised in the literature, the policy itself is severely limited as to coverage.

There are other signs that give such companies away. The elderly are victimized by names that sound as though they are associated with Medicare. The literature describes the benefits as "up to" and "as high as." "No medical examination is required and health is not a factor," but the application forces you to list all illnesses, and this gives the company an escape clause when payment is due, should you have forgotten one illness. The policy as advertised promises, for instance, that there is coverage of $1000 on a family of five, but it fails to mention, except in fine print in the policy, that the coverage is allocable, or divided, among all members of the family, thus, in this case, providing only $200 apiece for each of the five members.

Another strategem is sending you what appears to be an actual policy with your name on it, but which is not a policy, and is still only a form of advertising, which is to be read carefully.

The most important point in a policy is the kind of risk insured against, and what are the exclusions. If you read nothing else, read these sections, for it is too late to learn the details after you have paid premiums for several years. If the language is too difficult, have your friend take you to his insurance broker who will be glad to explain it to you, and after you have discounted as much of his advice as might be sour grapes or a salesman's natural pitch, you will still have a better idea of what you are being enticed into.

Similar indications of fraud are shown by official looking envelopes, especially directed at Veterans to look as if they came from VA-connected organizations, or if an IBM card is sent in an official-appearing envelope to those under Medicare. These latter items offer information as to Social Security benefits. Then, if you sign and return the punch card, you receive high pressure literature offering you insurance.

Care must be taken with regard to liberal-sounding accident and health plans, because many of the policies restrict the types of hospitals to which benefits will be paid so severely that 80 percent of American hospitals do not qualify. Similar literature usually uses thrilling terms, such as "guaranteed continuable," or "only you can cancel," but the odds are the policy will state differently.

Another trap is the advertisement claiming "lowest regular premium of any company." Aside from the fact that ultra-low rates do not guarantee honesty, and merely mean that most claims are rejected, the wording may mean that the low initial premium jumps up at a later time. Ask the company for a complete schedule of what the premium payments will be, and then compare the data (if they ever send it to you) with other companies.

If you have any doubts, check first with the insurance department of your own state (phone book or librarian) as to whether the company is licensed to do business in your state. If not, don't buy anything from the company, as your own officials could then be barred from intervening in any controversy you might have with the insurance company. You might also check with your local Better Business Bureau as to whether it has any bad reports or complaints about that particular company.

Assuming you buy insurance from the company, and it is registered in your state, and further assuming trouble on a claim and/or fraud, write your usual letter of complaint, giving all details succinctly, and attaching copies of all pertinent documents, to your state Department of Insurance, with copies to the insurance department in the state in which the company is based (your librarian will obtain this information for you); the Postal Inspector of the United States Postal Service (Appendix B); your state consumer organization (Appendix B); the Better Business Bureau (Appendix A); Consumers Union (Appendix C); and the Attorney General of your state and of the state in which the company is headquartered. Another agency to be notified is the Federal Trade Commission (Appendix B), which handles cases involving misleading and deceptive practices of mail order insurance sellers operating in states in which they are not licensed. Although the FTC has no authority over rates, the financial soundness of the company, settlement of claims, and the like, and although the agency cannot advise you as to the integrity or the liability of the company, knowledge by the insurance company that the FTC is involved may exert a positive subtle pressure to force the company to get you off its back. Another agency that should be notified is the United States Office of Consumer Affairs (Appendix B).

The list is endless of those areas in which man swindles man. Complaints against computer dating establishments, dance studios, and storage facilities should be handled in the same manner as any of the above-described frauds and/or problems. Notify your state consumer agency, your state Attorney General, your District Attorney, the Better Business Bureau, and all of the interested groups recommended above as most likely to intervene.

The minute you smell fraud, work fast!

CHAPTER
16

—— What the Future May Hold ——

In this imperfect world, we have become used to our hopes and expectations coming to nought. Thus, today, we see many plans proposed in Congress and elsewhere to benefit the consumer, many of which will eventually die. The mood of the country is such, however, that at least some of the following plans will come to fruition. Watch for them and use them, for if you are ignorant of what your rights are, you will lose them.

The formation of an agency is being pushed in Congress to act as a consumer partisan in the halls of government. This Consumer Protection Agency will not only serve as a voice for the consumer, but may be a force for action as well.

Bills for consumer protection are in the federal hopper similar to the "Truth in Lending" law.

Truth in Savings is also the subject of possible legislation, requiring banks to clearly advise depositors as to the annual percentage rate of interest, the minimum amount of time that the deposit must be left untouched in order to draw such interest, the annual true percentage you would receive (omitting false claims as juggled by accountants), the frequency of interest compounding, and the dates or times such interest is actually paid.

Further "truth" bills being considered involve "Truth in Life Insurance," as to the true cost, value, and benefits of policies, and "Truth in Advertising."

The future will probably see more advertising campaigns by the federal, state, and city governments to warn people of the dangers of certain products (such as aerosol sniffers), and to advise them of their consumer rights. It's good politics. Accompanying this, there will be a greater degree of power given to governmental consumer watchdogs to crack down on violators of such rights.

We may see Consumer's Courts instituted in more urban and/or enlightened parts of the country, dedicated to help the consumers in the never-ending battle against unfair and fraudulent sellers of goods and services, and against landlords. These may, in large measure, replace Small Claims Courts, which have proven ineffective.

On a regulatory level, we are likely to see a growing trend, on the state and local scene, toward licensing of auto mechanics, TV repairmen, and hearing-aid dealers in an attempt to correct the notorious abuses now present in these fields. From state to state, there will probably be a rise in the amount of wages held exempt from wage assignments, so that there will be less of an incentive to trap the consumer into signing such documents. There may be requirements imposed upon professionals, such as doctors, for periodic licensing so the professionals will have to stay abreast of current developments in their field.

Almost certainly, over and above federal action, most states will adopt bans on pyramid and chain schemes, as to dealerships and selling of unworthy merchandise.

More joint action by consumer groups will be in order, doing away with the unseemly scrambling by some of the groups for headlines, instead of devoting all efforts to helping the consumer.

As its use becomes popularized, more local television stations and other media will increase coverage of consumer frauds, a typical "muckraking" function of reporters for many decades.

The government and private self-help groups of consumers have been using local consumer volunteers to watch TV, newspapers, and magazines for fraudulent advertising, and to advise and counsel individual consumers on their problems. They will also be used to check stores as to sales of unsafe toys and the like. Certainly, this will remain a growing trend.

But all of these possibilities are in the future, and none will completely protect you. Your best defense, your best offense, is still to be found, not in a group, but within yourself. If you refuse to lose, you can't lose.

Congratulations. You're on your way to winning.

─── Better Business Bureau ───

Council of Better Business Bureaus, 1150 17th Street N.W., Washington, D.C. 20036

National Better Business Bureau, 230 Park Avenue, New York, N.Y. 10017

ALABAMA: Birmingham, Huntsville, Mobile

ARIZONA: Phoenix, Tucson

ARKANSAS: Little Rock

CALIFORNIA: Bakersfield, Fresno, Long Beach, Los Angeles, Oakland, Orange, Sacramento, San Bernardino, San Diego, San Francisco, San Jose, San Mateo, Santa Barbara, Stockton, Vallejo, Van Nuys, Walnut Creek

COLORADO: Denver

CONNECTICUT: Bridgeport, Hartford, New Haven, Stamford

DELAWARE: Wilmington

DISTRICT OF COLUMBIA: Washington

FLORIDA: Miami, West Palm Beach

GEORGIA: Atlanta, Augusta, Columbus, Savannah

HAWAII: Honolulu

IDAHO: Boise

ILLINOIS: Chicago, Peoria

INDIANA: Elkhart, Fort Wayne, Gary, Indianapolis, South Bend

IOWA: Des Moines, Sioux City

KANSAS: Topeka, Wichita

KENTUCKY: Lexington, Louisville

LOUISIANA: Baton Rouge, Lake Charles, Monroe, New Orleans, Shreveport

MARYLAND: Baltimore, Bethesda

MASSACHUSETTS: Boston, Springfield, Worcester

MICHIGAN: Detroit, Grand Rapids

MINNESOTA: Minneapolis, St. Paul

MISSISSIPPI: Gulfport, Jackson

MISSOURI: Kansas City, St. Louis, Springfield

NEBRASKA: Lincoln, Omaha

NEVADA: Las Vegas, Reno

NEW HAMPSHIRE: Concord

NEW JERSEY: Haddonfield, Newark, New Brunswick, Paramus, Trenton

NEW MEXICO: Albuquerque

NEW YORK: Buffalo, New York City (2), Rochester, Schenectady, Syracuse, Utica, Westbury, White Plains

NORTH CAROLINA: Asheville, Charlotte, Greensboro, Winston-Salem

OHIO: Akron, Canton, Cincinnati, Cleveland, Columbus, Dayton, Toledo

OKLAHOMA: Oklahoma City, Tulsa

OREGON: Portland

PENNSYLVANIA: Philadelphia, Pittsburgh, Scranton

PUERTO RICO: Santurce

RHODE ISLAND: Providence

TENNESSEE: Chattanooga, Knoxville, Memphis, Nashville

TEXAS: Abilene, Amarillo, Austin, Beaumont, Bryan, Corpus Christi, Dallas, El Paso, Fort Worth, Houston, Lubbock, Midland, San Antonio, Waco

UTAH: Salt Lake City

VIRGINIA: Norfolk, Richmond, Roanoke

WASHINGTON: Seattle, Spokane, Tacoma, Yakima
WISCONSIN: Milwaukee

CANADA

ALBERTA: Calgary, Edmonton
BRITISH COLUMBIA: Vancouver, Victoria
NEWFOUNDLAND and LABRADOR: St. John's
MANITOBA: Winnipeg
NOVA SCOTIA: Halifax
ONTARIO: Ottawa, Toronto
QUEBEC: Montreal, Quebec

—— Governmental Agencies ——

Federal Trade Commission
Bureau of Consumer Protection
Washington, D.C. 20580

FIELD OFFICES

11000 Wilshire Boulevard
Room 13209
Los Angeles, California 90024
or
450 Golden Gate Avenue
Box Number 36005
San Francisco, California 94102
or
730 Peachtree Street NE
Room 720
Atlanta, Georgia 30308
or
Room 486
U.S. Courthouse and Federal
Office Building

219 South Dearborn Street
Chicago, Illinois 60604
or
1000 Masonic Temple Building
333 St. Charles Street
New Orleans, Louisiana 70130
or
John F. Kennedy Federal
Building
Government Center
Boston, Massachusetts 02203
or
2806 Federal Office Building
911 Walnut Street
Kansas City, Missouri 64106
or
Federal Building
22nd Floor
26 Federal Plaza
New York, New York 10007

or

Federal Office Building
Room 1339
1240 East Ninth Street
Cleveland, Ohio 44199

or

450 West Broad Street
Falls Church, Virginia 22046

or

908 Republic Building
1511 Third Avenue
Seattle, Washington 98101

Interstate Commerce Commission

Washington, D.C. 20423
(Hotline: (202) 343-4761 or
(202) 343-4141 channels consumer calls to a central office
that supplies immediate answers, or can refer the consumer to the proper office to
make inquiries)

Food and Drug Administration

Department of Health, Education
and Welfare
5600 Fishers Lane
Rockville, Maryland 20852
(However, all violations should
be reported first to the nearest
Food and Drug Administration
office, the address of which
may be ascertained by looking
at your local telephone direc-

tory under, "United States—
Department of Health, Education and Welfare," or consulting the following list:

DISTRICT OFFICES

60 Eighth Street, N.E.
Atlanta, Georgia 30309

or

900 Madison Avenue
Baltimore, Maryland 21201

or

585 Commercial Street
Boston, Massachusetts 02109

or

850 Third Avenue
Brooklyn, New York 11232

or

599 Delaware Avenue
Buffalo, New York 14202

or

433 West Van Buren Street
Room 1222, Main Post Office
Chicago, Illinois 60607

or

Paul B. Dunbar Building
1141 Central Parkway
Cincinnati, Ohio 45202

or

3032 Bryan Street
Dallas, Texas 75204

or

513 U.S. Customhouse
Denver, Colorado 80202

or
1560 East Jefferson Avenue
Detroit, Michigan 48207

or
1009 Cherry Street
Kansas City, Missouri 64106

or
John L. Harvey Building
1521 West Pico Boulevard
Los Angeles, California 90015

or
240 Hennepin Avenue
Minneapolis, Minnesota 55401

or
970 Broad Street
Newark, New Jersey 07102

or
423 Canal Street, Room 222
U.S. Customhouse Building
New Orleans, Louisiana 70130

or
2nd and Chestnut, Room 1204
U.S. Customhouse Building
Philadelphia, Pennsylvania 19106

or
50 Fulton Street, Room 526
San Francisco, California 94102

or
P.O. Box 4427
Old San Juan Station
San Juan, Puerto Rico 00905

or
Federal Office Building
901 First Avenue, Room 5003
Seattle, Washington 98104

Chief Postal Inspector
United States Postal Service
Washington, D.C. 20260

United States Office of
Consumer Affairs
New Executive Office Building
Washington, D.C. 20506

Civil Aeronautics Board
Bureau of Enforcement or
Office of Consumer Affairs or
Office of the Consumer Advocate
Washington, D.C. 20428
   (Hot line: (202) 382-7735 or
   (202) 382-6376)

Department of Agriculture
Consumer and Marketing Service
Washington, D.C. 20250

Federal Communications
Commission
Washington, D.C. 20554

Office of Interstate Land Sales
Registration
Department of Housing and
   Urban Development
451 Seventh Street S.W.
Washington, D.C. 20410

Department of Justice
Washington, D.C. 20530
   (or report complaint to one of

local offices, as listed in your telephone directory)

National Highway Traffic Safety Administration
Department of Transportation
400 7th Street S.W.
Washington, D.C. 20590

U.S. Department of Labor
Employment Standards
  Administration
Wage and Hour Division
Washington, D.C. 20210

Social and Rehabilitation Service
Department of Health, Education
  and Welfare
Washington, D.C. 20201

Bureau of Complaints
Consumer Product Safety
  Commission
Department of Health, Education
  and Welfare
5401 Westbard Avenue
Bethesda, Maryland 20016
Toll Free: (800) 638-2666

Federal Housing Administration
Department of Housing and
  Urban Development
Washington, D.C. 20410

STATE CONSUMER AGENCIES

Alabama
Consumer Protection Officer
Office of the Governor
138 Adams Avenue
Montgomery, Alabama 36104

Consumer Services Coordinator
Office of the Attorney General
State Administration Building
Montgomery, Alabama 36104

Alaska
Assistant Attorney General
Office of the Attorney General
Pouch "K", State Capitol
Juneau, Alaska 99801

Arizona
Consumer Protection and
  Antitrust Division
Office of the Attorney General
159 State Capitol Building
Phoenix, Arizona 85007

Arkansas
Consumer Protection Division
Office of the Attorney General
Justice Building
Little Rock, Arkansas 72201

California
Department of Consumer Affairs
1020 N. Street
Sacramento, California 95814

Colorado
Office of Consumer Affairs
Office of the Attorney General
112 East 14th Avenue
Denver, Colorado 80203

Connecticut
Department of Consumer
  Protection
State Office Building
Hartford, Connecticut 06115

Assistant Attorney General for
  Consumer Protection
Office of the Attorney General
Capitol Annex
30 Trinity Avenue
Hartford, Connecticut 06115

Delaware
Consumer Affairs Division
Department of Community
  Affairs and Economic
  Development

201 West 14th Street
Wilmington, Delaware 19801

Deputy Attorney General
Consumer Protection Division
Department of Justice
Public Building
Wilmington, Delaware 19801

District of Columbia
Office of Consumer Affairs
1407 L Street, N.W.
Washington, D.C. 20005

Florida
Consumer Advisor to the
  Governor
Office of the Governor
State Capitol
Tallahassee, Florida 32304

Consumer Counsel, FTP Office
Department of Legal Affairs
State Capitol
Tallahassee, Florida 32304

Division of Consumer Affairs
Department of Agriculture &
  Consumer Services
106 W. Pensacola Street
Tallahassee, Florida 32301

Director for Consumer Protection
Office of the Comptroller
State Capitol

Tallahassee, Florida 32304
(with regard to consumer credit)

Room 204
Chicago, Illinois 60602

Georgia

Assistant Attorney General for
  Deceptive Practices
Office of the Attorney General
132 State Judicial Building
Atlanta, Georgia 30334

Georgia Consumer Services
  Program
618 Ponce de Leon Avenue N.E.
Atlanta, Georgia 30303

Hawaii

Director of Consumer Protection
Office of the Governor
250 S. King Street, 602
  Kamamalu Building
P.O. Box 3767
Honolulu, Hawaii 96811

Idaho

Deputy Attorney General for
  Consumer Protection
Office of the Attorney General
State Capitol
Boise, Idaho 83701

Illinois

Assistant Attorney General and
  Chief, Consumer Fraud Section
Office of the Attorney General
134 N. La Salle Street

Indiana

Division of Consumer Credit
Department of Financial
  Institutions
1024 Indiana State Office
  Building
Indianapolis, Indiana 46204

Office of Business Education
% Indiana Dept. of Commerce
336 State House
Indianapolis, Indiana 46204

Consumer Protection Division
Office of the Attorney General
215 State House
Indianapolis, Indiana 46204

Iowa

Assistant Attorney General
Consumer Protection Division
Iowa Department of Justice
220 East 13th Court
Des Moines, Iowa 50319

Kansas

Consumer Protection Division
Office of the Attorney General
State Capitol
Topeka, Kansas 66612

Kentucky

Consumer Protection Division
Office of the Attorney General
Room 34, The Capitol
Frankfort, Kentucky 40601

Louisiana

Consumer Protection Division
Office of the Governor
P.O. Box 44091
State Capitol
Baton Rouge, Louisiana 70804

Consumer Affairs & Promotion
  Office
Department of Agriculture
P.O. Box 44302, Capitol Station
Baton Rouge, Louisiana 70804

Consumer Protection and Com-
  mercial Fraud Prosecution
  Unit
Office of the Attorney General
234 Corola Avenue, 7th Floor
New Orleans, Louisiana 70112

Maine

Consumer Protection Division
Office of the Attorney General
State House
Augusta, Maine 04330

Maryland

Consumer Protection Division

Office of the Attorney General
One South Calvert Street
Baltimore, Maryland 21202

Massachusetts

Executive Office of Consumer
  Affairs
Consumer Complaint Division
State Office Building
100 Cambridge Street
Boston, Massachusetts 02202

Consumer Protection Division
Department of the Attorney
  General
State House, Room 167
Boston, Massachusetts 02133

Michigan

Consumer Protection & Anti-
  Trust Division
Office of the Attorney General
Law Building
Lansing, Michigan 48913

Michigan Consumer Council
414 Hollister Building
Lansing, Michigan 48933

Minnesota

Assistant Attorney General for
  Consumer Protection
Office of the Attorney General
102 State Capitol
St. Paul, Minnesota 55101

Office of Consumer Services
Department of Commerce
Metro Square, 5th Floor
St. Paul, Minnesota 55155

Mississippi
Consumer Protection Division
Office of the Attorney General
Gartin Justice Building
P.O. Box 220
Jackson, Mississippi 39205

Consumer Protection Division
Department of Agriculture &
Commerce
Jackson, Mississippi 39205

Missouri
Consumer Protection Division
Office of the Attorney General
Supreme Court Building
Jefferson City, Missouri 65101

Deputy Insurance Superintendent
and Director, Consumer Services Section
Division of Insurance
Department of Business &
Administration
Jefferson City, Missouri 65101

Montana
Department of Business
Regulation

805 North Main Street
Helena, Montana 59601

Nebraska
Assistant Attorney General for
Consumer Protection & Antitrust
Office of the Attorney General
State Capitol
Lincoln, Nebraska 68509

Nevada
Deputy Attorney General for
Consumer Affairs
Office of the Attorney General
Supreme Court Building
Carson City, Nevada 89701

Consumer Affairs Division
Department of Commerce
Coller Building, Room 219
1111 Las Vegas Boulevard South
Las Vegas, Nevada 89104

New Hampshire
Consumer Protection Division
Office of the Attorney General
State House Annex
Concord, New Hampshire 03301

New Jersey
Deputy Attorney General for
Consumer Protection
Office of the Attorney General

State Office Building
1100 Raymond Boulevard
Newark, New Jersey 07102

Division of Consumer Affairs
Division of Law & Public Safety
State Office Building
1100 Raymond Boulevard
Newark, New Jersey 07102

New Mexico
Consumer Protection Division
Office of the Attorney General
Supreme Court Building
Box 2246
Santa Fe, New Mexico 87501

New York
Consumer Protection Board
Office of the Governor
Twin Towers Office Building
99 Washington Avenue
Albany, New York 12210

Consumer Frauds and Protection
  Bureau
Office of the Attorney General
2 World Trade Center
New York, New York 10047

Consumer Frauds and Protection
  Bureau
Office of the Attorney General
State Capitol
Albany, New York 12225

North Carolina
Consumer Protection Division
Office of the Attorney General
Box 629, Justice Building
Raleigh, North Carolina 27602

North Dakota
Consumer Fraud Division
State Capitol
Bismarck, North Dakota 58501

Consumer Affairs Office
State Laboratories Department
Lock Box 937
Bismarck, North Dakota 58501

Ohio
Consumer Frauds & Crimes
  Section
Office of the Attorney General
154 State Office Tower
Columbus, Ohio 43215

Division of Consumer Protection
Department of Commerce
33 North Grant Avenue
Columbus, Ohio 43215

Oklahoma
Assistant Attorney General for
  Consumer Protection
Office of the Attorney General
112 State Capitol
Oklahoma City, Oklahoma 73105

Governor's Advisor on Consumer
  Affairs
3033 North Walnut Avenue
Oklahoma City, Oklahoma 73105

Oregon
Consumer Protection Division
Department of Justice
1133 S.W. Market Street
Portland, Oregon 97201

Consumer Officer
Oregon Department of
  Agriculture
Agriculture Building
Salem, Oregon 97310

Consumer Services Division
Department of Commerce
Salem, Oregon 97310

Pennsylvania
Bureau of Consumer Protection
Department of Justice
23A South Third Street
Harrisburg, Pennsylvania 17101

Rhode Island
Chief Assistant for Consumer
  Affairs
Department of the Attorney
  General
250 Benefit Street
Providence, Rhode Island 02903

Rhode Island Consumers'
  Council
365 Broadway
Providence, Rhode Island 02902

South Carolina
Office of Citizens Service
Governor's Office
State House
Columbia, South Carolina 29211

Assistant Attorney General for
  Consumer Protection
Office of the Attorney General
Hampton Office Building
Columbia, South Carolina 29211

South Dakota
Commissioner of Consumer
  Affairs
Office of the Attorney General
State Capitol
Pierre, South Dakota 57501

Tennessee
Assistant Attorney General for
  Consumer Protection
Office of the Attorney General
Supreme Court Building
Nashville, Tennessee 37219

Office of Consumer Affairs
Department of Agriculture
P.O. Box 40627, Melrose
  Station
Nashville, Tennessee 37204

Texas
Antitrust and Consumer
  Protection Division
Office of the Attorney General
P.O. Box 12548, Capitol Station
Austin, Texas 78711

Utah
Assistant Attorney General for
  Consumer Protection
Office of the Attorney General
State Capitol
Salt Lake City, Utah 84114

Department of Business
  Regulation
Trade Commission
330 East 4th South Street
Salt Lake City, Utah 84111

Administrator of Consumer
  Credit
10 West 3rd South, Suite 331
Salt Lake City, Utah 84101

Vermont
Assistant Attorney General
Consumer Fraud Division
200 Main Street
Box 981
Burlington, Vermont 05401

Virginia
Office of the Attorney General

Room 401, 203 N. Governor St.
Richmond, Virginia 23219

Director of Consumer Affairs
Department of Agriculture &
  Commerce
825 East Broad Street
Richmond, Virginia 23219

Washington
Consumer Protection and
  Antitrust Division
Office of the Attorney General
1266 Dexter Horton Building
Seattle, Washington 98104

West Virginia
Office of the Attorney General
State Capitol
Charleston, West Virginia 25305

Consumer Protection Division
Department of Agriculture
Charleston, West Virginia 25305

Consumer Protection Division
Department of Labor
1900 Washington Street, East
Charleston, West Virginia 25305

Wisconsin
Consumer Affairs Coordinator
Department of Justice
State Capitol
Madison, Wisconsin 53702

Bureau of Consumer Protection
Trade Division
Department of Agriculture
801 West Badger Road
Madison, Wisconsin 53713

Assistant Attorney General for
Consumer Protection
Department of Justice
State Capitol
Madison, Wisconsin 53702

Wyoming
Consumer Affairs Division
Office of the Attorney General
Capitol Building
Cheyenne, Wyoming 82002

State Examiner & Administrator
Consumer Credit Code
State Supreme Court Building
Cheyenne, Wyoming 82001

Commonwealth of Puerto Rico
Department of Consumer Affairs
P.O. Box 13934
Santurce, Puerto Rico 00908

Virgin Islands
Consumer Services
Administration
P.O. Box 831, Charlotte Amalie
St. Thomas, Virgin Islands
00801

 **GOVERNMENT TELEPHONE NUMBERS
TO CALL FOR HELP**

Alabama: (205) 269-7002
Alaska: (907) 586-5391
Arizona: (602) 271-5911
Arkansas: (501) 371-2007
California: (213) 620-2655
Colorado: (303) 392-8501
Connecticut: (203) 566-4206
Delaware: (302) 658-9251
Florida: (904) 488-4444
Georgia: (1800-toll free)
282-8900
Hawaii: (808) 548-2560 or
(808) 531-5995

Idaho: (208) 384-2400
Illinois: (312) 793-3580
Indiana: (317) 633-6276
Iowa: (515) 281-5926
Kansas: (913) 296-3751
Kentucky: (502) 564-6607
Louisiana: (504) 529-1636
Maine: (207) 289-3716
Maryland: (301) 383-3713
Massachusetts: (617) 727-8400
Michigan: (517) 373-1140
Minnesota: (612) 296-3353
Mississippi: (601) 354-7130

Missouri: (314) 751-3321
Montana: (406) 449-3163
Nebraska: (402) 471-2211
Nevada: (702) 385-0344
New Hampshire: (603)
271-3658
New Jersey: (201) 648-3537
New Mexico: (505) 827-5237
New York: (212) 488-4141
North Carolina: (919) 829-7741
North Dakota: (710) 224-2215
Ohio: (1800-toll free) 282-1960
Oklahoma: (405) 521-5636
Oregon: (503) 229-5522

Pennsylvania: (717) 787-7109
Rhode Island: (401) 831-6850
South Carolina: (803) 758-8384
South Dakota: (605) 224-3215
Tennessee: (803) 342-8385
Texas: (512) 475-3288
Utah: (801) 328-6445
Vermont: (802) 864-0111
Virginia: (804) 770-2042
Washington: (1800-toll free)
552-0700
West Virginia: (304) 348-2021
Wisconsin: (608) 266-1852
Wyoming: (307) 777-7797

Non-Governmental
——————Organizations——————

**Major Appliance Consumer
Action Panel (MACAP)**
20 North Wacker Drive
Chicago, Illinois 60606
(Call Collect: (312) 236-3165)

**National Retail Merchants
Association**
100 West 31st Street
New York, New York 10001

**National Association of
Discount Merchants**
50 Central Park West
New York, New York 10023

**Furniture Industry Consumer
Advisory Panel (FICAP)**
209 South Main Street

High Point, North Carolina
27261

**National Association of
Furniture Manufacturers**
8401 Connecticut Avenue
Suite 911
Washington, D.C. 20015

**National Society of Interior
Decorators**
315 East 62nd Street
New York, New York 10021

**American Institute of Interior
Designers**
730 Fifth Avenue
New York, New York 10019

Mail Order Action Line Service
Direct Mail Advertising
Association
230 Park Avenue
New York, New York 10017

**Direct Mail Marketing
Association, Inc.**
6 East 43rd Street
New York, New York 10017

Associated Credit Bureau
6767 Southwest Freeway
Houston, Texas 77036

Direct Selling Association
1730 M Street N. W.
Washington, D.C. 20036

Jewelers Vigilance Committee
919 Third Avenue
New York, New York 10022

**American Society of Travel
Agents**
360 Lexington Avenue
New York, New York 10017

**International Fabricare
Institute**
Room 5623
Empire State Building
New York, New York 10001

**American Veterinarian Medical
Association**
600 South Michigan Avenue
Chicago, Illinois 60605

**Joint Commission on
Accreditation of Hospitals**
875 North Michigan Avenue
Chicago, Illinois 60611

American Hospital Association
840 North Lake Shore Drive
Chicago, Illinois 60611

American College of Surgeons
55 East Erie Street
Chicago, Illinois 60611

American Nurses Association
10 Columbus Circle
New York, New York 10019

**American Nursing Home
Association**
1025 Connecticut Avenue N.W.
Washington, D.C. 20036

American Medical Association
535 North Dearborn Street
Chicago, Illinois 60610

American Dental Association
211 East Chicago Avenue
Chicago, Illinois 60611

International Chiropractors Association
1801 "K" Street N.W.
Washington, D.C. 20006

American Chiropractic Association (Legal Officer)
1735 De Sales Street N.W.
Washington, D.C. 20036

American Podiatry Association
20 Chevy Chase Circle N.W.
Washington, D.C. 20015

American Bar Association
1155 East 60th Street
Chicago, Illinois 60637

Chrysler Center
P.O. Box 1086
Detroit, Michigan 48231
(In Canada, write to **Chrysler Center,** Windsor, Ontario)

Ford Marketing Corp.
Ford Customer Service
   Division
Box 1514
Dearborn, Michigan 48121

Buick Motor Division
Flint, Michigan 48550

Cadillac Motor Car Division
2860 Clark Avenue
Detroit, Michigan 48232

Chevrolet Motor Division
General Motors Building
Detroit, Michigan 48202

Oldsmobile Division
Lansing, Michigan 48921

Pontiac Motor Division
Pontiac, Michigan 48053

American Motors Corp.
14250 Plymouth Road
Detroit, Michigan 48232
(In Canada, 350 Kennedy Road
South, Brampton, Ontario)

Sears Roebuck
No central office to contact. The company policy is that you must call or write to the Customer Service Department of the store nearest you, no matter where the item was purchased. This also applies to purchases made through a catalog.

General Electric Company
Manager of Customer Care
   Service
GE Appliance Park
Louisville, Kentucky 40225

Maytag Co.
Consumer Information Center
Newton, Iowa 50208

Caloric
Topton, Pennsylvania 19561

These three firms have hot lines:

Westinghouse
(800) 245-0600. Round-the-clock
toll-free complaints. A consumer
relations representative is
available for direct consultation
between 8:00 A.M. and 5:00 P.M.

Whirlpool Corp.
Round-the-clock toll-free service
on complaints, at
(800) 253-1301.

Admiral Corp.
The consumer relations
department may be reached at
(201) 933-9000. If the complaint
is not resolved, there is a hot line
to company headquarters, toll-
free, (800) 447-1305.

National Canners Association
Department of Consumer Affairs
1133 20th Street N.W.
Washington, D.C. 20036

American Meat Institute
Department of Consumer Affairs
1600 Wilson Boulevard
Arlington, Virginia 22209

General Foods
Consumer Services
250 North Street
White Plains, New York 10625

Consumers Union
256 Washington Street
Mount Vernon, New York 10550

**Consumer Federation of
America**
1012 14th Street N.W.
Washington, D.C. 20005

National Consumers League
1029 Vermont Avenue N.W.
Washington, D.C. 20005

National Consumer Congress
2000 "P" Street N.W.
Suite 503
Washington, D.C. 20036

Center for Auto Safety
1346 Connecticut Avenue N.W.
Washington, D.C. 20036

National Consumer Federation
815 16th Street N.W.
Washington, D.C. 20006

International Consumer Credit Association
375 Jackson Avenue
St. Louis, Missouri 63130

National Foundation for Consumer Credit
1819 "H" Street
Washington, D.C. 20006

National Safety Council
425 North Michigan Avenue
Chicago, Illinois 60611

Consumer Association of Canada
100 Gloucester Street
Ottawa 4, Canada

Family Service Association of America
44 East 23rd Street
New York, New York 10010

Small Claims Study Group
c/o John H. Weiss
Room 1
Quincy House
Cambridge, Massachusetts 02138

——Product-Related Injuries——

The following is a list of injuries associated with the top 15 injury-producing types of products (with adjustments made to give added weight to injuries in children under 10), as listed by the United States Consumer Product Safety Commission:

Ranking—Number 1
Bicycles and bicycle equipment including add-on features (baskets, horns, nonstandard seats, handbrakes)
Injuries: Concussion, fractures, lacerations, amputations, broken teeth, bruises.

Ranking—Number 2
Stairs, ramps and landings; indoors and outdoors
Injuries: Lacerations, contusions, abrasions, fractures, dislocations, strain/sprains, hematomas.

Ranking—Number 3
Doors, other than glass doors, including folding, swinging, garage and screen doors.

Injuries: Lacerations, crushing, contusions, abrasions, fractures, strain/sprains, hematomas.

Ranking—Number 4
Cleaning agents, caustic compounds
Injuries: Chemical burns, poisonings, inhalation of dangerous fumes, swallowing

Ranking—Number 5
Tables, nonglass
Injuries: Lacerations, contusions, abrasions, fractures, strain/sprains, hematomas

Ranking—Number 6
Beds, including springs, box springs, and frames
Injuries: Fractures, cuts, bruises, concussion, lacerations, contusions, abrasions, strain/sprains, hematomas, burns

Ranking—Number 7
Football, activity, and related equipment and apparel
Injuries: Fractures, muscle and joint injuries, bruises, concussions, broken teeth, and other injuries.

Ranking—Number 8
Swings, slides, seesaws, and climbing apparatus
Injuries: Concussions, fractures, bruises, lacerations, amputations

Ranking—Number 9
Liquid fuels, kindling or illuminating (including gasoline, kerosene, lighter fluid, charcoal starter)
Injuries: Swallowing, bad burns, carbon monoxide poisoning

Ranking—Number 10
Architectural glass, including doors, tub enclosures, shower enclosures, windows
Injuries: Punctures, severe lacerations

Ranking—Number 11
Power lawn mowers, including rotary and reel, gas and electric; riding and non-riding
Injuries: Amputations, fractures, cuts, bruises, electric shock

Ranking—Number 12
Baseball, activity, related equipment, and apparel
Injuries: Cuts, bruises, head and leg injuries, fractures

Ranking—Number 13
Nails, carpet tacks, screws, and thumb tacks
Injuries: Puncture wounds, lacerations, swallowing

Ranking—Number 14
Bath tub and shower structures, other than doors and panels, including tub, walls, hand-grips, etc.
Injuries: Bruises, cuts, fractures from falls, scalds, electric shock

Ranking—Number 15
Space heaters and heating stove
Injuries: Burn injuries, resulting from clothing ignition, explosion and hot surfaces; carbon monoxide poisonings

Index

(Does not include references to form letters or appendixes)